CREATIVE DIRECTOR'S SOURCEBOOK

CREATIVE DIRECTOR'S SOURCEBOOK

NICK SOUTER • STUART NEWMAN

FOREWORD
BY
JOHN
HEGARTY

Macdonald Orbis

A Macdonald Orbis Book.
Copyright © 1988
Quarto Publishing plc.
First published in Great
Britain in 1988 by
Macdonald & Co
(Publishers) Ltd London
and Sydney.
A member of Maxwell
Pergamon Publishing
Corporation plc.

British Library
Cataloguing in
Publication Data.
Souter, Nick
   Creative director's
   sourcebook.
   1. Advertising, history
   I. Title II. Newman,
   Stuart
   659.1'09.

ISBN 0-356-17192-2

This book was designed
and produced by Quarto
Publishing plc,
The Old Brewery,
6 Blundell Street,
London,
N7 9BH.

Project Director
Alastair Campbell
Editors
Maria Pal
Robert Stewart
Designers
Penny Dawes
Vincent Murphy
Picture Researcher
Valya Alexander
Art Director
Moira Clinch
Editorial Director
Carolyn King

Typeset by
QV Typesetting Ltd.
Manufactured in Hong
Kong by Regent
Publishing Services Ltd.
Printed by Leefung-Asco
Printers Ltd, Hong Kong.

Macdonald & Co
(Publishers) Ltd, Greater
London House,
Hampstead Road,
London NW1 7QX.

"IF I HAVE SEEN FURTHER, IT IS BECAUSE I HAVE BEEN ABLE TO STAND ON THE SHOULDERS OF OTHER GREAT MEN." *SIR ISAAC NEWTON*

For those without such vision I can seriously recommend purchasing this book. By standing on it you will certainly see further.

For those with vision and prone to reading, open it up and you will be rewarded by the ingenuity and the history of advertising.

This remarkable book is a testament to the skills that made that happen. Skills that reveal the aspirations and concerns of previous generations. In a unique and memorable way.

We're very good at plundering our past, we're not very good at applauding it. This book can put a little of that to rights.

Use it as a reference book and as a source of inspiration. Remember you don't have to be tall to see further, although this book will do that for you too.

John Hegarty

JOHN HEGARTY
CREATIVE DIRECTOR
BARTLE BOGLE HEGARTY

CREATIVE DIRECTOR'S SOURCEBOOK

IF YOU HAVE EVER worked in the creative department of an advertising agency or design group you will know the acute frustration of finding that the mind is as blank as the layout pad at which your eyes are staring. Sometimes this agony will be compounded by another—the futile ransacking of the department in search of last year's awards annual, a search that will inevitably broaden to include any awards annual or advertising reference work and that will just as inevitably fail. These books are as elusive as the Muse herself, and for good reason. They have been stolen. By whom? Those same friends and colleagues who could not help you find them. Because they too have discovered that these tomes contain not only the fruits, but also the seeds, of inspiration. So it was with this scenario in mind—the clench-fisted art director or copywriter standing before the desecrated shelves of the department library—that the idea for this publication was conceived: the creative director's sourcebook—a 320-page, international, decade-by-decade history of advertising since the year 1850. A library between the covers of a single book.

From the outset we decided to exclude television and radio. It is impossible to treat these media fairly on the printed page. Scripts and storyboards rarely capture more than the basic idea. That left us with newspapers and magazines, posters and some point-of-sale material.

Our search began with a mailshot to advertising agencies in the major cities of the world. In return we received many enthusiastic and encouraging replies, but no real leads. No one knew of any archives that contained advertising from before the 1970s. The industry, we concluded, had little or no sense of its own history and we would have to look elsewhere.

Our first discovery was Gordon Philips and the History of Advertising Trust in London. There we received a daunting sense of the project's scale and an invaluable list of names. One contact leads to another and so it was that either directly or indirectly through Gordon we found the many people who helped us to compile this book. There is not space to name and thank them all, but some deserve special mention. Stacey Flaherty and her staff at the National Museum of American History at the Smithsonian Institute in Washington worked at breakneck speed to locate and photograph the material we required. Ted Shepherd at Shell and Peter Bullstrode at Guinness threw open the doors of their archives and took time out to help us. And when all else failed Margaret Dunlop at Gallaher came up with a near-complete set of Benson and Hedges posters.

The main problem with ads is that they are intrinsically disposable—they end up in the same bin as the newspaper or magazine that printed them. And posters are either pasted over or torn from the hoardings. So we were relieved to discover the Ephemera Society in London and through it a group of zealous and dedicated individuals who unearth and collect the very things that everyone else throws away.

Robert Opie, who runs his own Packaging Museum in Gloucester, supplied more than

100 ads and spent many hours helping us to date some of the more obscure ones. We have tried, wherever possible, to include credits for each campaign but, more often than not, this information has disappeared for good.

The Russian Revolution posters are all from a collection compiled and held by David King, who also struggled with his dictionary to translate the headlines. And in the last stages of the project we had the luck to stumble upon Colin MacArthur. Colin lent us some exquisite advertisements from his collection of *Punch* magazines and managed to trace some of the Volkswagen work for which we had searched in vain.

Through the efforts of these people and many others we found ourselves confronted with a mountain of transparencies and the problem of sorting them out. It is not possible to judge old advertisements by the criteria we use at work today. Back in the twenties and thirties no one had defined such concepts as the 'Unique Selling Proposition' or such creative philosophies as the 'Relevant Unexpected'. Initially, we used a very straightforward selection procedure. We simply sifted through the work and set aside those ads that grabbed our attention. Crude as it may seem, this is the test all advertising has to pass when it first appears. Stage two involved a closer scrutiny. We wanted every ad to have some element that was original and inspiring—typography, photography, illustration, copy or concept, it did not matter which.

By the time we had finished we were down to about 1,000 transparencies. We then arranged them by decade. This proved to be preferable to dividing the work into product categories, because it is easier to understand and appreciate the ads when you see them in a historical context alongside their contemporaries.

Inevitably, some decades are more full than others. We found relatively little that we liked in the years 1850-1879 and so we made them into a single chapter. On the other hand, we could not bring ourselves to pare down the 1930s any further, since that decade contained so much of our favourite material.

The 1970s and 1980s were a problem. We have tried to downweight them as these are the decades that everyone remembers and their advertising tends to follow philosophies established in the mid-sixties. That is not to say that the work was not great—we were inundated with award-winning ads. But something had to go and we wanted to place the emphasis on lesser-known campaigns. We hope that we have struck the right balance and that the book acts as both a record and a reference work that details the various styles and techniques that have emerged during the last 130 years. A friend recently described it as a 'swipefile'. It is a description that misses the point. The purpose of this book is to provoke inspiration, not imitation. Unfortunately, it may also inspire theft. Whatever you do, do not leave it lying on your desk.

NICK SOUTER
SENIOR COPYWRITER
CREATIVE GROUP HEAD
LEO BURNETT LTD.

STUART NEWMAN
ART DIRECTOR
CREATIVE GROUP HEAD
LEO BURNETT LTD.

CREATIVE DIRECTOR'S SOURCEBOOK

IN HIS BOOK, 'Understanding Media', Marshall McLuhan wrote that 'the historians and archaeologists will one day discover that the ads of our times are the richest and most faithful daily reflections that any society ever made of its entire range of activities'. Appropriately enough, his words have become sloganised and reduced to a catch-phrase: 'Advertising is the cave art of the twentieth century'. Some would disagree with his statement and argue that, in creating artificial product superiorities, advertising is simply a lie and that, in attempting to create need out of desire, it has paid little heed to reality and has instead invented a parallel world in which ideals are the norm—women are beautiful, men are strong and everyone smiles at breakfast.

True, one could say that even these images are a 'reflection' of the world, providing a poignant insight into our dreams and fears. But sometimes it is easier to interpret them in the way one would photographic negatives—as they depict what people are encouraged to want and not what they actually have. No doubt, as you look through the chapters, you will find evidence to support advertising's sternest critics. But, at the same time, you will see much to support the claim that advertising is more than a craft—it's an art. Thousands of ads have combined exquisite design, illustrations or photography with great wit, flair and inventiveness. Certainly, in this book you will find examples of the work of some of the greatest artists, photographers, designers and typographers of the last 120 years.

What they have created, to a greater or lesser extent, bears the imprint of history—the Industrial Revolution, two World Wars, the Russian Revolution, the depression of the thirties, the prosperity of the fifties, the social revolution of the sixties and the backlash of the seventies and eighties. But the purpose of this book is not to use advertising to examine the politics, economics, and ideology of the last 120 years. Quite the reverse. This is a gallery of advertising images that uses history only as a backdrop to create a sense of time and place.

We decided to start in 1850, but advertising was much in evidence before then. As long ago as 500BC, the Greeks were engraving announcements for the theatre in stone. And 400 years later, in Rome, it was commonplace to find advertisements for the Arena painted on walls throughout the city. The Romans were ingenious and creative in their use of media—prostitutes hammered nails into the soles of their sandals so that they printed the words 'Follow me' into the dusty streets. Much later, in 1477, William Caxton produced the first printed advertisements to promote his publication, 'The Pyes of Salisbury'. The ad was somewhat less interesting than the event itself which could be said to mark the birth of modern advertising. However, nearly another 150 years passed before the first newspaper advertisements started to appear. A measure of their success in England was the publication in 1657 of 'The Publicke Advertiser', a quarterly newsbook devoted entirely to advertisements.

Throughout the next two centuries, both in England and America, advertising made its slow infiltration into commerce and culture. But it was not until the middle of the 19th century that society had organised itself in such a way as to make advertising an essential and integral part of developing economies. By 1850 the Industrial Revolution was transforming societies beyond recognition. Mass manufacture was leading to an age of abundance and the increasing automation of agricultural machinery had caused a migration to the towns and the rapid growth of commercial centres where advertising could be used to regulate demand.

Throughout the latter half of the century the efficacy of advertising was greatly increased by rapid advances in printing technology. Off-set litho brought high-quality colour reproduction and the poster boom of the 80s. Newspapers and magazines became cheaper and therefore a more accessible and far-reaching medium. In the aftermath of the Industrial Revolution the world became a smaller place or, to borrow another McLuhanism, a 'global village'. And this led naturally to the development of a global market.

Advertising played a crucial role in the development of that market. In its symbiotic relationship with mass manufacture, it managed to create perceived differentials in virtually identical products—especially cheap, repeat-purchase household items. No longer an oddity or novelty, it was to become one of the most effective tools in a new field of human endeavour—marketing. All of which presented a golden opportunity to the manufacturers, who started to advertise without restraint. Outrageous claims were made for products—particularly patent medicines—with no fear of prosecution.

But eventually criticism and complaint led to the formation of regulatory bodies and manufacturers began to fear that blatant overclaims would drive disappointed customers to try competitive brands. It became clear that a more subtle language of persuasion was required.

Advertising agencies and consultants started to appear in the 1880s and by 1900 there were colleges in America that specialised in teaching copywriting skills. That year also saw the publication of the first of many treatises called 'the psychology of advertising'. The title alone acknowledged that advertising expertise in the future would require an intimate understanding of human desires, fears and motivations.

What has ensued is a complex language of images and symbols that has played upon our basic emotions. It has managed to connect our feelings about such issues as sex, fame and power with a diverse range of consumer products and services. You will find that every decade has its own style—Edwardian elegance, the prettiness of the 1920s, the artiness of the thirties and so on. But the principles and ploys of persuasion have barely changed—hyperbole, testimonial, negative sell, fair comparison, before and after, knocking copy. They have all been around since the early days of the business.

Perhaps the real art of advertising is that, with these same devices, it still produces work that is stunningly original, ads that grab and hold our attention. The best of them not only reflect our tastes, they help to form them.

CHAPTER ONE

ADVERTISING WITHOUT MEDIA? It would be like music without sound. And so, the thirty years covered in this chapter were, perhaps, most significant for the development of the newspaper as an advertising medium. During this period, the printing industry rapidly employed the techniques of mass manufacture and automation that had been the driving force of the Industrial Revolution. As a result, there was a dramatic increase in the number of copies printed and a sharp drop in price. Whereas previously newspapers had been borrowed and shared, now everyone could afford to buy one. At the same time, there was a fantastic growth in the number of women's magazines. In England in 1850 there were only four such publications; by the turn of the century there were more than fifty.

Suddenly, the new industrialists had acquired a means by which they could address and control the markets they had watched develop and expand in the early decades of the century. Needless to say, they did not hesitate to use it.

However, while the media were developing at a pace, advertising itself was still finding its feet. Most of the ads in this chapter could be just as well described as announcements. Each one announces a product or service and its price. Some elaborate on quality or function. Others give details as to where a purchase can be made. But none really conforms to the view of advertising we have today: no advertising strategies or attempts at branding; no knocking copy in among the superiority claims. And the typographic style was in most cases supplied by the publication and does not represent any effort on the part of the manufacturer to carve out his own aesthetic niche.

But in spite of, or perhaps because of, these limitations and constraints the period has its own particular style and the ads have an immediate, naive and honest sort of charm.

TAYLOR BROTHERS MARAVILLA COCOA MILLS

LONDON

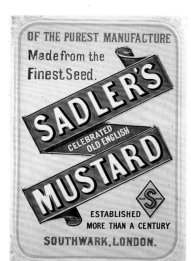

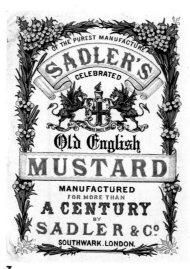

POSTERS, MAGAZINE INSERTS,
SHOWCARDS AND HANDBILLS, UK

1 *CLIENT:* TAYLOR BROTHERS

2 *CLIENT:* BROWN AND POLSON

3 *CLIENT:* T. & H. SMITH

4 *CLIENT:* J. S. FRY AND SONS

5 *CLIENT:* GOODALL BACKHOUSE
AND COMPANY

6 *CLIENT:* SADLER AND COMPANY

7 *CLIENT:* SADLER AND COMPANY

8 *CLIENT:* KEEN'S MUSTARD

There was no concept of an advertising
strategy at the time these ads were made and
they are included here simply as examples of
the illustrative and typographic styles of the
time. However, it's interesting to see a special
panel in the Keen's Mustard poster for the
insertion of the retailer's name and address.
Today this would be considered a ploy to
encourage the retailer to stock the product.
But then it was just as much the case of
giving credibility and respectability to the
manufacturers via association with a well
established shop.

*Although the printing on all of these
examples is very fine, you'll notice that the
colours are flat tones and are not overprinted
to create a full colour effect. This technique
would come later after the influence of Jules
Cheret.*

THE PATENT CIRCULAR-FRONT COOKING RANGE, with Hot-Closet, Steam Kettles, and Roasting Screens.

1

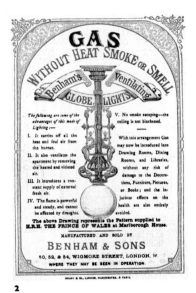

2

3

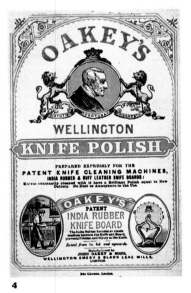

4

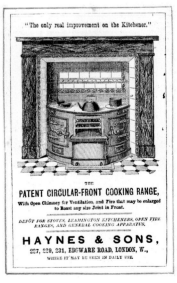

5

6

7

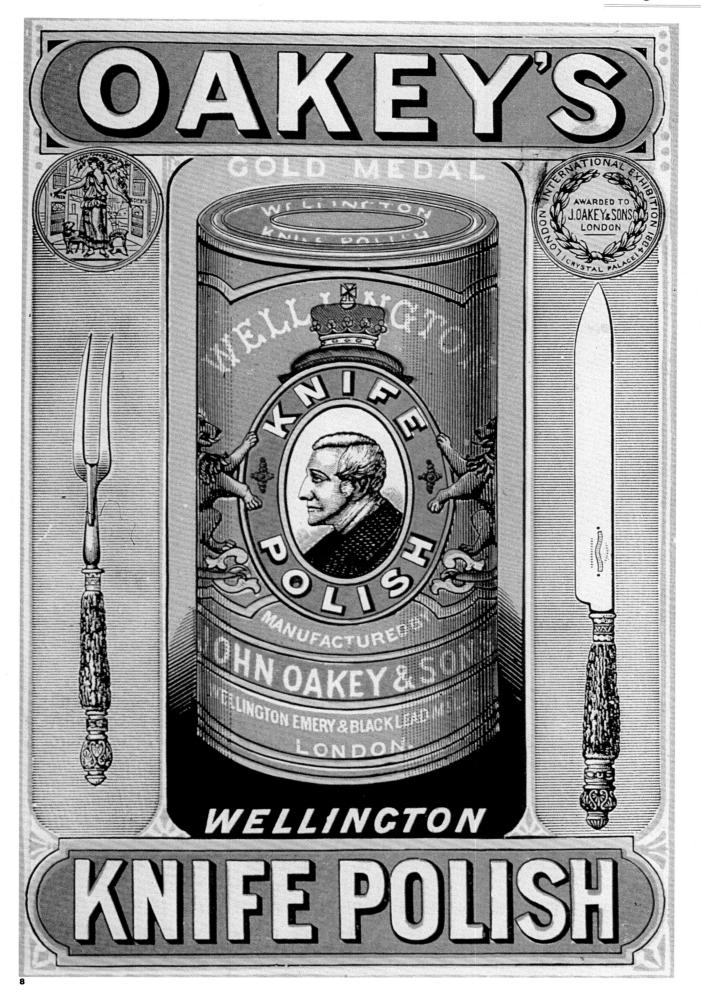

8

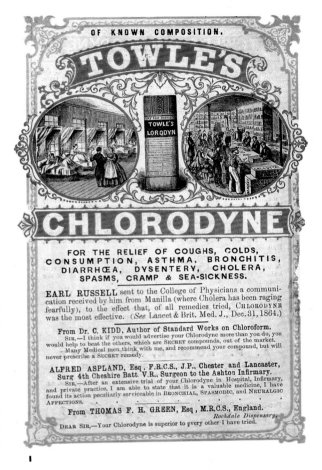

1

2

3

4

5

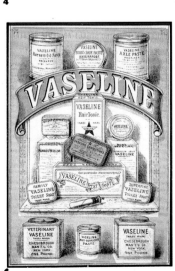

6

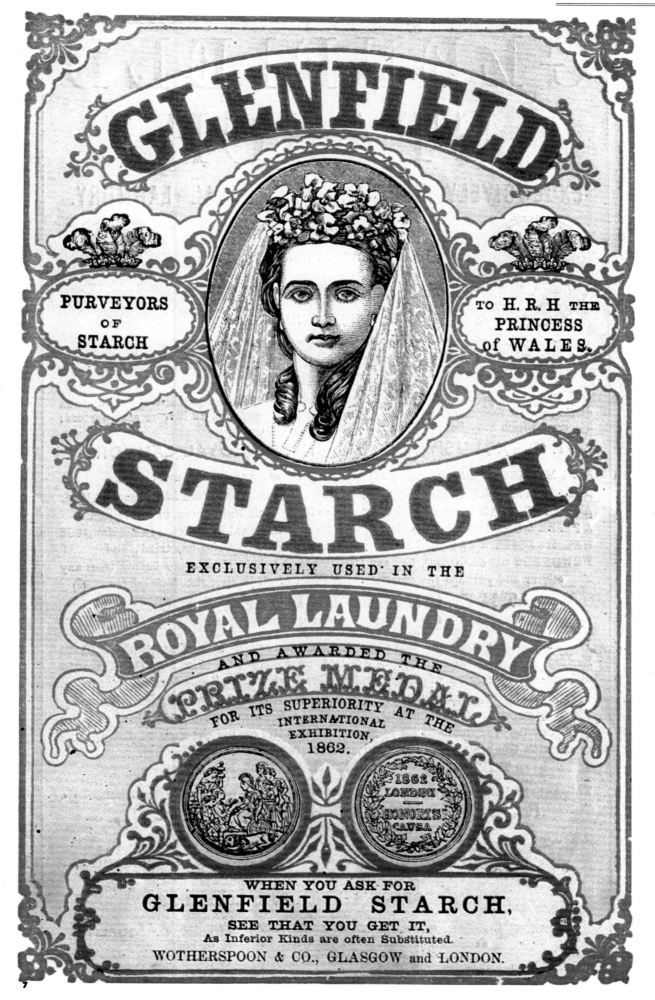

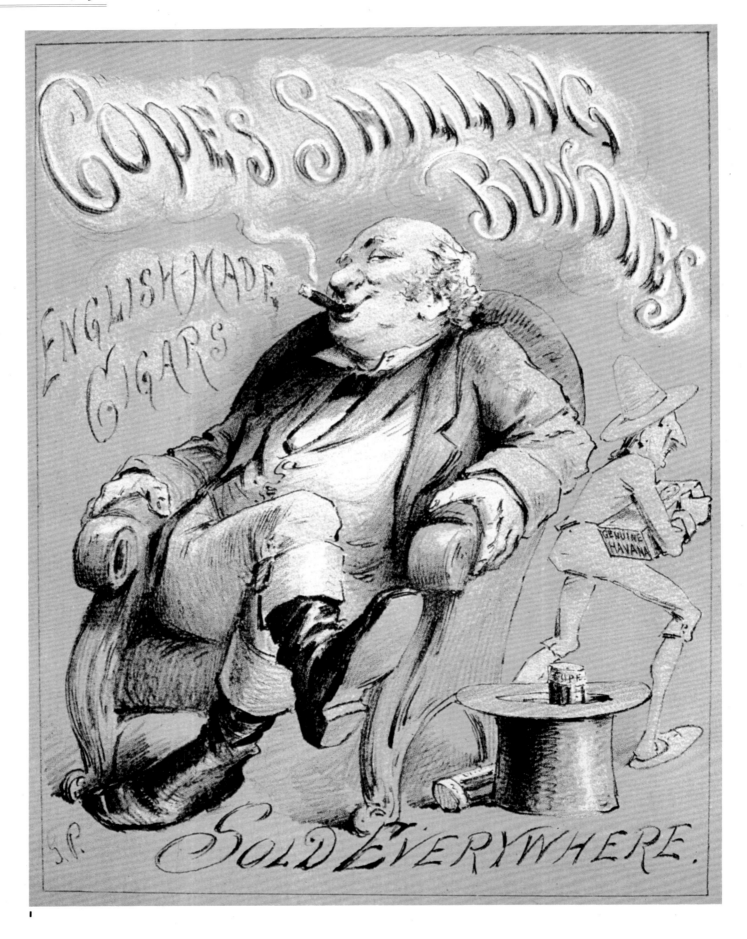

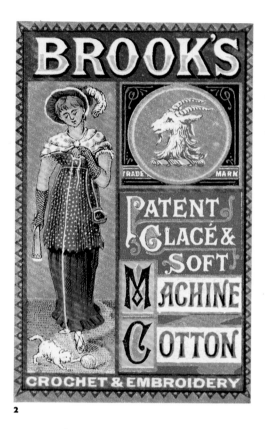

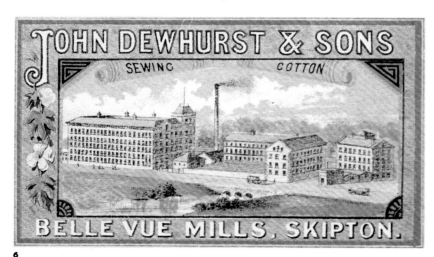

1 *ALMANAC COVER, 1856, UK*
CLIENT: RIMMEL'S PERFUMERY

2-5 *POSTERS, 1860s, UK*
CLIENT: RIMMEL'S PERFUMERY

6 *POSTER, 1860s, UK*
CLIENT: PIESSE AND LUBIN

7-8 *POSTERS, 1862, UK*
CLIENT: RIMMEL'S PERFUMERY

It has now become quite rare to see perfume advertising that doesn't feature women but in the middle of the last century these products were sold with floral imagery that was intended to evoke a sense of fragrance and not of sophistication.

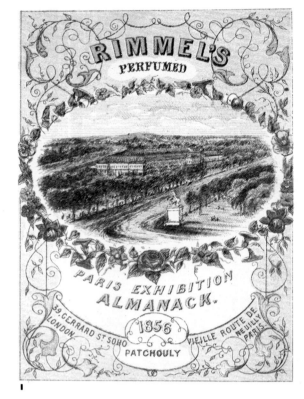

1

2

3

4

5

6

7

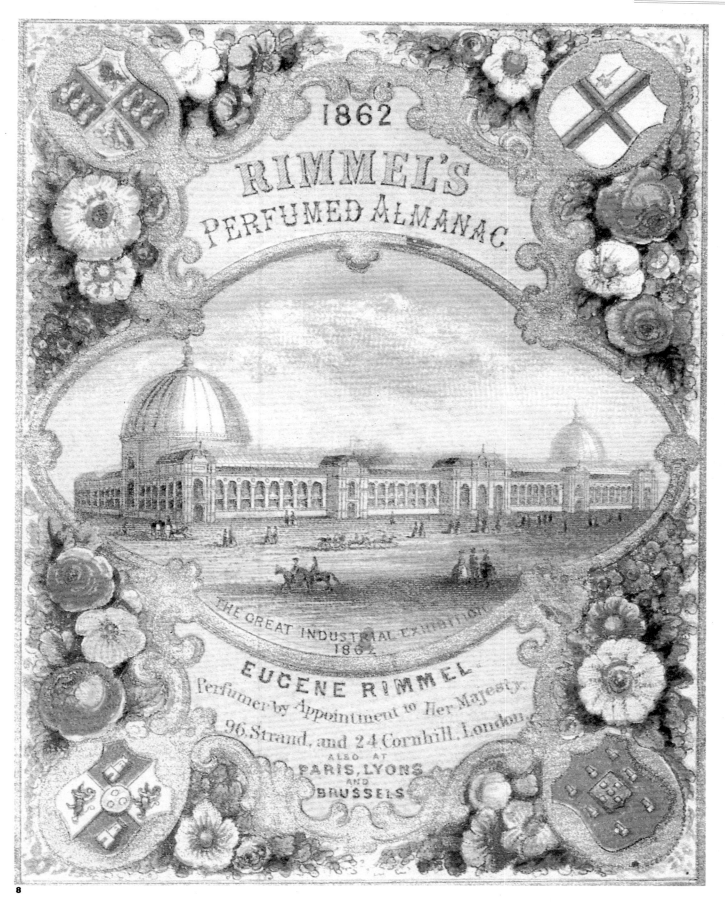

1862

RIMMEL'S
PERFUMED ALMANAC

THE GREAT INDUSTRIAL EXHIBITION
1862

EUGENE RIMMEL
Perfumer by Appointment to Her Majesty.
96, Strand, and 24 Cornhill, London.
ALSO AT
PARIS, LYONS
AND
BRUSSELS

8

1

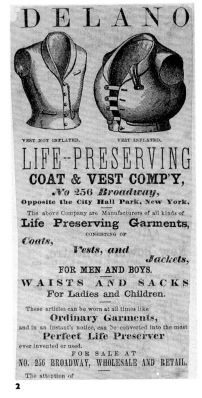

2

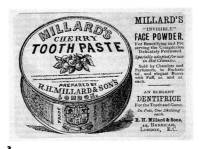

3

4

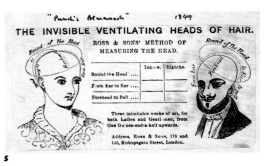

5

6

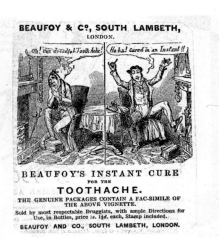

7

Width.	Length.	Tinned Wire.	Brass Wire.
2ft. 6in.	1ft. 4in.	£3 15 0	£4 15 0
3ft. 0in.	1ft. 6in.	4 12 0	5 12 0
3ft. 6in.	1ft. 6in.	6 0 0	7 5 0

W. MYERS & CO.
Wire Workers and Manufacturers,
132 Euston Road, LONDON.

CATALOGUES ON APPLICATION.

8

ICE SAFES.

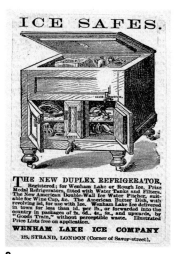

THE NEW DUPLEX REFRIGERATOR,
Registered; for Wenham Lake or Rough Ice. Price Medal Refrigerators, fitted with Water Tanks and Filters. The New American Double-Wall Ice Water Pitcher, suitable for Wine Cup, &c. The American Butter Dish, with revolving lid, for use with Ice. Wenham Lake Ice delivered in town for less than 1d. per lb., or forwarded into the country in packages of 2s. 6d. 4s., 5s., and upwards, by "Goods Train," without perceptible waste. Illustrated Price Lists free on application.

WENHAM LAKE ICE COMPANY
125, STRAND, LONDON (Corner of Savoy-street).

9

Wedding Trousseaux complete, from the most inexpensive to the richest. One of the Largest Stocks in the Kingdom to choose from.

Embroidered Pocket Handkerchiefs, from 10s. 6d. to 21s. the dozen, specially worked for this house.

The distinguishing features of the Establishment are, Excellence in the Quality of the Materials used, beauty of Needlework, and Moderation in Prices.

Every article necessary for the Layette.

Short Coating at moderate prices.

Mrs Young herself superintends the business, and is assisted by experienced assistants in every department.

Every requisite for India. Ladies assisted in their choice by some valuable hints from a Resident.

MRS. T. G. YOUNG.
LADIES OUTFITTING AND BABY LINEN WAREHOUSES
128 & 129 OXFORD ST. W.
ONE GUINEA.

MRS. YOUNG'S "ONE GUINEA" DRESSING GOWNS.
ILLUSTRATIONS & PATTERNS POST FREE.

CLOAKS HOODS & PELISSES LISTS POST FREE

BABY LINEN IN SETS FROM 5 TO 50 GUINEAS.

WEDDING OUTFITS FROM 20 TO 100 GUINEAS.

INDIAN OUTFITS FROM 25 TO 100 GUINEAS.

TROUSSEAUX & INDIAN OUTFITS.
PRICE LISTS POST FREE.

128 & 129, OXFORD-STREET, LONDON, W.

10

BOULEVARD D'ORNANO, 11, 13 & 15
Tout par l'épargne!
Crédit a tout le monde
CRESPIN AINÉ
DE VIDOUVILLE
Bᵈ d'Ornano.

— Perdu! Sans espoir et sans crédit, que vais-je devenir avec mes six enfants?
— Eh bien, tu retravailleras, et avec du courage et mon crédit, tu reconstitueras ton capital.

11

c.1960.

FOR GENTLEMEN.

The largest assortment of materials, adapted either for morning or for evening wear, may be inspected at H. J. and D. Nicoll's warerooms. Cutters are employed for each specialty, and perfection in the fit and general appearance of each garment is thus attained. By the employment of many hundreds of workpeople, military outfits and liveries may be obtained with very short notice. The prices vary from two guineas, but for the lounging or travelling suit, and to which the sketch refers, the price will be regulated by the nature of the material selected. H. J. and D. NICOLL, 114, 116, 118, 120, Regent-street, and 22, Cornhill, London.

12

THE SHEFFIELD FURNISHING WAREHOUSE.
J. JONES & SON,
SILK MERCERS,
WHOLESALE & RETAIL
DRAPERS,
63, MARKET-PLACE.
ILLUSTRATED CATALOGUES BY POST

13

25

CHAPTER TWO

IN THE LAST twenty years of the 19th century the world was bombarded with the effects of the Industrial Revolution. Developments in transportation were rapidly changing our sense of scale—a train could cross America in as little as six days, Karl Benz and Gottlieb Daimler were building prototype motor cars and the bicycle was becoming a common sight. 'The Age of Invention' had by then given us the telephone, the phonograph and the electric light bulb. And while the camera was becoming a craze in American households, the Lumière brothers were already pioneering the first cinema films.

All of these events were reflected in the world of advertising, which was then enjoying a period later to be described as 'The Golden Age of the Poster'. Posters were adorning city streets long before the 1880s. (They take their name from the wooden roadside posts to which the bills were originally attached.) In fact, in 1851, there were more than 150 bill-stickers in London posting around 90,000 bills every week.

Throughout the second half of the century the poster evolved from a typographical to a visual medium, with the textual element reduced to a bare minimum. This emphasis on imagery was enhanced by the development of lithography, which made possible the gradation of colour and tone.

Both aesthetically and technically the real pioneering work took place in the late 1870s in Paris where the artist, Jules Chéret, and his printer, Chaix, refined the lithographic process to the point where long print-runs became commercially viable. Chéret's posters for the Folies-Bergère were the talk of the town and critical acclaim led to the involvement of other 'serious' artists such as Mucha and Henri de Toulouse-Lautrec. However, Lautrec's Japanese-influenced work was never as popular as Cheret's sparkling girls, who were known locally as the 'Chérettes'.

In England the first poster, in the modern sense, was for a production of *The Woman in White* in 1871. But the English infatuation with posters didn't begin until 1886 and the unveiling of the Pears' campaign. When Thomas J. Barratt bought Sir John Everett Millais' portrait of his young grandson and then added a bar of Pears' Soap to the painting, he outraged the art world. But the general public did not share these wounded sensibilities and 'Bubbles' was a sensational success. As other manufacturers followed Barratt's lead in exploiting the arts, poster-collecting became a popular pastime and there was even a magazine devoted to the subject. Similar developments were taking place in America, where Will Bradley and Maxfield Parish, both influenced by Aubrey Beardsley, were working in a style comparable to that found in Europe.

Fortunately, the craze for collecting means that many of the originals have survived intact. They bear witness to that moment when art and advertising first shook hands.

1 *POSTER, 1893, FRANCE*
CLIENT: FOLIES BERGÈRES
ARTIST: JULES CHERET

2 *POSTER, c.1890, FRANCE*
CLIENT: UNKNOWN
ARTIST: LOUIS GALICE

3 *POSTER, 1884, FRANCE*
CLIENT: FOLIES BERGÈRES
ARTIST: UNKNOWN

4 *POSTER, 1891, FRANCE*
CLIENT: ZIDLER, MOULIN ROUGE
ARTIST: HENRI DE TOULOUSE-
LAUTREC

The history of the poster owes a great deal to Cheret and Lautrec. Certainly Lautrec's Art Nouveau style work for the Moulin Rouge gave great credibility to the poster as an art form. But without Cheret's pioneering development of chromolithography it is unlikely that the mass reproduction of posters would have been possible at this time.

1

2

3

1 *POSTER, FRANCE*
CLIENT: NOUVEAU THEATRE
ARTIST: JULES CHERET

2 *POSTER, FRANCE*
CLIENT: THEATRE NATIONAL DE
L'OPERA
ARTIST: JULES CHERET

3 *POSTER, FRANCE*
CLIENT: MOULIN ROUGE
ARTIST: JULES CHERET

*Three examples from the 1890s that display
Cheret's pioneering development of printing
techniques.*

4

5

6

7

4 *POSTER, 1896, FRANCE*

CLIENT: THEATRE DE LA
RENAISSANCE

ARTIST: ALPHONSE MUCHA

5 *POSTER, 1895, FRANCE*

CLIENT: SARAH BERNHARDT'S
AMERICAN TOUR

ARTIST: ALPHONSE MUCHA

6 *POSTER, 1897, FRANCE*

CLIENT: SOCIETE POPULAIRE DES
BEAUX ARTS

ARTIST: ALPHONSE MUCHA

7 *POSTER, 1896, FRANCE*

CLIENT: SALON DES CENTS

ARTIST: ALPHONSE MUCHA

*Art Nouveau, which originated in London
and then spread to the continent, was a
reaction to the academic historicism of the
late 19th century. It was most commonly
found in practical and applied arts and
these four posters by Mucha are classics of
the style.*

ARTIST: HENRI DE TOULOUSE LAUTREC

Seven posters that reveal Lautrec's superb artistry and the subtleties that printers were achieving in the late 1890s.

1 *POSTER, 1893, FRANCE*

CLIENT: VICTOR JOZE'S PUBLISHING HOUSE

2 *POSTER, 1893, FRANCE*

3 *POSTER, 1893, FRANCE*

CLIENT: JARDIN DE PARIS

This is regarded as one of Lautrec's most adventurous pieces — the framing of the dancer, the treatment of the music sheets, the distortion of the double bass, the strange shape of the player's head, all illustrate how he was breaking away from the conception of the pretty poster. Jane Avril was a dancer who sat for him many times as a model.

4 *POSTER, 1899, FRANCE*

5 *POSTER, FRANCE*

CLIENT: EXHIBITION POSTER

6 *POSTER, 1896, FRANCE*

CLIENT: INTERNATIONAL POSTER EXHIBITION

7 *POSTER, 1892, FRANCE*

CLIENT: VICTOR JOZE'S PUBLISHERS

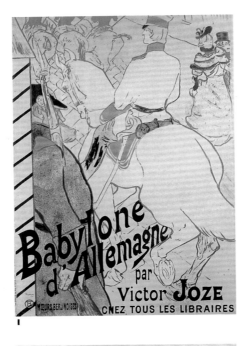

1

2

3

4

5

6

7

CLIENT: JEROME B. RICE AND
COMPANY

*POSTER CAMPAIGN, 1887-89,
USA*

*This campaign was way ahead of its time. It
must be one of the first and finest examples
of taking the product and giving it a human
form. And, as well as beautiful typography
and illustration, there is even the occasional
pun.*

1

2

3

4

The poster for Snag-proof boots is a wonderful example of early advertising at its best. The drawing, which is presumably a reference to the tale of the Elves and the Shoemaker, combines a beautiful portrayal of the boot with a humorous demonstration of its benefits. There is an element of hyperbole in all of these ads which has perhaps gone a little too far in the poster for Silver Pine Healing Oil.

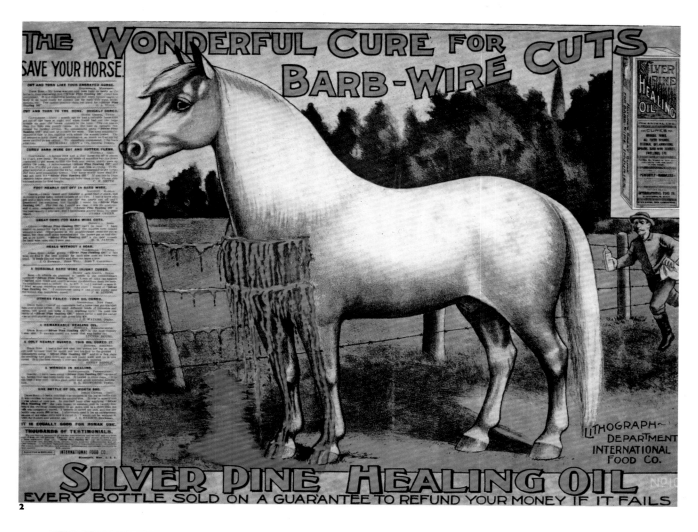

2

3

4

2

3

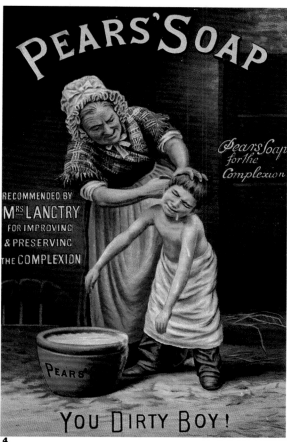

4

5

CLIENT: PEARS' SOAPS

POSTERS AND MAGAZINE INSERTS,
UK

When, in 1862, Thomas J. Barratt joined
the company of A. & F. Pears he instigated a
publicity campaign that has led many to
refer to him as the 'Father of Modern
Advertising'. As well as securing the
endorsements of prominent doctors, skin-care
specialists and even Lillie Langtry, he
managed to purchase the painting 'Bubbles'
by Sir John Everett Millais for £2200 and
persuade the artist to permit the addition of
a clear bar of Pears' soap. Millais was the
most popular artist of the day and his
painting set the style of an unashamedly
sentimental advertising campaign that
featured women, children and flowers and
which continues until this day in the form of
the Pears' Girls Portraits.

CLIENT: PEARS' SOAPS

1-4 *POSTERS, INSERTS, UK*

As was the case with much of advertising from this period, many of these images appeared in different media and sizes. The company considered itself philanthropic in that the Pears Annual made previously unattainable works of art available to the public at an easily affordable price. Certainly the quality of reproduction was extraordinary, considering that the chromolithographic process involved printing from 24 different colour blocks.

CLIENT: MAYPOLE DYES

5-8 *POSTERS AND MAGAZINE INSERTS, UK*

Maypole used the entire colour spectrum in both their illustrations and typography to suggest the wide range of dyes that they manufactured. The exception here is plate 8, in which the message is more concerned with the wash-resistant nature of the product.

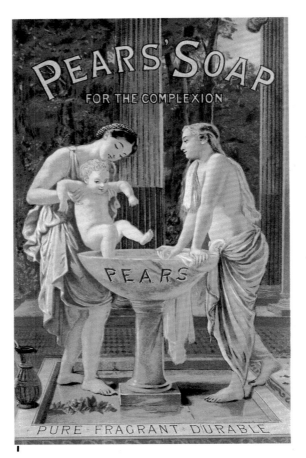

1

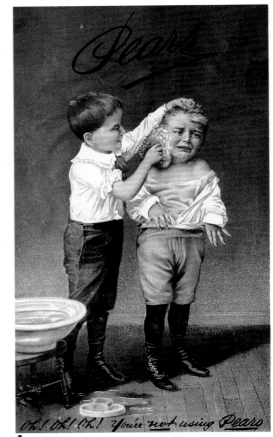

2

3

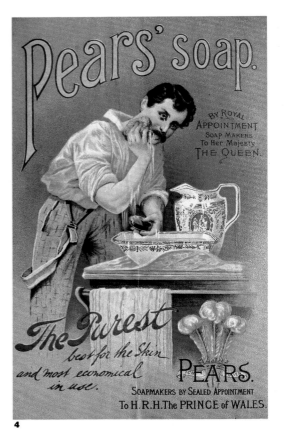

4

5

6

7

8

1

2

3

4

POSTERS AND SHOWCARDS, USA

1 *CLIENT:* J. & P. COATS AND COMPANY

2 *CLIENT:* J. R. LEESON AND COMPANY

3 *CLIENT:* WHEELER AND WILSON

4 *CLIENT:* A. L. ELIEL

5 *CLIENT:* AYER'S CATHARTIC PILLS

6 *CLIENT:* WOONSOCKET SHOES

7 *CLIENT:* BUCHAN'S CARBOLIC SOAP

The poster boom of the eighties and nineties was as evident in America as it was in the UK. We've chosen seven here that illustrate the range and subtlety of colour that was already being achieved.

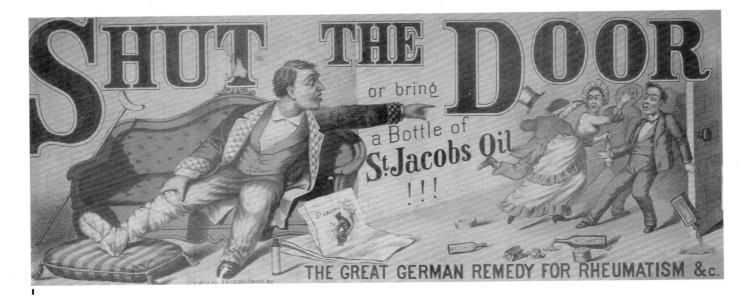

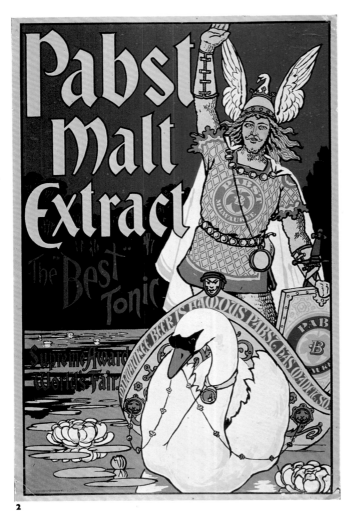

4

5

1 *POSTER, USA*

CLIENT: ST JACOB'S OIL

2 *POSTER, 1896, USA*

CLIENT: PABST MALT EXTRACT

3 *POSTER, 1886, USA*

CLIENT: AYER'S HAIR VIGOR

4-5 *POSTERS, 1890s, USA*

CLIENT: MRS WINSLOW'S
SOOTHING SYRUP

6 *SHOWCARD, 1887, USA*

CLIENT: E. W. HOYT AND COMPANY

7 *POSTER, 1890s, USA*

CLIENT: EAGLE BRAND MILK

*These posters are typical of their period but
the St Jacob's Oil ad is unusual in that
typographically it places the emphasis on an
idea and not the brand name.*

6

7

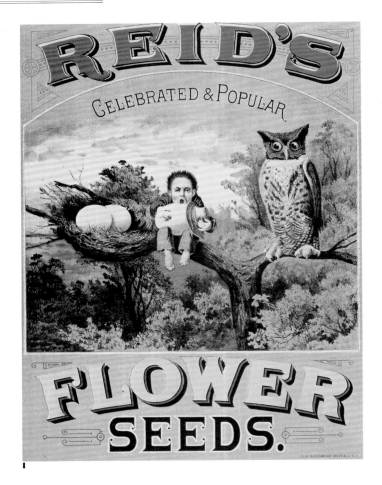

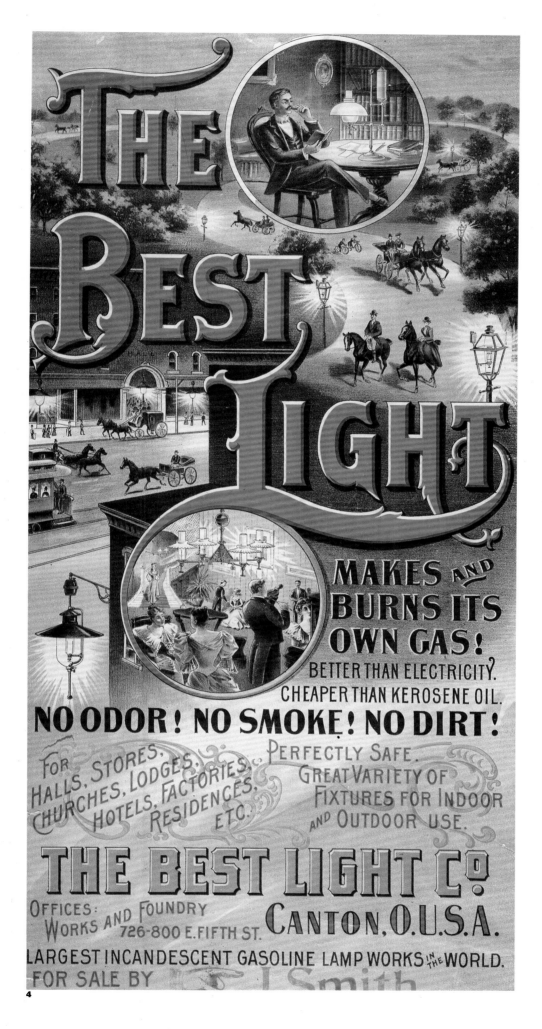

1 *POSTER, 1895, USA*

CLIENT: REID'S FLOWER SEEDS

2 *POSTER, USA*

CLIENT: D. M. FERRY AND
COMPANY

3 *POSTER, USA*

CLIENT: DUNLAP'S FLOWER SEEDS

4 *POSTER, USA*

CLIENT: THE BEST LIGHT
COMPANY

*You can see the extent to which advertising
posters had become a popular art form in the
ad for D. M. Ferry Flower Seeds. In return
for 10 cents or seed packets to the value of 50
cents, the company offered copies of the
poster without the wording.*

47

CLIENT: BOVRIL

POSTERS, LEAFLETS AND
MAGAZINE INSERTS, UK

Bovril was first sold in Canada in 1874 and then imported to England by its inventor, John Johnston, in 1886. The imagery of the advertising covered every possible claim that could be made for a beef extract — from gastronomic delights, quickness and convenience, caring motherhood, and strength-building to patriotism.

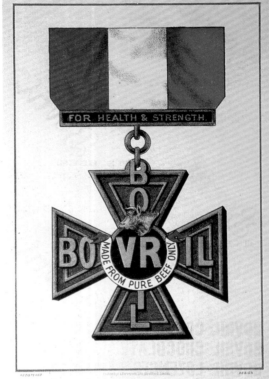

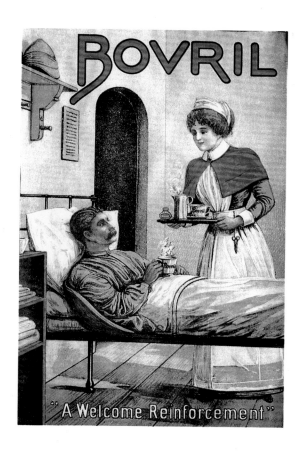

"A Welcome Reinforcement"

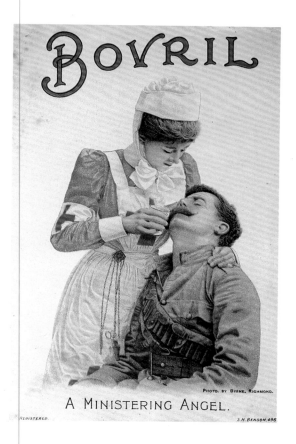

A MINISTERING ANGEL.

CLIENT: CADBURY AND COMPANY

*POSTERS AND TRADE CARDS, 1890s,
UK*

*The Cadbury company were quick to
develop a campaign theme within their
advertising. Despite the differing
typography and illustrative styles, their
posters and trade cards shared a
commonality of design and all re-stated the
same product benefit — purity.*

1

2

3

4

5

6

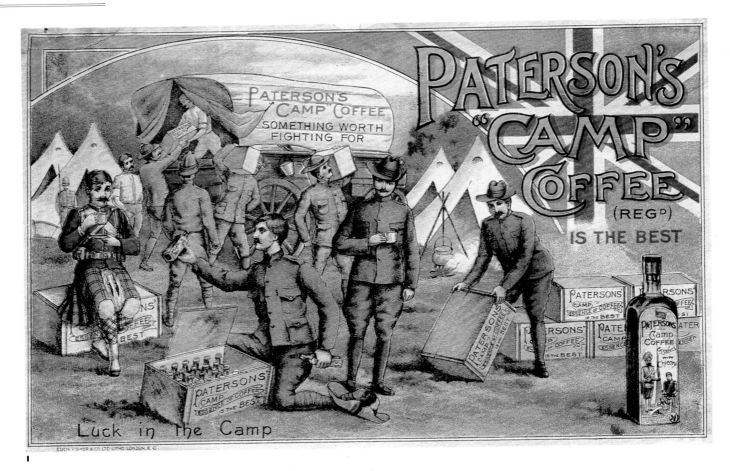

1

2

3

4

5

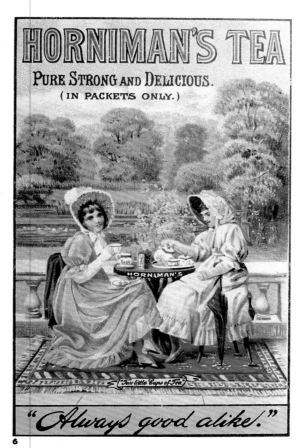

6

7

CLIENT: CAMP COFFEE

1/7 *SHOWCARDS AND POSTERS, UK*

CLIENT: HORNIMAN'S TEA

2-6 *SHOWCARDS, UK*

Although each advertisement is beautiful in itself, the Horniman's series has no graphic consistency either within each ad or within the campaign as a whole. These years are well in advance of branding and typography is essentially decorative.

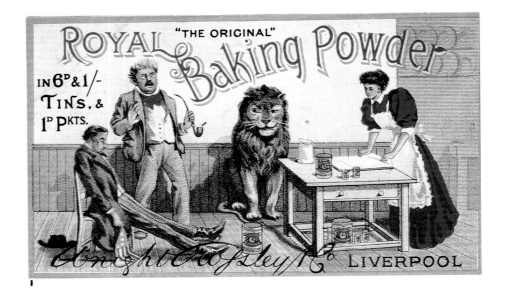

Posters number 6 and 7 are particularly interesting as they are among the first that Oxo produced. Before this date the product was called Liebig Company's Extract.

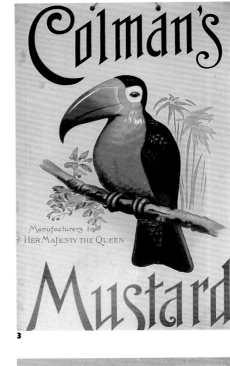

6

7

8

9

INSERTS, HANDBILLS
AND SHOWCARDS, UK

1 CLIENT: PEEK, FREAN BISCUITS

2 CLIENT: HOVIS BAKERY

3 CLIENT: ENO'S FRUIT SALT

4 CLIENT: ROSE'S LIME CORDIAL

5 CLIENT: KOPS CREAM DRINK

6 CLIENT: COOPER COOPER & CO'S TEAS

7 CLIENT: FRY'S COCOA

8 CLIENT: MASON'S WINE ESSENCES

9 CLIENT: MASON'S EXTRACT OF HERBS

10 CLIENT: HUNTLEY & PALMERS BISCUITS

These ten inserts, handbills and showcards all typify the pictorial style of the age but it is interesting to note that only the Eno's Fruit Salt ad has consistent typography that is representative of the brand.

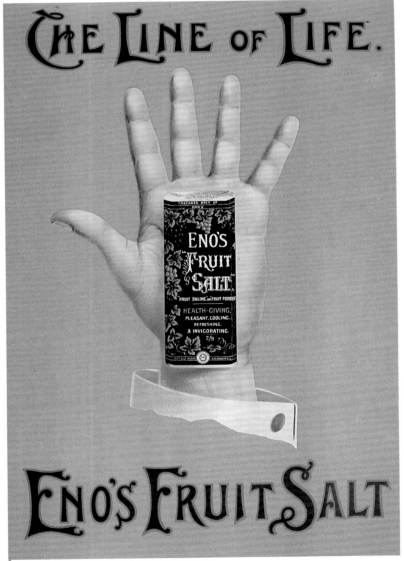

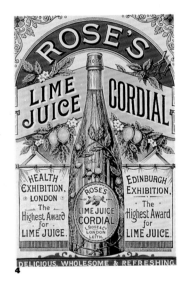

COOPER COOPER & C⁰'s
TEAS

6

7

8

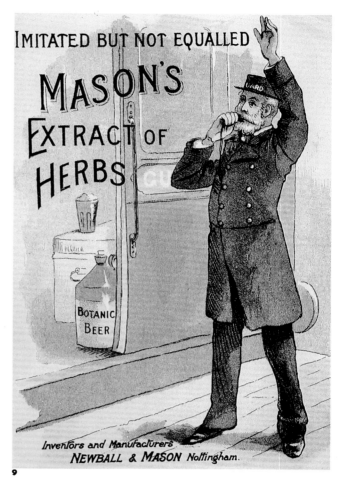

9

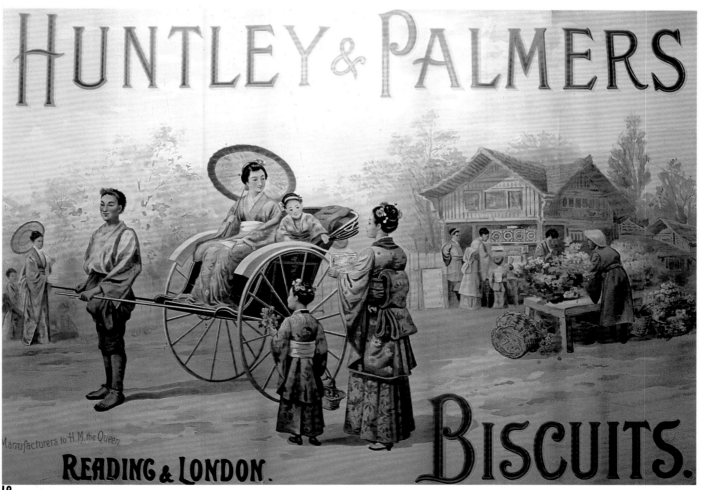

10

1 *POSTER, 1892, FRANCE*
CLIENT: CHOCOLAT MEXICAIN
MASSON
ARTIST: EUGENE GRASSET
2 *POSTER, 1890, ITALY*
CLIENT: G. BUTON AND COMPANY
3 *POSTER, FRANCE*
CLIENT: A.H.F.

4 *POSTER, 1898*
CLIENT: NADIR CIGARETTES
ARTIST: LOUIS CORINTH

1

2

3

4

CHAPTER THREE

IF THE INDUSTRIAL REVOLUTION made the world a smaller place, it did not bring a greater sense of unity. At the turn of the century there were distinctly contrasting moods on each side of the Atlantic. For the Americans this was an era of great hope and optimism—their country had a strong economy and an abundance of natural resources and labour. In 1901 the promise of prosperity and the absence of income tax attracted more than 450,000 immigrants. Ten years later the figure was closer to a million.

But in England the prevalent feelings were of uncertainty. The Boer War was unpopular and incurred foreign hostility. There was civil unrest in Ireland, labour disputes at home and the first inklings of a social revolution as the suffragettes went to ever greater extremes to advance their cause. In 1901 Queen Victoria died and England lost a monarch whose name, over the previous sixty years, had become synonymous with national progress and security. She was succeeded by Edward VII, whose love of refinement was reflected in the elegance of the period in which he ruled.

In 1903 the Wright Brothers took to the air and it was only six years later that Blériot flew across the English Channel in just twenty-six minutes. At the same time, Henry Ford introduced his Model T, the first mass-produced motor car. It would be hard to overestimate the impact of these events on advertising—the motor and aviation industries have been consistently high spenders for the last sixty years.

The first decade of the century also saw the establishment of other long-term advertisers. Lever Brothers, Bisto, Cadbury's, Wills Tobacco, to name but a few, have all maintained high-profile campaigns since that period.

The poster continued to enjoy a craze of popularity in Europe and America and was developing as an advertising medium. In the 1890s much poster imagery had been irrelevant to the product and designed only to catch the eye. Thomas Barratt had mounted a campaign based on optical illusions in London for this exact purpose and many printers stored images to which they simply added the client's name. But after 1900 we find an increasing number of visual themes in support of manufacturer's claims.

The predominant influence from the art world was still Art Nouveau, with its emphasis on decoration, line and the non-representational use of colour.

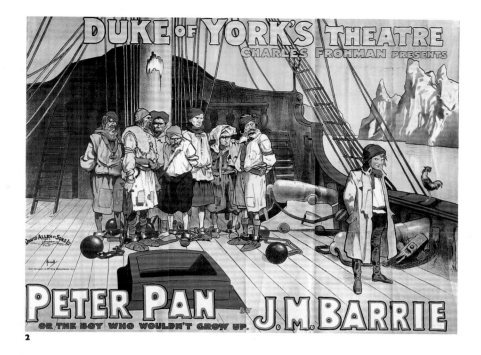

1 *POSTER, 1908, UK*

CLIENT: GREAT NORTHERN RAILWAY

ARTIST: JOHN HASSALL

No collection of advertising art would be complete without Hassall's famous poster for Skegness. We have put it here alongside four examples of the many posters he did for the theatre.

2 *POSTER, 1904, UK*

CLIENT: DUKE OF YORK'S THEATRE

3 *POSTER, 1900, UK*

CLIENT: DRURY LANE THEATRE

4 *POSTER, UK*

CLIENT: DRURY LANE THEATRE

5 *POSTER, UK*

CLIENT: DALY'S THEATRE

MEETING D'AVIATION NICE
10=25 AVRIL 1910

Ch. BsoR

4

One of our favourite posters in this book. Every element — the style of the drawing, the subject, the lighting and the chiselled typography — is suggestive of power, strength and speed.

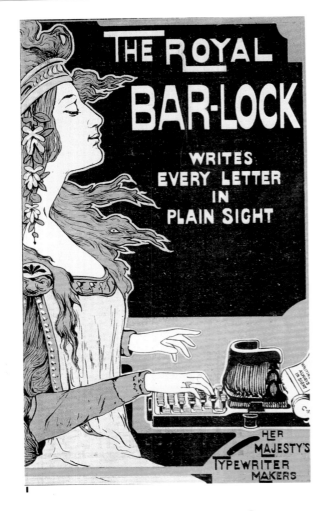

1

2

3

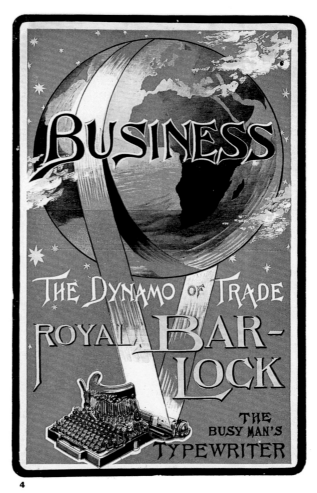

4

CLIENT: ROYAL BARLOCK
TYPEWRITERS

MAGAZINE INSERTS, UK

*The advent of the typewriter was a
significant moment in the history of the
Women's Movement, as it led women out of
the home and into the office. The imagery in
three of these plates is feminine rather than
business-orientated and there is some
influence of the Art Nouveau style.*

1-2 *POSTERS, 1905, UK*
CLIENT: LEVER BROTHERS
PRODUCT: LUX SOAP
ARTIST: JOHN HASSALL
3-4 *POSTERS, UK*
CLIENT: LIFEBUOY SOAP

1

2

3

4

CLIENT: CADBURY'S COCOA

ARTIST: CECIL ALDIN

5 PRESS AD, 1902, UK

6 PRESS AD, 1900, UK

7 PRESS AD, 1901, UK

Advertising strategies change and the Cadbury's Cocoa campaign is a good example. Nowadays we think of cocoa as a relaxing bed-time drink but at the turn of the century it was known as a stimulant that was both refreshing and invigorating.

Dobson, Molle & Co Ltd
Edinburgh
Glasgow & London.

2

I *POSTER, 1904, UK*

CLIENT: DOBSON MOLLE AND COMPANY

PRODUCT: BISTO

ARTIST: JOHN HASSALL

This ad precedes Will Owen's Bisto Kid poster and is shown here in the artwork version before the type was added.

2 *POSTER, 1904, UK*

CLIENT: VERITAS MANTLES

ARTIST: JOHN HASSALL

3 *POSTER, 1908, UK*

CLIENT: RICHMOND GAS FIRES

ARTIST: JOHN HASSALL

4 *POSTER, UK*

CLIENT: CAMERON'S COALS

5 *POSTER, UK*

CLIENT: RASHLEIGH ELECTRIC LAMPS

3

4

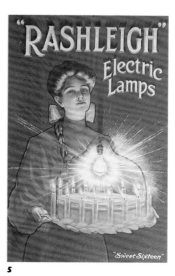

5

1 POSTER, 1902, SWITZERLAND
CLIENT: NESTOR CIGARETTES
ARTIST: SIEGM VON SUCHODOLSKI

2 POSTER, 1903, SWITZERLAND
CLIENT: VAUTIER CIGARETTES
ARTIST: EDMOND BILLE

3 POSTER, 1907, UK
CLIENT: W. D. AND H. O. WILLS
PRODUCT: CAPSTAN NAVY CUT
ARTIST: JOHN HASSALL

1

2

3

4 *POSTER, 1907, SWITZERLAND*
CLIENT: STERNENBERG BREWERY
ARTIST: BURKHARD MANGOLD
5 *POSTER, 1903, FRANCE*
CLIENT: KLAUS CHOCOLATE
ARTIST: LEONETTO CAPPIELLO
6 *POSTER, 1901, FRANCE*
CLIENT: LA TOURAINE BISCUITS
ARTIST: FIRMIN BOUISSET

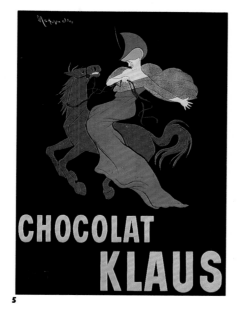

1

2

3

4

5

6

1-3 *POSTERS, 1900, USA*

CLIENT: ROBERT PORTNER
BREWING COMPANY

4 *POSTER, 1900, USA*

CLIENT: F. HOLLENDER AND
COMPANY

5 *POSTER, 1900, USA*

CLIENT: VINCENT HATHAWAY AND
COMPANY

6 *POSTER, 1900, USA*

CLIENT: W. A. GAINES AND
COMPANY

*The imagery in the Robert Portner posters
may seem sexist to some and irrelevant to
others. However, the development of off-set
litho had led to a craze for reproducing
'works of art', on which many advertisers
simply put their names.*

It is very hard to be precise about the exact medium in these examples as it was commonplace at the time to use the same artwork for posters, handbills, leaflets and trade cards.

If you scrutinize the label on a Colman's Mustard tin, you'll find that the product can also be used to soothe aching feet. This famous poster was topical, as it depicted a prospector returning from the Klondyke Gold Rush.

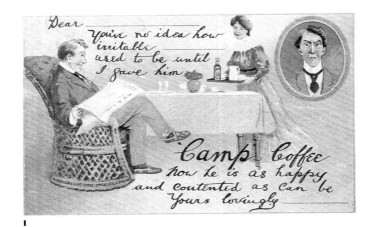

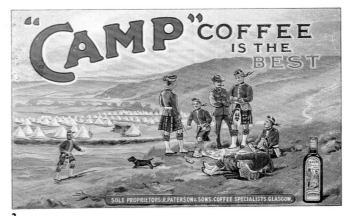

"KASSAMA"

CORN FLOUR

6

*J. W. Beggarstaff was, in fact, the
pseudonym for the illustration partnership
of James Pryde and William Nicholson.*

CHAPTER FOUR

FEW DECADES have witnessed such innovation and upheaval as the years from 1910 to 1919, when change was truly the only constant. While painters struggled to gain public acceptance of Fauvism, Futurism, Expressionism and Cubism, the Russian Ballet under Diaghilev took the world by storm. It visited London in 1911 and New York in 1916. Sets by Picasso and Chagall, music by Debussy and Ravel, the dancing of Nijinski—it was a spectacle the likes of which had never been seen before. A new musical form was also emerging—jazz. Although confined in its early years within the narrow limits of Ragtime, it was soon to develop and challenge popular notions of harmony and melody in much the same way that abstract painting was confronting conventions of representational art. But, without doubt, the major cultural event was the arrival of cinema. A novelty act in 1903, fifteen years later motion pictures were the most popular form of public entertainment and Hollywood a new capital in the world of art.

It is hard to imagine such a chaos of creativity prevailing at a time when the drama on the political stage was so grim and hopeless. Two murders changed the course of history. In 1914 World War I began after the Archduke Franz Ferdinand, heir to the Austrian Empire, was assassinated. In 1917 the Bolsheviks killed the Russian Czar and his family and started the Russian Revolution. Advertising had a 'good war'. By this time advertising agencies had organised themselves into the departments you find today and they were well prepared to handle the responsibilities of producing government advertising. They also enjoyed the status that this new role conferred upon them. World War I was good for business. Up until the paper-shortage, many advertisers took advantage of the rise in newspaper circulation and from a creative point of view it was a chance for the industry to sharpen the tools of persuasion.

From the posters of World War I and the Russian Revolution, advertising learned a great deal about the techniques of manipulating emotions. As well as playing on feelings of patriotism, honour and love of family, they took caricature and hyperbole to new extremes in the evocation of fear, guilt and hatred. This use of negative emotions has been put to effective use by advertising ever since and is now most obvious in the device of 'negative sell'—in which an ad depicts the tragic consequences of failing to buy the product.

SCHLITTENFAHRT

1

❀ EISLAUF. ❀

2

DAVOS

WINTERKUREN

GRAPH. ANSTALT J.E. WOLFENSBERGER ZÜRICH

3

❀ SKILAUF. ❀

4

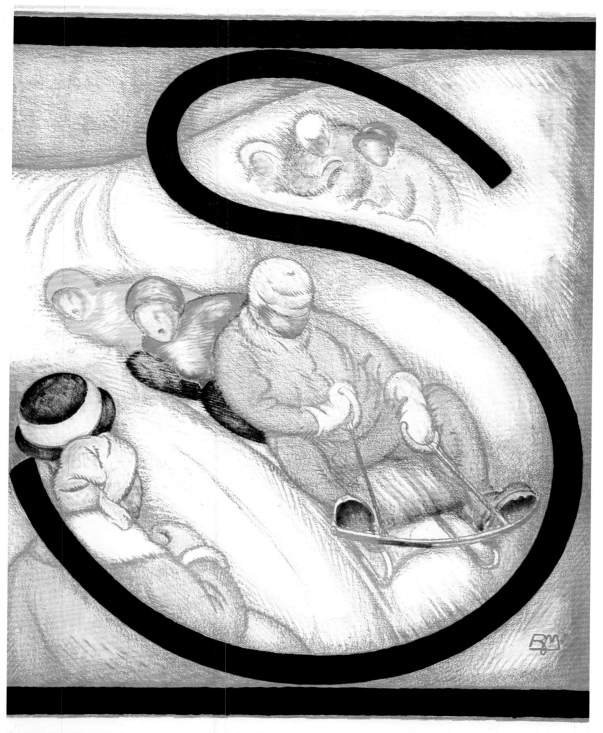

5

SCHLITTENSPORT

CLIENT: DAVOS TOURIST OFFICE
POSTERS, 1916, SWITZERLAND
ARTIST: BURKHARD MANGOLD
1 *HEADLINE:* 'SLEDGING'
2 *HEADLINE:* 'ICE SKATING'
3 *HEADLINE:* 'HEALTH SPA'
4 *HEADLINE:* 'SKI-ING'
5 *HEADLINE:* 'TOBOGGANING'

Side by side these five posters all spell out the name Davos, a winter holiday resort, and each one illustrates and titles one of the amenities that were available there.

1 *POSTER, 1914, NETHERLANDS*
CLIENT: H.Y.S.M.
ARTIST: WILLY GLUITER

2 *POSTER, 1917, HUNGARY*
CLIENT: BUDAPEST MILITARY
AIRCRAFT EXHIBITION
ARTIST: BELA MOLDOVAN

3 *POSTER, 1911, GERMANY*
CLIENT: LIMETREE CABARET
ARTIST: JO STEINER

1

2

CLIENT: LEVER BROTHERS

POSTERS, UK

1-5 *PRODUCT:* LUX SOAP

6-11 *PRODUCT:* SUNLIGHT SOAP

1/2/3/4/10/11 *ARTIST:* WILL OWEN

6 *ARTIST:* LAWSON WOOD

7 *ARTIST:* JOHN HASSALL

8 *ARTIST:* TOM B

3

4

5

6

"WHY GO SOUTH FOR SUNLIGHT
WHEN YOU CAN HAVE IT AT HOME?"

7

8

9

THAT'S WHAT MOTHER USES

11

10

1-6 *POSTERS, UK*
CLIENT: LEVER BROS.

Lever Bros. invested heavily in advertising for their soap products and this is a fairly representative sample of the work they produced.

1

Old time Courtesy.

2

3

4

5

6

7 POSTER, 1914, UK
CLIENT: COLMAN'S MUSTARD
8 PRESS AD, 1916, UK
CLIENT: OXO
9 PRESS AD, 1910, UK
CLIENT: KELLOGG'S CORNFLAKES

When Kellogg's first went into production each packet was signed as proof of authenticity. As production increased they tried to retain this idea by having a printed logo that resembled the original signature.

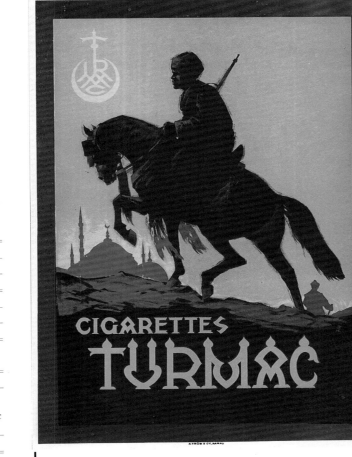

I *POSTER, 1915, EUROPE*

CLIENT: TURMAC CIGARETTES

ARTIST: JVAN E. HUGENTOBLER

2 *POSTER, 1914, EUROPE*

CLIENT: GERBER CIGARETTES

ARTIST: JULIUS KLINGER

3 *POSTER, 1914, EUROPE*

HEADLINE: 'THE TWENTIETH ANNIVERSARY OF THE RE-ESTABLISHMENT OF THE OLYMPIC GAMES, 1894-1914'

ARTIST: EDOUARD ELZINGRE

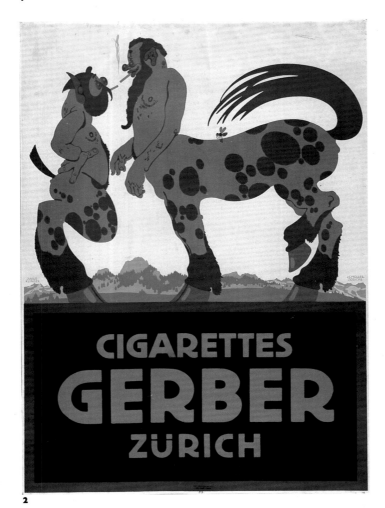

CLIENT: THE WHITE COMPANY

1-3 *PRESS ADS, 1913, USA*

ARTIST: OTHO CUSHING

These mythological drawings, in which the Gods were tempted by White automobiles, appeared in Town and Country in 1913 and represent an interesting attempt by the designers to create a branding device out of the 'white' style of drawing and layout.

CLIENT: STEVENS-DUREYA COMPANY

4-6 *PRESS ADS, 1913, USA*

ARTIST: WILLIAM H. FOSTER

Fascination

The WHITE BERLINE, even to the naturally prejudiced owner of a car of another make, has an irresistible attraction, once its quality is inquired into and its performance known. Where sentiment for another car has not prevented investigation, it will be found that the WHITE BERLINE *alone* possesses *all* of the correct and fundamental features of construction, and wealth of appointments, without which, a car of this type is today practically obsolete.

THE WHITE COMPANY
CLEVELAND

The allurement of the White Berline causes Neptune and Amphitrite to forsake their sea-home.

1

Alone

For its absolute correctness of construction, for the perfect control and noiselessness of its power, for its inspiring dignity of appearance, and for the studied attention to every smallest detail that provides complete comfort and relaxation, the White Berline stands unequalled.

THE WHITE COMPANY
CLEVELAND

2

Grace

THE WHITE coupé is the car she has always wished for—light, beautiful, swift and far running. Here are found the safety and simple operation of the electric vehicle, combined with the flexible speed and touring possibilities which only the gasoline roadster can give. Primarily *her* car for *all* purposes, its power and convenience also make the White coupé the preferred car for *his* town and winter use.

THE WHITE COMPANY
CLEVELAND

3

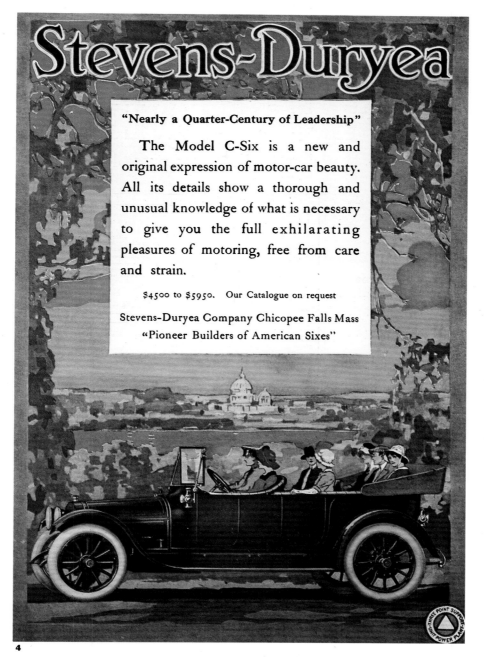

Stevens-Duryea

"Nearly a Quarter-Century of Leadership"

The Model C-Six is a new and original expression of motor-car beauty. All its details show a thorough and unusual knowledge of what is necessary to give you the full exhilarating pleasures of motoring, free from care and strain.

$4500 to $5950.   Our Catalogue on request

Stevens-Duryea Company Chicopee Falls Mass
"Pioneer Builders of American Sixes"

4

5

6

Not only has the Pierce-Arrow turned the tide of imported cars so that there are today far less in proportion than some years ago—not only that, but the Pierce-Arrow in American hands has invaded Europe, giving greater satisfaction to its owners than a native car on its native heath.

The Pierce-Arrow Motor Car Company, Buffalo, N. Y.

1

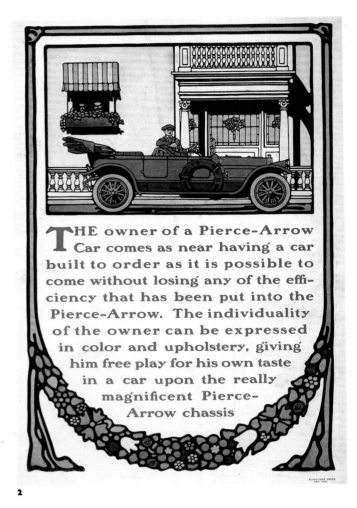

THE owner of a Pierce-Arrow Car comes as near having a car built to order as it is possible to come without losing any of the efficiency that has been put into the Pierce-Arrow. The individuality of the owner can be expressed in color and upholstery, giving him free play for his own taste in a car upon the really magnificent Pierce-Arrow chassis

2

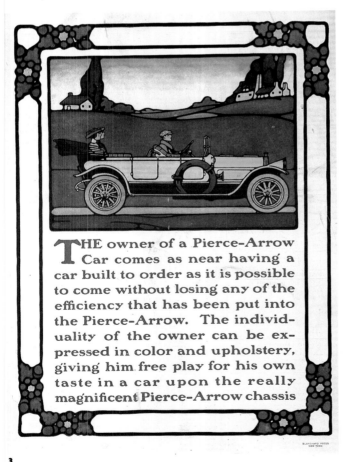

THE owner of a Pierce-Arrow Car comes as near having a car built to order as it is possible to come without losing any of the efficiency that has been put into the Pierce-Arrow. The individuality of the owner can be expressed in color and upholstery, giving him free play for his own taste in a car upon the really magnificent Pierce-Arrow chassis

3

THE PIERCE-ARROW CAR has that beauty which comes from perfect adaptability to its purpose. To this has been added the taste of the designer, making a car that is both flexibly responsive to the will of its owner, and the acme of luxury and comfort.

The Pierce-Arrow Motor Car Company, Buffalo, New York

4

5

6

7

1-4 *PRESS CAMPAIGN, USA*

CLIENT: PIERCE ARROW MOTOR
CAR COMPANY

*Another fine example of cars being sold for
their style value. At one point the copy reads,
'The individuality of the owner can be
expressed in color and upholstery...'*

5-7 *POSTER CAMPAIGN, USA*

CLIENT: BETHLEHEM MOTOR
TRUCKS

AGENCY: ATLAS ADVERTISING,
NEW YORK

*We found this campaign in the
Smithsonian's Warshaw collection and chose
it for its exquisite use of duotone.*

CLIENT: PACKARD MOTOR CARS

PRESS CAMPAIGN, USA

ARTIST: E. HORTER

While foreign travel was still the most glamorous of pursuits, Packard used European settings to accentuate further the stylishness of their product. Absolutely no information is given about the car, but the overall tone of confidence is clearly summed up in the endline.

The Packard Phaeton-Runabout in Paris — From etching by E. Horter

1

2

3

PACKARD

ASK THE MAN WHO OWNS ONE

Packard "38" Phaeton. Rome.   From the etching by E. Horter.

4

Firestone

GOAL!

THE goal that every tire user seeks to make is Most Miles per Dollar, with the utmost riding luxury and the least worry and expense.

Firestone Teamwork brings this goal within easy reach. The efficient training of the greatest army of tire specialists, gathered into one institution, international distribution, the "backs" ready to pass you Firestone Service everywhere every moment, all work together to give you the goal, Most Miles per Dollar.

FIRESTONE TIRE AND RUBBER CO.
"America's Largest Exclusive Tire and Rim Makers"
Akron, Ohio   Branches and Dealers Everywhere

1

WHEREVER representative Americans gather—for sport or business—Firestone Tires predominate. For originality of design and reliable performance, for safety with speed and economical going—all who demand the highest standards of travel look for the "Word of Honor," the name "Firestone."

The Firestone Tire and Rubber Co., Akron, O.—Branches and Dealers Everywhere

Firestone Tires

FIRESTONE TIRES have all the qualities of the thoroughbred; sure footing with instant response, stamina and speed. These qualities make your motor car of universal use, practical on all roads, in every season. They explain why Firestone Tires are unanimously given high rank for a valued public servant.

FIRESTONE TIRE AND RUBBER COMPANY, AKRON, OHIO

Firestone

2   3

Right
Makes
Might

RIGHT from the start—leading the way along the Quality course to the goal of maximum tire value at lowest possible cost.

This has made the MIGHT of Firestone success—a success without rival in rapid and consistent increase of sales and industrial prestige. Right in design; Right in materials; Right in workmanship; Right in service.

Ride on Firestones for luxurious comfort —insurance against delay or accident— the economy of Most Miles per Dollar.

FIRESTONE TIRE & RUBBER CO., AKRON, OHIO
"America's Largest Exclusive Tire and Rim Makers"
BRANCHES AND DEALERS EVERYWHERE

Firestone

4

1 *POSTER, 1919, GERMANY*

CLIENT: ADLER

ARTIST: AUGUST HAJDUK

2 *POSTER, 1919, GERMANY*

CLIENT: DER HERRENFAHRER

ARTIST: JUPP WIERTZ

3 *POSTER, 1913, SWITZERLAND*

CLIENT: MOTORWERKE BERNA AG

ARTIST: EMILE CARDINAUX

4 *POSTER, 1911, GERMANY*

CLIENT: OPEL

ARTIST: HANS RUDI ERDT

In this decade only the rich could afford motor cars and the marketing platform was one of style and fashionability. So it is interesting to see that the poster for Berna lorries, which are of course commercial vehicles, differs in that it employs a visual that suggests a product benefit — strength and loadbearing capacity.

1

2

3

4

5

*POSTERS FROM THE RUSSIAN
REVOLUTION*

Some of the most powerful advertising ever
produced has been propaganda. We have
chosen these posters from the Russian
Revolution for the power of their imagery
which, by comparison, makes most
advertising hyperboles look like
understatements.

1 *POSTER, 1919, USSR*

HEADLINE: 'WOMEN WORKERS
AND PEASANTS FORM RANKS WITH
MEN UNDER THE RED BANNER.
TERRIFY THE BOURGEOISIE'

2 *POSTER, 1919, USSR*

ARTIST: VICTOR DENI

HEADLINE: 'CAPITALISTS OF THE
WORLD UNITE'

3 *POSTER, 1919, USSR*

HEADLINE: 'THE MENCHEVIK
COUNTER REVOLUTIONARIES'

4 *POSTER, 1919, USSR*

ARTIST: DAVID MOOR

*The poster shows two White Army generals
having their heads torn off. On the arms are
the words 'DICTATORSHIP OF THE
PROLETARIAT.'*

5 *POSTER, 1919, USSR*

ARTIST: DAVID MOOR

HEADLINE: 'DEATH TO WORLD
IMPERIALISM'

6 *POSTER, 1919, USSR*

ARTIST: VICTOR DENI

HEADLINE: 'CAPITAL'

7 *POSTER, 1918, USSR*

ARTIST: APSIT

HEADLINE: 'TSAR, POPE AND THE
RICH'

6

7

105

The platform of the Labour Party has always been one of identification with the working man, the unemployed and the homeless. Such is the timeless quality of these posters, they were reprinted and used again in 1971.

"LANDLESS"

PUBLISHED BY THE LABOUR PARTY. 33,Eccleston Square, London, S.W. & PRINTED BY VINCENT BROOKS, DAY & SON,LTD 48,Parker St. Kingsway,London.WC.2

1

"WORKLESS"

PUBLISHED BY THE LABOUR PARTY. 33,Eccleston Square, London, S.W. & PRINTED BY VINCENT BROOKS, DAY & SON,LTD 48,Parker St. Kingsway,London.WC.2

2

STEP INTO YOUR PLACE

3

Daddy, what did _YOU_ do in the Great War?

CLIENT: US GOVERNMENT
POSTER CAMPAIGN, 1918, USA
1 *ARTIST:* A. RALEIGH
2 *ARTIST:* WALTER WHITEHEAD
3 *ARTIST:* C. W. LOVE
4 *ARTIST:* ELLSWORTH YOUNG
5 *ARTIST:* R. H. PARTEOUS

Both visually and verbally, wartime recruitment and bond advertising is relentlessly emotional in its appeal. These five posters are intended to excite feelings of anger, hatred, guilt, fear, manly and maternal pride.

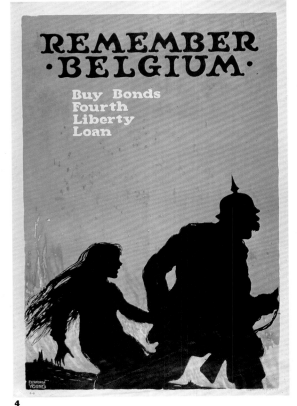

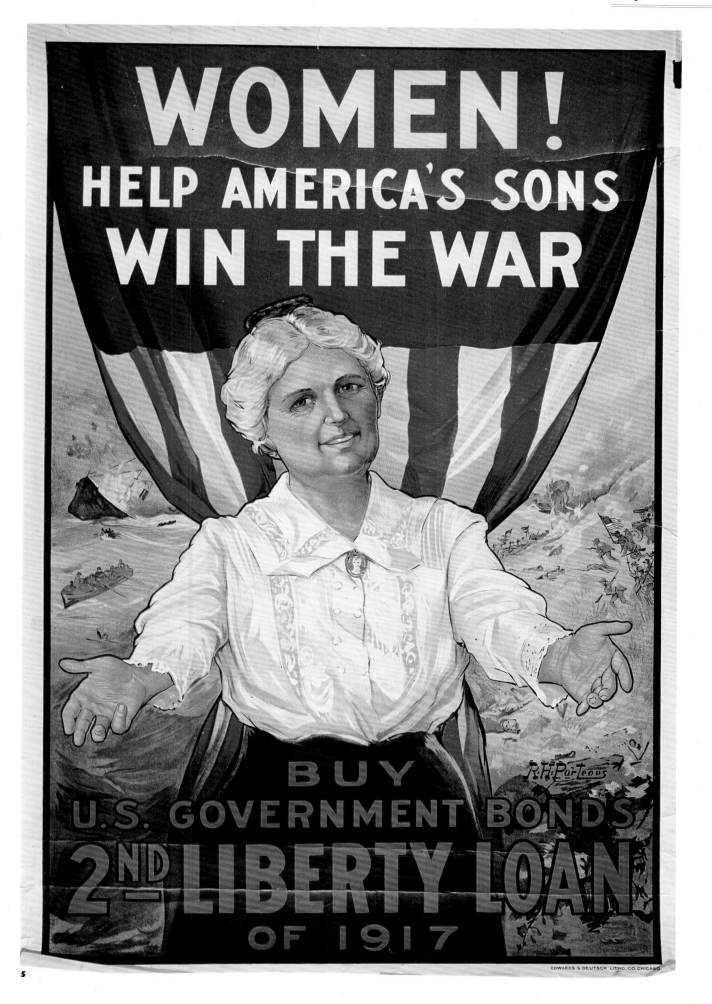

CHAPTER FIVE

THE 'JAZZ AGE'—ten years when the world turned its back on the memories of a bloody and costly war and decided to have a good time—had a character and atmosphere more distinctive than that of any other decade of the century. It was a time when England and America moved culturally and commercially closer to one another, although the twenties definitely 'roared' louder in the States. Perhaps, as Scott Fitzgerald believed, it was due to the unspent energy left over from the war. England was to enjoy only two years of prosperity before slumping into depression; the American economy did not founder until the Wall Street crash of 1929.

There was a party spirit in all areas of social activity both in Europe and on the other side of the Atlantic, where the introduction of Prohibition in 1920 merely increased the number of speakeasies in which the fast set could enjoy the pleasures of illicit drinking.

Fashions changed at a furious rate—the bob, the Eton crop, the cloche hat, the short skirt, plucked eyebrows and scarlet lips in the shape of a cupid's bow. Earrings were long, as were cigarette holders and necklaces. The corset was abandoned and, forty years before it was burned, the bra was born.

Suddenly jazz music was the rage and the miracle of radio brought live dance music into everybody's front room. The Charleston, invented in South Carolina in 1913 and described as 'the first and easiest step to Hell', was introduced in 1925 to England, where it was considered vulgar until the Prince of Wales became one of its most agile exponents.

In the world of literature it is impossible to overestimate the significance of these years. James Joyce, Ernest Hemingway, Aldous Huxley, D.H. Lawrence, Noel Coward, Virginia Woolf, Evelyn Waugh and Scott Fitzgerald were all at the height of their powers.

Transport technology continued to surge forward. Passenger air-travel across the Atlantic became possible with the German Graf Zeppelin in 1928 and in the same year Bert Hinkler flew from London to Sydney in just over 180 hours.

But this decade really belonged to the motor car. In America in 1919 there were six million cars, a figure which rose to twenty-three million in the following ten years. And in England the increase in car ownership was even higher. It had an effect on every aspect of life—from social mobility to the sex-life of the young and even crime (the getaway car).

For advertising these were boom years. Fortunes were spent on promoting rival products and competition was intense, especially as the introduction of hire-purchase had increased the number of potential consumers. Inevitably the ads were influenced by Art Deco, but style was assuming a different and less central role in advertising, as agencies struggled to find new persuasive devices such as product-endorsement by the film stars that Hollywood was busy creating.

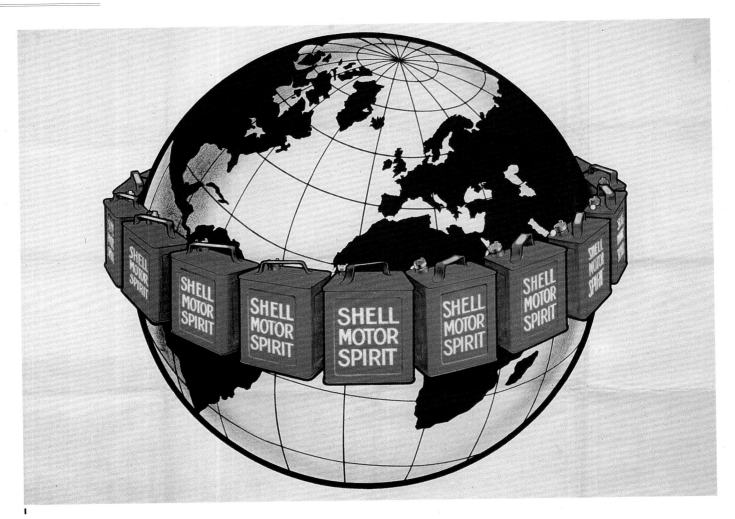

1

2

3

4

5

A SOUND INVESTMENT

'BANK' ON SUPER SHELL MOTOR LUBRICATING OIL

6

THE QUICKSTARTING PAIR

SHELL OIL AND PETROL

7

The SHELL HILL CLIMB TEAM ARE COMING!

Look out for them

SHELL MOTOR CYCLE OILS

SEE LOCAL PRESS FOR FULL DETAILS

8

The Perfect Power Pair

SHELL OIL & SHELL PETROL

9

CLIENT:	SHELL OIL, UK
1 *LORRY BILL, 1924, UK*	
ARTIST: NORMAN KEENE	
2 *LORRY BILL, 1929, UK*	
ARTIST: FINN	
3 *LORRY BILL, 1926, UK*	
ARTIST: BURTON	
4 *LORRY BILL, 1926, UK*	
ARTIST: SEP E. SCOTT	
5 *LORRY BILL, 1924, UK*	
ARTIST: VIC	
6 *LORRY BILL, 1928, UK*	
ARTIST: SEP E. SCOTT	
7 *LORRY BILL, 1927, UK*	
ARTIST: JEAN D'YLEN	
8 *LORRY BILL, 1926, UK*	
ARTIST: SEP E. SCOTT	
9 *LORRY BILL, 1929, UK*	
ARTIST: NUNNEY	

Up until the arrival of the road tanker in 1954, Shell petrol was delivered to garages in cans. Ingeniously, the company used the delivery trucks as a mobile advertising medium and pasted 'Lorry Bills', measuring 30" ×45", slightly behind and on either side of the driver's cab. This was entirely in keeping with Shell's philosophy of environmental protection and in 1930 they received a commendation from the Design & Industries Association for their 'stand against roadside advertising.'

1

2

3

4

5

6

7

8

9

115

1 *POSTER, 1922, ITALY*

AGENCY: A. C. D'ITALIA

ARTIST: ALDO MAZZA

2 *POSTER, 1924, SWITZERLAND*

CLIENT: MARTINI

HEADLINE: 'MARTINI THE
MOUNTAIN CLIMBER'

ARTIST: OTTO BAUMBERGER

3 *POSTER, 1925, SWITZERLAND*

CLIENT: ACS SCHWEIZ

ARTIST: KARL BICKEL

4 *POSTER, 1922, SWITZERLAND*

CLIENT: CHRYSLER

ARTIST: OTTO ERNST

5 *POSTER, 1921, GERMANY*

CLIENT: GRUNEWALD MOTOR
RACE

ARTIST: RUDOLF DIEDERICH

6 *POSTER, 1925, FRANCE*

CLIENT: BUGATTI

ARTIST: RENE VINCENT

7 *POSTER, 1923, SPAIN*

CLIENT: BARCELONA
INTERNATIONAL AUTO-RACE

ARTIST: I. SEFRELLES

*Some of the artists on this page seem to have
been influenced by the Futurists, whose
manifesto predated this work by 10 or 15
years. However, as most of these posters are
advertising motor races, it may just be the
subject matter that forces the comparison.*

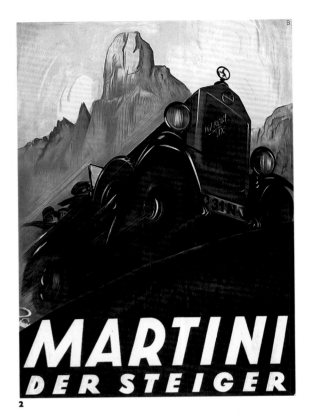

5

Auto-
Rennen
Grunewald
24./25.Sept.

6

BUGATTI

7

AUTODROMO
NACIONAL
SITGES-BARCELONA

1923
1ª. GRAN SETMANA INTERNACIONAL
28 OCTUBRE. GRAN PREMI VOITURETTE/ 29 OCTUBRE. GRAN PREMI MOTO/
1 NOVEMBRE. " " AUTOCICLE/ = 4 NOVEMBRE. " " COTXE/
200.000 PE//ETE/ DE PREMI/
RIEUSSET = BARCELONA

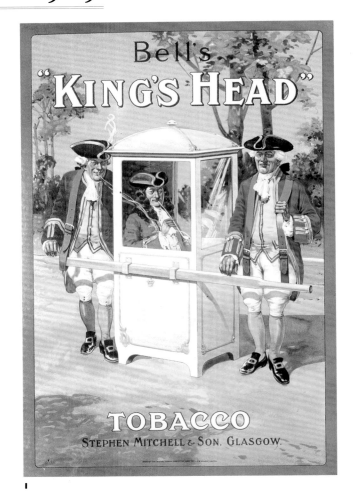

1

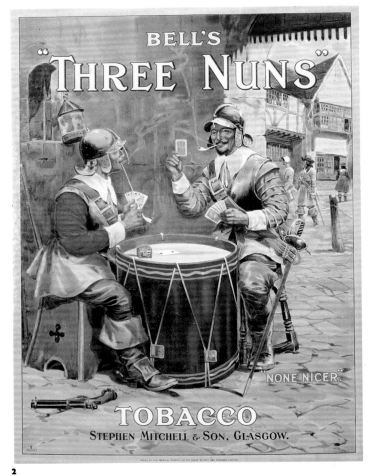

2

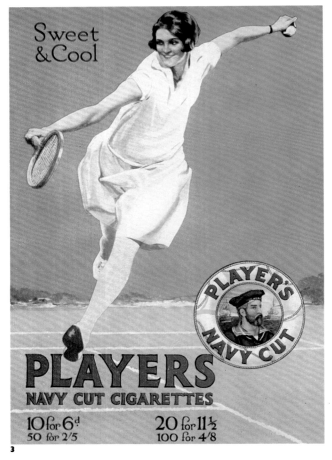

3

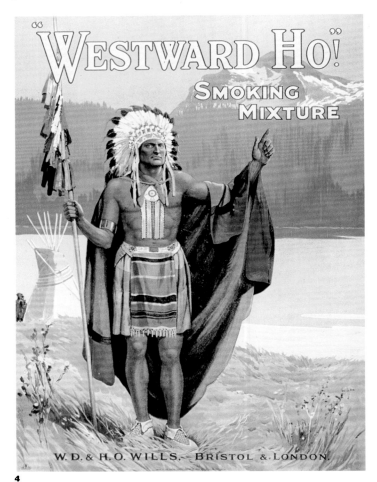

4

LEADING **LIGHTS**

& ABDULLA

ABDULLA SUPERB CIGARETTES.

A RULER OF MEN.

Bolito, born with a brain of steel, has suffered a Strong Man's fate ;
The Nation begs him with tearful pride to trample—command—dictate.
A spotted Pard on his office desk sits purring intense applause
As Bolito shatters stenographers with drafts of despotic laws.

He props his head on the telephone for a ten minutes' doze each night,
His Staff drop dead and are swept away—but Bolito is always bright.
And the latest rule for his Country's good—more stringent than all the rest—
Is that every soul—from the Highest down—must savour ABDULLA'S Best.

F. R. HOLMES.

5

I *POSTER, 1920s, UK*
CLIENT: BELL'S KING'S HEAD TOBACCO
2 *POSTER, 1920s, UK*
CLIENT: BELL'S THREE NUNS TOBACCO
3 *POSTER, 1920s, UK*
CLIENT: PLAYERS NAVY CUT
4 *POSTER, 1920s, UK*
CLIENT: WESTWARD HO TOBACCO
5-7 *PRESS ADS, 1925, UK*
CLIENT: ABDULLA CIGARETTES
ARTIST: NERMAN
WRITER: F. R. HOLMES

*There are not many examples of flat spot
colour in this book but it works particularly
well in this campaign for Abdulla cigarettes.*

LEADING **LIGHTS**

& ABDULLA

ABDULLA SUPERB CIGARETTES.

THE WOMAN EXPLORER.

Paulina Fibster makes a hit
In her Parisian trekking kit
  When daintily exploring :
Shy zebras stare with wistful eyes,
Gorillas register surprise,
  And hippos cease from snoring.

Outshining Orpheus and his lute,
She subjugates the savage brute
  Of every shape and colour.
They gather round her at a run
Despite the fashionable gun,
  Bewitched by her ABDULLA.

F. R. Holmes.

6

LEADING **LIGHTS**

& ABDULLA

ABDULLA SUPERB CIGARETTES.

THE RAIDER.

He crashes from a skylight, or bursts through triple doors,
Or bounces from the cellars to catch us breaking laws,
So gallantly he pens us within the prison van
We lose our hearts to Robert—a Raider and a Man.
But, when a trifle weary of planking down a fine,
We proffer him politely the Cigarette Divine,
Viewed through ABDULLA'S Smoke wreathes it grows sublimely clear
Our " Naughty Naughty " Night Club is run on—ginger-beer.

F. R. Holmes.

7

1 *POSTER, 1920, GERMANY*

CLIENT: MUNICH RAILWAY
STATION

HEADLINE: 'THE LITTLE BAR ON
THE RAILWAY STATION IN MUNICH

ARTIST: KNAB-KOCH

2 *POSTER, 1922, SWITZERLAND*

CLIENT: GENEVA BALLOONING
EVENT

ARTIST: H. LOUTANS

3 *POSTER, 1924, PORTUGAL*

CLIENT: DALIA TOOTHPASTE

ARTIST: ROBERTO

4 *POSTER, 1925, SPAIN*

CLIENT: CARMEN SOAP

ARTIST: OTTO BAUMBERGER

5 *POSTER, 1929, GERMANY*

CLIENT: KALODERMA

HEADLINE: 'SHAVING SOAP IN A
TUBE'

ARTIST: LUDWIG HOHLWEIN

1

2

3

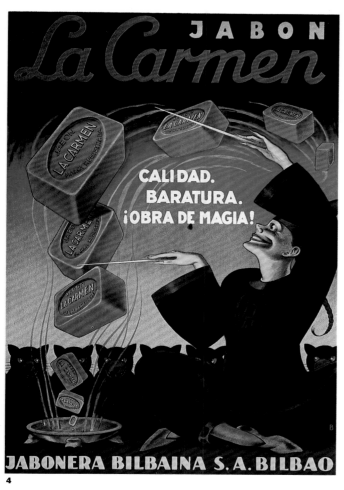

4

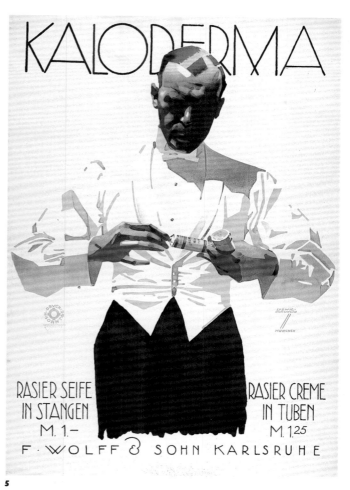

5

CLIENT: BOVRIL
1-7 POSTERS, UK
7 ARTIST: H. H. HARRIS

The promise of Bovril has always been that it contains the goodness of beef in concentrated form and therefore provides strength and energy. After the austerity of the war years Bovril's advertising became more humorous. In 1920 artist H. H. Harris created their most famous poster of all — the carefree pyjama man astride the sea-borne jar of Bovril. The line 'prevents that sinking feeling' had been written some years previously and withheld through fear of causing offence after the Titanic disaster.

1

2

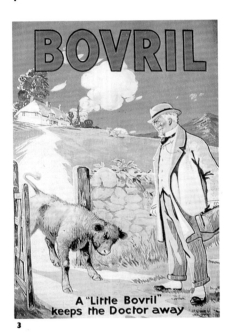

3

4

5

6

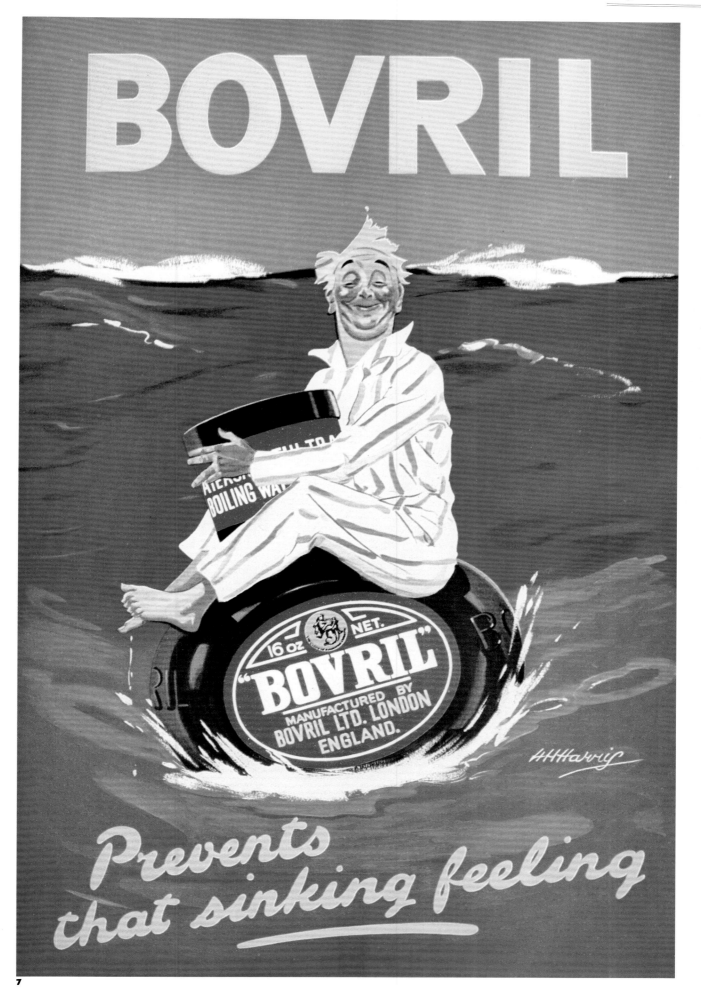

7

8

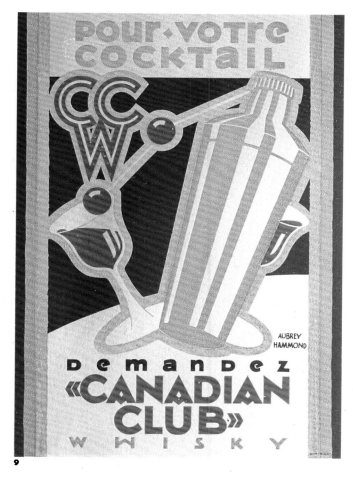

9

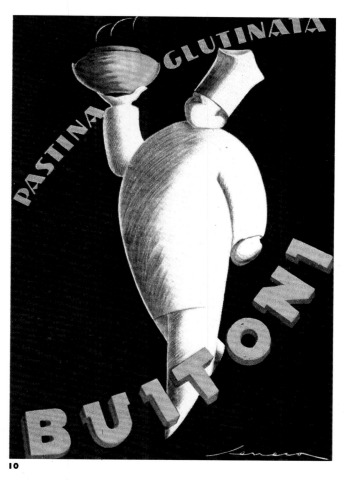

10

1

2

3

4

CLIENT: OXO

1-4 *POSTERS AND MAGAZINE INSERTS, UK*

In 1899 Liebig's Extract became Oxo in liquid form and the cube was introduced in 1910. Thereafter Oxo became a part of the British way of life and its advertising reflected the issues and concerns of the day. During peacetime it projected images of health, beauty and nourishment and during the war years advertised itself as an invaluable recuperative aid.

5 *SHOWCARD, UK*

CLIENT: MINERAL WATERS

ARTIST: J. BIGGAR

6 *SHOWCARD, UK*

CLIENT: BURROW'S TABLE WATER

7 *SHOWCARD, UK*

CLIENT: DUNVILLE'S WHISKY

ARTIST: EDWARD COLE

8 *SHOWCARD*

CLIENT: PARKINSON'S BAKING POWDER

1

2

3

4

5

6

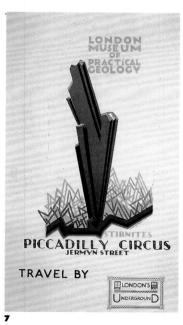

7

1 POSTER, 1924, USSR

ARTIST: A. STRACHOV

HEADLINE: 'LENIN 1870-1924'

2 POSTER, 1922, USSR

HEADLINE: 'WITH MARX TO INTERNATIONAL COMMUNISM'

3 POSTER, 1927, USSR

ARTIST: STENBERG BROTHERS

Poster for the film 'In Springtime'

4 POSTER, 1920, USSR

ARTIST: LEBEDEV

HEADLINE: 'WORK NEEDS RIFLES AROUND'

5 POSTER, 1925, USSR

ARTIST: ALEXANDER RODCHENKO

A poster for the Lengiz publishing house

6 POSTER, 1925, USSR

ARTIST: UNKNOWN

HEADLINE: 'HYGENIC WORKING CONDITIONS INCREASE PRODUCTIVITY'

7 POSTER, 1927, USSR

ARTIST: UNKNOWN

HEADLINE: 'SUNSHINE IS A CHILD'S BEST FRIEND'

8 POSTER, 1922, USSR

ARTIST: UNKNOWN

Famine relief poster

9 POSTER, 1925, USSR

ARTIST: UNKNOWN

A Red Cross poster encouraging children to work hard, play hard and take care of their personal hygiene.

5

6

7

8

9

POSTERS, UK

1 *CLIENT:* LONDON AND NORTH EASTERN RAILWAY

ARTIST: GREGORY BROWN

2 *CLIENT:* LONDON TRANSPORT

ARTIST: CHARLES PAINE

3 *CLIENT:* LONDON AND NORTH EASTERN RAILWAY

ARTIST: V. L. BANVERS

4 *CLIENT:* LONDON TRANSPORT

ARTIST: DOROTHY DIX

5 *CLIENT:* LONDON TRANSPORT

ARTIST: E. L. BAMFORD

6 *CLIENT:* LONDON TRANSPORT

ARTIST: NOEL ROOKE

7 *CLIENT:* LONDON TRANSPORT

ARTIST: CHARLES PAINE

8 *CLIENT:* LONDON TRANSPORT

ARTIST: CHARLES PAINE

9 *CLIENT:* LONDON AND NORTH EASTERN RAILWAY

ARTIST: SPURRIER

10 *CLIENT:* LONDON AND BRIGHTON AND SOUTHERN REGION

ARTIST: E. A. COX

Throughout the twenties and during the economic recovery from the first world war, the LNER commissioned these posters and promoted tourism within the British Isles to encourage more people to use the railways.

1

2

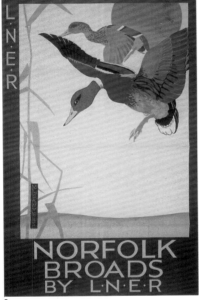

3

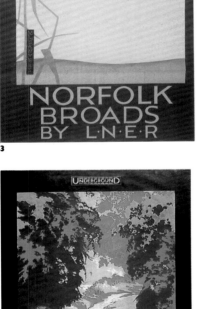

4

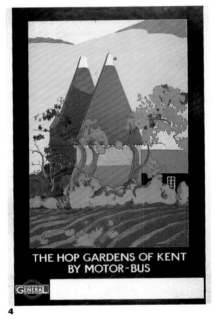

5

6

KINGSTON BY TRAM

CPAINE

7

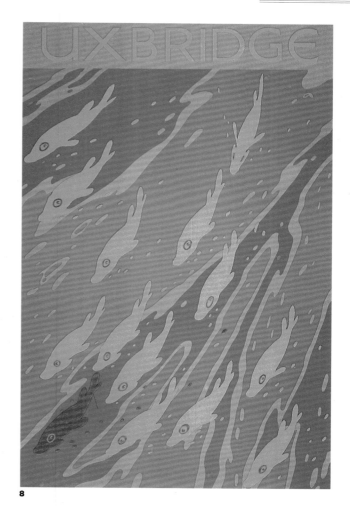

UXBRIDGE

8

YORKSHIRE

Illustrated Holiday Booklet, and if desired,
Lodgings Guide. Post Free on application to
Passenger Manager (A1) London & North Eastern Railway, York.

9

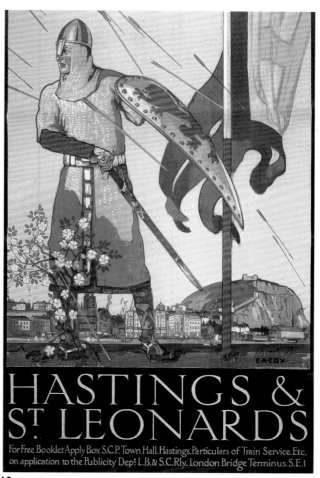

HASTINGS &
St LEONARDS

For Free Booklet Apply Box S.C.P. Town Hall, Hastings. Particulars of Train Service, Etc.
on application to the Publicity Dep! L.B.& S.C. Rly, London Bridge Terminus, S.E.1

10

1

2

3

1 *POSTER, 1927, FRANCE*
CLIENT: BELGIAN RAILWAYS
ARTIST: A. M. CASSANDRE
2 *POSTER, 1927, FRANCE*
CLIENT: BELGIAN RAILWAYS
ARTIST: A. M. CASSANDRE
3 *POSTER, 1925, HOLLAND*
CLIENT: HOLLAND-AMERIKA LINIE
ARTIST: ADRIAAN JOH VAN 'T HOFF

CHAPTER SIX

THE ECONOMIC OUTLOOK at the beginning of the 1930s was bleak and the effervescent style of the twenties had given way to a more sombre mood. America was in the grip of the Great Depression that succeeded the Wall Street crash of 1929 and Great Britain, to a lesser extent, was in a financial slump. However, Roosevelt came to power in 1933 with promises of a 'New Deal' for the American people, a system of social security was instigated and Prohibition was ended. Britain, too, struggled to pull itself out of the doldrums and during the decade went on to produce some of the finest advertising ever seen on either side of the Atlantic.

As usual, the advertising industry was in a state of flux. New areas of expertise were emerging—namely, planning and research. In origin these were American developments, but the European agencies soon followed suit, encouraged by the influence of American marketing personnel who were on the continent. Also, advertising was being closely scrutinised to ensure that the claims it made were honest. In England, in 1935, agencies were made legally responsible for their output and could be sued for misrepresentation. Some publications started independently to vet the ads they carried. *John Bull* made a point of analysing all food advertising and the *Radio Times* employed a medical panel to check all pharmaceutical campaigns.

But these pressures from both outside and inside the business were, perhaps, less significant than the influence of certain key individuals. It is to them that advertising owes its reputation for having gone through a particularly arty period in the 1930s.

Frank Pick, who worked for the London Under-ground, was one of the first to appreciate the value of art to advertising. As far back as 1914 he had commissioned such artists as Frank Brangwyn and Spencer Pryce and was responsible for the discovery of Edward McKnight Kauffer. Their posters for the tube trains set a trend that was followed by British Rail and during the 1930s the public enjoyed the work of Fred Taylor, Tom Purvis, Austin Cooper and Francis Marshall.

Jack Beddington, who was the advertising manager of Shell from 1932 to 1939, was another great patron of the arts. The work he commissioned from Graham Sutherland, Fouqueray, Paul Nash and Duncan Grant was a contribution to the development of British landscape painting and part of a move away from Impressionism. Beddington, who had a brother in the art world, employed artists of wildly differing styles—from the Surrealist-influenced Hans Schleger (Zero) to the cartoon-like John Reynolds, with whom he created one of the most famous advertising campaigns of all time: 'That's Shell—that was'

Although the first Guinness ad appeared in 1928, it was during the thirties that their agency, S.H. Benson, really set the campaign in motion. What followed was twenty years of outrageous puns and parodies, illustrated by John Gilroy's charming menagerie of Guinness-guzzling animals. Many artists of diverse styles worked for Guinness—John Nash, Quentin Blake, Antony Groves-Raines, H.M. Bateman—and only a few of the great British cartoonists failed to receive a commission from the company.

This decade also saw photography make inroads into advertising and the emergence of such famous names as Edward Steichen, Herbert Matter and Martin Munkacsi. But colour photography was still in its infancy and the thirties really belonged to the illustrators.

HELLO JOE . . . have one of your Camels . . . we've covered women, politics, religion, marriage, ideals, philosophy, women. . . . Have you birds been at my carton of Camels? . . . Sure . . . you can't keep a good bull session going on hot air alone . . . a little Camel now and then. . . . All right—I admire your taste . . . as well as your nerve . . . but speaking of women. . . .

CLIENT: R.J. REYNOLDS AND COMPANY

PRODUCT: CAMEL CIGARETTES

PRESS CAMPAIGNS, 1930, USA

Camel cigarettes developed a sort of schizophrenic brand personality when Reynolds ran both of these campaigns in the first three months of 1930. The first three ads ran in college magazines and were designed with their primary colours and 'Bull Session' scenarios to appeal to young men. The second campaign, which ran in mags such as Cosmopolitan, True Stories and Smart Set, positioned Camel as the cigarette for sophisticated young women.

If all the Camels smoked at all the "bull sessions" were piled in a heap, you'd see an impressive monument to the pleasure of good talk and good tobacco.

COME ON, let's get going . . . now these essayists . . . who wrote Sartor Resartus? . . . Who cares? —Have a Camel. . . . You'll care . . . when you hit the exam tomorrow . . . curfew shall not ring tonight . . . somebody bring a pot of coffee from the Greek's . . . and another deck of Camels . . . thank heaven, the Camels never fail us. . . . Come on, let's get going. . . .

Earnest seekers after knowledge learn in the wee, small hours that Camel's goodness never palls; that the last Camel is as good as the first.

BETTER Prom than last year . . . look at that something in the blue dress. . . . Hey, Tubby . . . you passed my Camels to the whole stag line. . . . Never mind . . . another carton in the booth. . . . Hello, Jack . . . why the fatigue? . . . This committee racket's no cinch . . . been trying to keep the boys from crashing the gate . . . I need a breathing spell. . . . You need a Camel . . . have one. . . .

When they tell you they smoke Camels "just because they're good," they mean that Camel is a better cigarette.

'Vantage In

Swift and breathless, those final moments of thrilling play. Too swift and breathless to last. But there's an after-thrill that's even better: The quiet satisfaction of a good cigarette . . . so fragrant and rich, so mild, so incomparably mellow that it could only be a Camel. . . . And that's your advantage, too.

Siesta

Sometimes in the whirl of existence one likes a moment apart . . . a moment of reflection and tranquillity . . . siesta. Camels fit this mood of introspection. They are so fragrant and delightful; so unobtrusive and so satisfying. No other cigarette, at any price, gives quite so much of pleasure. . . . And no other has been so generously accepted by smokers the world over.

Sophisticate

You have the world at your finger-tips. Ashore or afloat, you get pretty much what you want. In cigarettes (we point with pride) you've shown a striking preference for Camels. For there's something about them . . . a golden fragrance, a delicacy and mellow mildness . . . which appeals to people of instructed taste. And it is this capacity for choosing the good things of life . . . whether a perfume, an evening gown, or a cigarette . . . which constitutes the best and highest type of sophistication.

If winter comes

You go south, Fortunate Lady, when the cold winds blow. You live graciously, in accordance with a high tradition, in a well-appointed world. And it is therefore a matter of particular interest that you, who can afford anything, have chosen to smoke Camels. . . . It is simply one more confirmation of the fact that there is no cigarette anywhere, at any price, so fragrant . . . so delicately and mildly mellow . . . so filled with downright *pleasure*.

This Players campaign seems to be extraordinary for its time — no use of sex, no packshot and no images of people enjoying the cigarette. However, the drawings are very entertaining and the consistency of style and repetition of the word 'Player's' in the speech bubbles makes it an involving and well-branded campaign.

1

2

3

5

6

1 *POSTER, 1936, GERMANY*

ARTIST: WURBEL

Poster for the Berlin Olympics

2 *POSTER, 1936*

ARTIST: LUDWIG HOHLWEIN

Poster for the Winter Olympics at Garmisch-Partenkirchen

3 *POSTER, 1937, SPAIN*

ARTIST: MORREL

A poster announcing a day of books and reading in Barcelona on 23 April 1937.

1

3

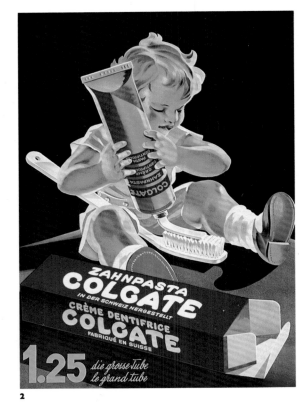

1

2

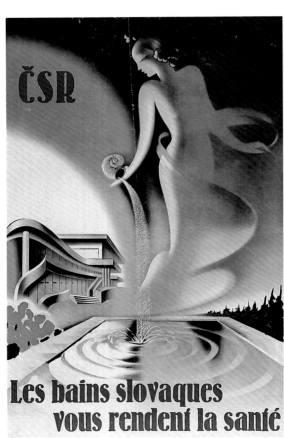

3

4

1 *POSTER, 1930, SWITZERLAND*
CLIENT: KOHLER
ARTIST: CHARLES KUHN

2 *POSTER, 1935, SWITZERLAND*
CLIENT: COLGATE
ARTIST: MARTIN PIEKERT

3 *POSTER, 1932, FRANCE*
CLIENT: SLOVAK BATHS
HEADLINE: 'SLOVAK BATHS
RESTORE YOUR HEALTH'

4 *POSTER, 1935, SWITZERLAND*
CLIENT: TRESAVON
HEADLINE: 'YES, I AM BEAUTIFUL,
BECAUSE I USE TRESAVON'

5 *POSTER, 1932, SWITZERLAND*
CLIENT: CLERMONT ET FOUET
HEADLINE: FOR HEATHLY TEETH
ARTIST: RENO

1 *POSTER, 1936, EUROPE*

CLIENT: SUNLIGHT

PRODUCT: LUX SOAP

HEADLINE: 'LUX TOILET SOAP FOR MY COMPLEXION'

2 *POSTER, EUROPE*

CLIENT: SILBERHALS SHAMPOO

ARTIST: HANS HANDSCHIN

HEADLINE: 'HAIR AS SOFT AS SILK WITH SILBERHALS SHAMPOO'

3 *POSTER, 1937, EUROPE*

CLIENT: ZURICH INTERNATIONAL AIRSHOW

ARTIST: OTTO BAUMBERGER

1

2

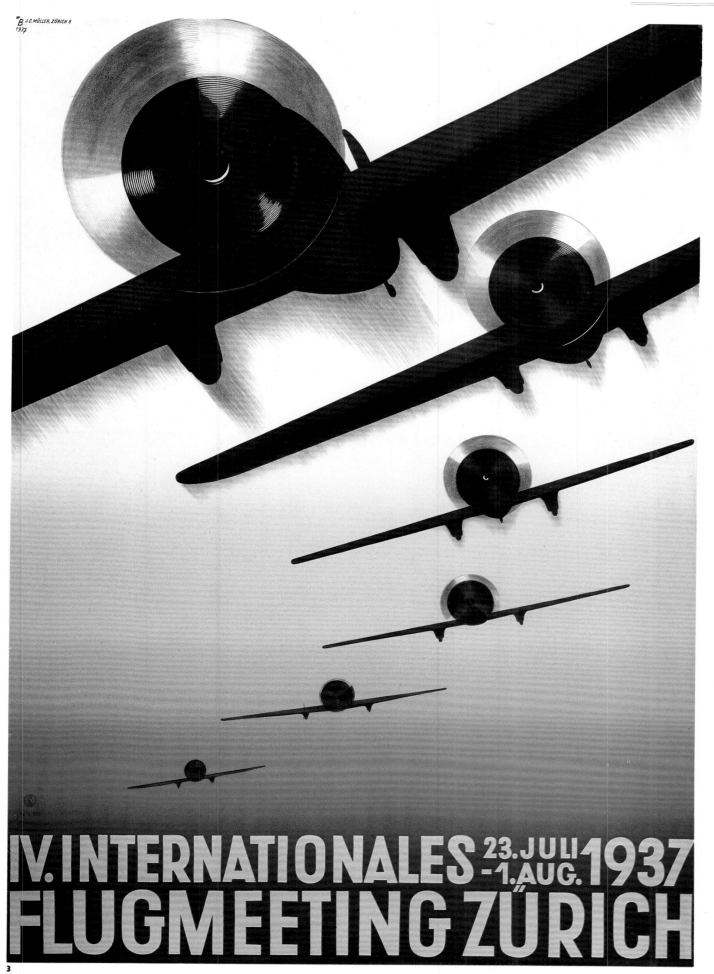

1

2

3

4

5

6

7

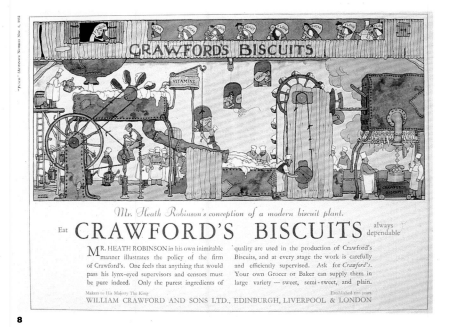

8

9

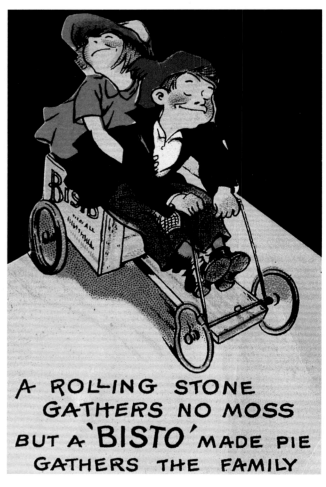

CLIENT: BISTO

POSTERS, UK

The Bisto kids have been with us now for over 50 years and are one of the earliest examples of advertising creating a brand property — a communication device that is unique, relevant, memorable and inextricably linked to one brand and no other. The only change the campaign has seen took place in 1976, when the Kids were redrawn to look slightly less raffish.

CLIENT: ARTHUR GUINNESS SON
AND COMPANY

The Guinness advertising which started in 1928 developed into one of the most popular campaigns ever to run in the United Kingdom. The original copy line 'Guinness is good for you' was felt to be too feminine in its appeal and so in 1932 they created the 'Guinness for Strength' slogan and produced their most memorable poster — the man carrying the girder.

1 *POSTER, 1932, UK*

2 *POSTER, 1934, UK*

ARTIST: JOHN GILROY

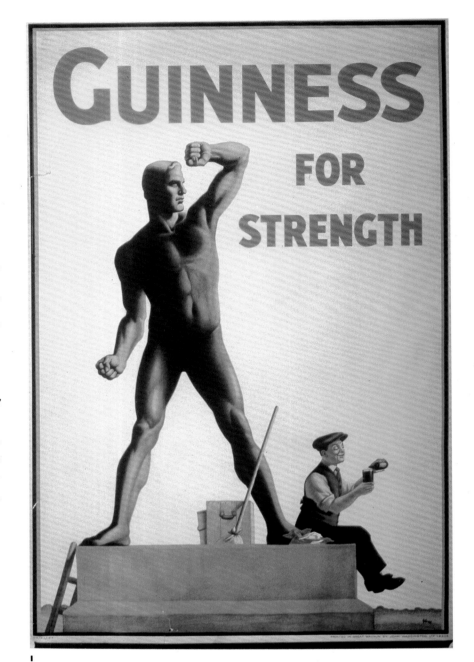

1

2

3

CLIENT: ARTHUR GUINNESS SON
AND COMPANY

*John Gilroy conceived of the Guinness
menagerie after a visit to the circus. The first
poster featured a sea-lion balancing a pint of
Guinness on the end of his nose and
introduced the headline 'My Goodness My
Guinness'. But his most famous creation was
the Toucan. This bird, which started life as a
pelican and was changed by Dorothy L.
Sayers, became one of the most successful and
lovable brand symbols of all time. It
survived four decades and finally made it
into TV in 1979.*

3 *POSTER, 1935, UK*

4 *POSTER, 1939, UK*

5 *POSTER, 1935, UK*

ARTIST: JOHN GILROY

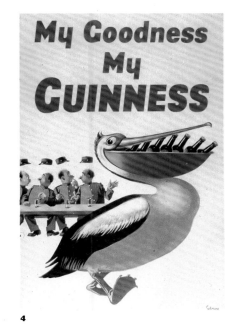

4

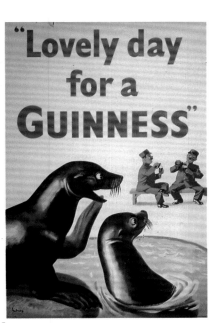

5

1

2

3

1

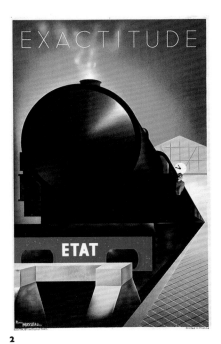

2

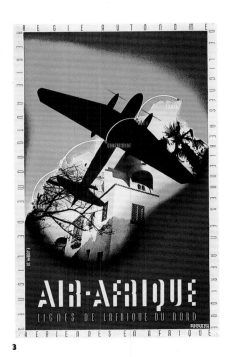

3

4

5

6

1 *POSTER, 1936, GERMANY*

CLIENT: DEUTSCHE ZEPPELIN-
REEDEREI

ARTIST: JUPP WIERTZ

2 *POSTER, 1932, FRANCE*

CLIENT: UNKNOWN

ARTIST: PIERRE MASSEAU

3 *POSTER, 1938, FRANCE*

CLIENT: AIR-AFRIQUE

ARTIST: F. JOSEPH

4 *POSTER, 1934, FRANCE*

CLIENT: ITALIA COSULICH

ARTIST: F. ROMOLI

5 *POSTER, 1935, HOLLAND*

CLIENT: DUTCH SHIPPING
COMPANY

HEADLINE: 'MADEIRA. THE LAND
OF FLOWERS AND SUNSHINE'

ARTIST: LUDWIG HOHLWEIN

6 *POSTER, 1930, FRANCE*

CLIENT: P.L.M. PARIS LYON
MEDITERRANEE

ARTIST: CHAUFFARD

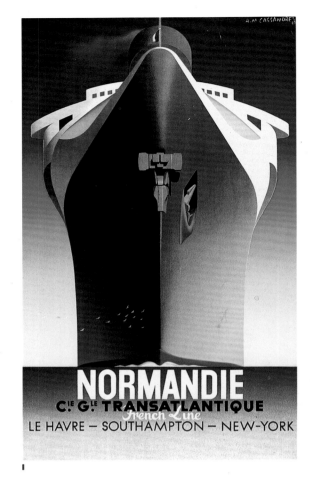

1

2

3

KONINKLIJKE NEDERLANDSCHE
STOOMBOOT MAATSCHAPPIJ

4

1 *POSTER, 1934, FRANCE*

CLIENT: BRITISH TOURISM

ARTIST: A. M. CASSANDRE

2 *POSTER, 1933, FRANCE*

CLIENT: MEDITERRANEAN CRUISES

ARTIST: A. M. CASSANDRE

3 *POSTER, 1934, UK*

CLIENT: LONDON TRANSPORT

ARTIST: E. MCKNIGHT KAUFFER

4 *POSTER, 1937, UK*

CLIENT: UNKNOWN

ARTIST: E. MCKNIGHT KAUFFER

5-8 *PRESS ADS, 1933, UK*

CLIENT: MANSION POLISH

ARTIST: HARRY ROUNTREE

Harry Rountree was one of the first artists to illustrate Brer Rabbit and we chose this campaign for Mansion Polish mainly for the quality of the drawings.

"Hullo Jack! got a prize from school?"
"Yes Dad-teacher asked,'What is it so wonderful that bees make'?
I wrote down 'Wax for Mansion Polish' remembering what a lovely
polish it gives to our floors and furniture. All the other boys said 'Honey'."

MANSION POLISH

**FOR STAINED OR PARQUET FLOORS & FURNITURE
POLISHES AND PRESERVES LINOLEUM**

'Dark Mansion' is specially made for dark Oak and all dark woods
In tins 6d., 10½d & 1/9. Large family tin 3/- containing 2 lbs. nett
THE CHISWICK POLISH CO.,LTD. CHISWICK. W.4.

5

A SPRING CLEANING
INCIDENT

"Oh Dad, do come and look! Mansion Polish has
made the floor so bright that you can see your
portrait in it. It looks just as though you are
making ugly faces at yourself."

MANSION POLISH

for Stained or Parquet Floors, Linoleum and Furniture

use **MIN** FOR THE PIANO AND ALL HIGHLY POLISHED SURFACES · In tins 6d., 10½d & 1/9. Also large household tin containing 2 lbs. net 3/-
CHISWICK PRODUCTS LTD. CHISWICK, LONDON. W.4.

6

"Between you and me Ethel, the long
and short of it is that you can't equal
this 'Mansion' for brightening the
home. It's made this floor look lovely
and that oak sideboard looks as
different again since you got busy
on it with that Dark Mansion."

MANSION POLISH

For Stained or Parquet floors,
Linoleum and Furniture. For
Dark woods use Dark Mansion.

In Tins 6d., 10½d. & 1/9. Large household tin containing 2 lbs. nett. 3/-
CHISWICK PRODUCTS LTD. CHISWICK. W.4.

7

Teddy adds to the
enjoyment of a game
of leap-frog by making
funny faces in the floor
that has been made so
bright with "Mansion".

MANSION POLISH

the easy and economical polish for Stained or Parquet
floors and linoleum... For Dark woods use Dark Mansion.

Tins 6d., 10½d. & 1/9. Large household tin containing 2 lbs. nett 3/-
CHISWICK PRODUCTS LTD. CHISWICK. W.4.

8

1 POSTER, 1930, FRANCE
CLIENT: CHEMIN DE FER DU NORD
ARTIST: A M CASSANDRE

2 POSTER, 1934, FRANCE
CLIENT: MINISTRY OF COMMERCE
AND INDUSTRY
ARTIST: A M CASSANDRE

3 POSTER, UK
CLIENT: GREAT WESTERN RAILWAY

4 POSTER, UK
CLIENT: LONDON UNDERGROUND
ARTIST: E MCKNIGHT KAUFFER

5 POSTER, 1930, ITALY
CLIENT: NAVIGATION SOCIETY
ARTIST: M DUDOVICH

6 POSTER, USSR
CLIENT: TOURIST OFFICE

7 POSTER, ITALY
CLIENT: TOURIST OFFICE

1

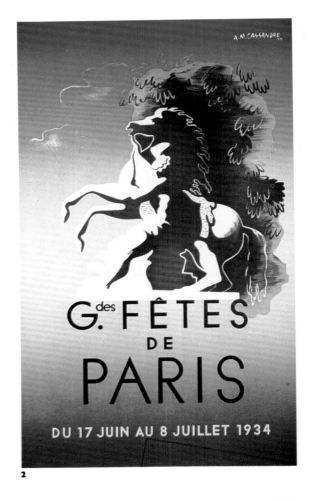

2

3

4

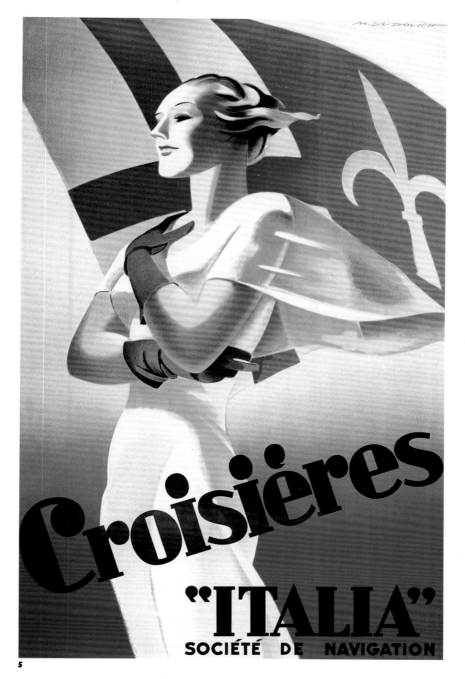

5

6

7

SCHWEIZ

DAS
BERGRENNEN
EUROPAS.

VIII. INTERNATIONALES
KLAUSENRENNEN
A.C.S.   9.10. AUGUST 1930   U.M.S.

1

X. INTERNATIONALES
KLAUSENRENNEN
DAS BERGRENNEN EUROPAS   5. AUGUST 1934

2

II. GROSSER
PREIS DER SCHWEIZ
FÜR AUTOMOBILE

BERN 25. AUGUST 1935

3

GROSSER PREIS
DER SCHWEIZ 15.-16.
AUG.
BERN 1931

4

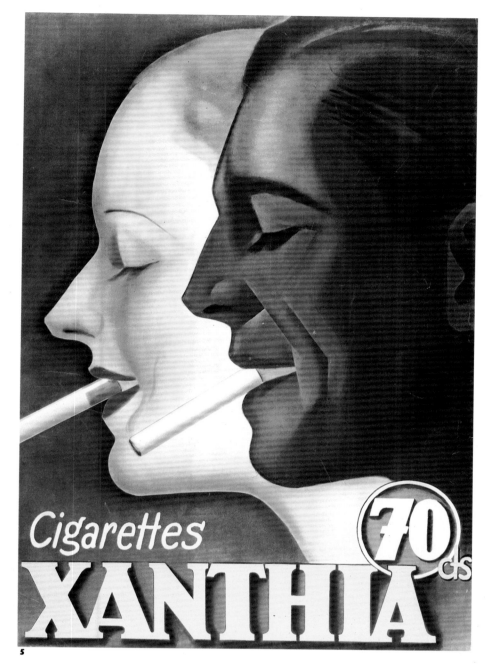

Cigarettes **XANTHIA** 70 cts

5

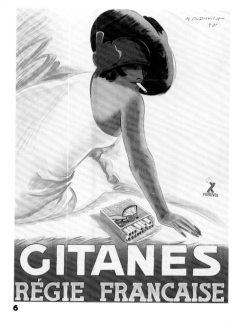

GITANES
RÉGIE FRANCAISE

6

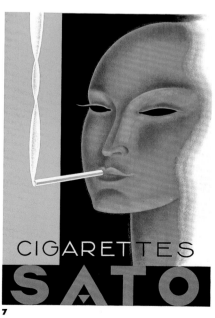

CIGARETTES
SATO

7

CLIENT: LINCOLN-ZEPHYR MOTOR
CARS

1-3 *PRESS ADS, 1939, USA*

*These three press ads, which appeared in
Country Gentleman and The Saturday
Evening Post, clearly illustrate the direction
that car advertising was taking in the late
thirties. Although the photo-realistic
airbrush drawing exaggerated the style and
beauty of the cars, the copy is now longer
and the emphasis is on engineering design
and product features.*

LET'S SPEAK OF VALUE BENEATH THE STYLE

Asked to name the one car responsible for today's handsome designs, most people would say Lincoln-Zephyr. They would be right. The influence of this car has been great. It ushered in a new style era—started the trend in a new direction.

But ask more than twenty Lincoln-Zephyr owners which feature of the Lincoln-Zephyr they most admire, and "style" will not predominate. This group, perhaps the most enthusiastic ever loyal to one car, values the Lincoln-Zephyr for its combination of features unique among all cars! Owners understand by personal experience value beneath the style.

From the beginning, the Lincoln-Zephyr has pioneered. The first forward-looking feature that set the car apart was the unit-body-and-frame. In all closed types there is no chassis, as that term is understood. Body and frame are a unit—a framework of steel trusses to which steel panels are welded. The results are efficient, economical operation (excess weight is eliminated) and great safety. These trusses have the rigid, unyielding qualities of a bridge of steel.

From the beginning, the Lincoln-Zephyr has been the only car at medium price to offer the smooth, sure performance of a V-type 12-cylinder engine. It

proved that great power and economy could go hand in hand. Owners report 14 to 18 miles per gallon!

And, from the first, the Lincoln-Zephyr has been an easy car to ride in and to drive. Many factors contribute to this: the distribution of car and passenger weight "amidships" . . . low center of gravity . . . soft transverse springs . . . roomy interiors . . . high visibility . . . hydraulic brakes. These, too, are a part of the sound value that lies beneath the Lincoln-Zephyr's startling beauty. Why not join those who enjoy a car modern in all its ways? Lincoln Motor Company—division of Ford Motor Company.

THE STYLE LEADER

1 page, 4 colors bleed   Saturday Evening Post   March 4,

I

THERE'S ONLY ONE WAY TO GET ALL THAT LINCOLN-ZEPHYR OFFERS!

Set down, if you will, all the qualities you would like in your new car. Use your imagination! Compromise with no desire! We have an idea your ideal car is here, and that you can well afford it.

Modern styling? Three years ago the Lincoln-Zephyr established the vogue of today.

But you are sensible enough to consider what lies beneath style. You like to drive—enjoy mastery over a powerful engine—have perhaps dreamed of a "twelve." The Lincoln-Zephyr has a smooth, efficient V-type 12-cylinder engine—the only "twelve" in the medium-price field.

You keep account of your running expenses and must watch the bills. *The Lincoln-Zephyr's 12 cylinders give 14 to 18 miles to the gallon.* To low first cost, you can add low cost of operation.

You pride yourself on knowing something about automobile engineering, are impressed by sound and original design. In all closed types, the body and frame of the Lincoln-Zephyr are a unit—steel panels welded to steel trusses. This is the arch-bridge construction, which results in light weight (for efficient operation) and rigid, unyielding strength (for great safety).

Your wife drives much—and you think often of her security. In addition to the strength of the unit-body-and-frame, many other Lincoln-Zephyr features contribute to safety—low center of gravity, hydraulic brakes, passenger position "amidships," soft transverse springs, and clear visibility through a wide windshield.

There are now more than 64,000 enthusiastic Lincoln-Zephyr owners. They say to you: There is only one way to get all that Lincoln-Zephyr offers. Get a Lincoln-Zephyr! Lincoln Motor Company, Division of Ford Motor Company.

THE STYLE LEADER

2

WHERE HAVE THE BAD ROADS GONE?

THOUGH it is not yet recorded on the maps, most roads in America are now first-class. Secondary routes have disappeared. By-paths have leveled off — their ruts and chuck-holes are somehow filled. It's easier now to drive wherever you please!

All this happens when you buy a Lincoln-Zephyr!

A unique combination of features, not to be matched at any price, is responsible for this car's great comfort and safety. First of these is the truss-type construction. Body and frame in closed models

are a unit — a rigid, unyielding framework of steel to which steel panels are welded. The whole is then gently cradled on soft transverse springs.

Other features make their distinct contributions to comfort: chair-high seats . . . large interiors (this is a big car) . . . high visibility . . . low center of gravity (steadiness around turns) . . . equal distribution of car weight and passenger weight . . . position of passengers toward the center (where shocks and jolts from the road are less likely to reach).

The V-type Lincoln-built engine is the only "twelve" in the medium-price field. It offers smooth power for all travel. And it is a thrifty "twelve" — under many conditions and many weathers.

You have admired the Lincoln-Zephyr's outward beauty. This *is* the car that set the styles for the industry! Discover now, on roads you once thought closed to travel, the comfort, power, economy and safety *beneath* the Lincoln-Zephyr's style! Lincoln Motor Company, Division of Ford Motor Company.

BENEATH ITS OUTWARD BEAUTY

A combination of features that makes it the only car of its kind. **1.** *Unit-body-and-frame—steel panels welded to steel trusses.* **2.** *V-type 12-cylinder engine—smooth, quiet, economical power.* **3.** *High power-to-weight ratio—low center of gravity.* **4.** *Comfort for six, "amidships" in chair-high seats—gliding ride—direct entrance—high visibility.* **5.** *Hydraulic brakes.*

Lincoln-Zephyr V·12

THE STYLE LEADER

3

1

2

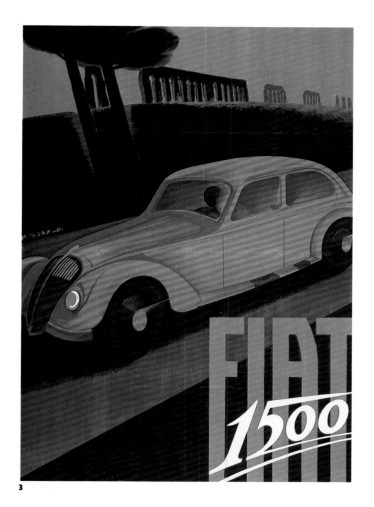

3

4

5

6

CLIENT: DUNLOP TYRES

1 PRESS AD, 1933, UK

2 PRESS AD, 1936, UK

3 PRESS AD, 1934, UK

4 PRESS AD, 1933, UK

5 PRESS AD, 1934, UK

6 PRESS AD, 1933, UK

Back in the thirties, those who could afford a car could indulge in the luxury of driving for pleasure. We chose this campaign because it so perfectly captures that sensation with a series of duotones that are not cluttered with unnecessary copy.

7 PRESS AD, 1930, UK
CLIENT: MORRIS MINOR

8 PRESS AD, 1930, UK
CLIENT: HUMBER

9 PRESS AD, 1930, UK
CLIENT: HILLMAN

10 PRESS AD, 1930, UK
CLIENT: MORRIS ISIS

1

2

3

4

5

6

MORRIS MINOR

A true conception of economical Motoring. 8 h.p., o.h.v. engine, generous seating accommodation, fine coachwork, 40-50 m.p.g., over 50 m.p.h. with excellent road-holding, completely equipped with every desirable accessory.

PRICES (O.H.V. type):
TWO-SEATER (*Fabric*) £125; TOURER (*Coachbuilt*) £130; SALOON (*Fabric*) as illustrated £135; SALOON (*Coachbuilt*) with folding head £140. *Prices ex works.*

TRIPLEX GLASS   CHROMIUM FINISH
STANDARD

BUY BRITISH AND BE PROUD OF IT

7

It was the directors' decree—

the new Humbers *must* be the world's finest car value in the quality class. The word went round. Efficiency was the order of the day. Rationalisation. Perfect organisation. And in the 1931 Humbers this wonderful ideal is realised to the full. You are invited to send for the new art catalogue which describes and illustrates these fine cars.

| "16/50" Saloon | "Snipe" Saloon | "Pullman" 7-Seater Saloon |
| £425. | £485. | £695. |

Triplex Glass on all models.

HUMBER

OVERSEAS REPRESENTATIVES—
Australia and New Zealand—Mr. C. E. Blayney, Rootes Ltd., Herald Buildings, Pitt Street, Sydney.
India and Ceylon—Mr. H. H. Lilley, P.O. Box 803, Bombay, India.
South Africa—Mr. H. C. Leon, Rootes Ltd., 40/40a, North British Buildings, C/R Commissioner and Simmonds Street, Johannesburg.
Burma, Malay and Far East—Mr. A. T. Sanderson, P.O. Box 505, Singapore.
Europe—Mr. R. Escudier, Devonshire House, Piccadilly, London, W.1.
South America Mr. R. W. H. Cook, Banca Anglo-Sud-Americana, Buenos Aires.

HUMBER LTD., COVENTRY.
London Showrooms and World Exporters:—
Rootes Ltd., Devonshire House, Piccadilly, W.1.

AGAIN—SUCH CARS AS EVEN HUMBER NEVER BUILT BEFORE.

8

The Car of Supreme Smoothness

Smoothness is the keynote of the Hillman "Straight Eight." In its smooth-running and its smooth-riding qualities it is supreme at its price. Its eight cylinders produce an effortless flow of power that only eight cylinders can produce; its remarkably fine suspension smooths out the worst of roads. Altogether, it is a car offering value entirely out of the ordinary. The saloon at £445 is a particularly fine example and should be seen and tried by every motorist. Write to-day for the colour-illustrated catalogue.

THE HILLMAN MOTOR CAR CO. LTD.,
COVENTRY.
World Exporters:
ROOTES LTD., Devonshire House, Piccadilly, W.1.

HILLMAN

STRAIGHT EIGHT	
Tourer	£430
Safety Tourer	£445
Saloon	£445
Safety Saloon	£495
*6-Light Weymann Saloon	£485
*Segrave Model	£495
Drop-Head Coupé	£510

FOURTEEN	
Tourer	£310
Safety Tourer	£325
Saloon	£325
Safety Saloon	£375
*6-Light Weymann Saloon	£375
*Segrave Model	£395
Drop-Head Coupé	£415
* Sunshine Roof £10 extra.	

Overseas Representatives:
AUSTRALIA: Mr. C. E. Blayney, Rootes Ltd., Herald Buildings, Pitt Street, Sydney.
NEW ZEALAND: Mr. Frank A. Beau, N.Z. Automobile Chambers, 30, Taranaki Street, Wellington.
SOUTH AFRICA: Mr. H. C. Leon, Rootes Ltd., 47/49a, North British Buildings, Cr. Commissioner and Simmonds Street, Johannesburg.
INDIA, BURMA and CEYLON: Mr. H. H. Lilley, P.O. Box 803, Bombay, India.

9

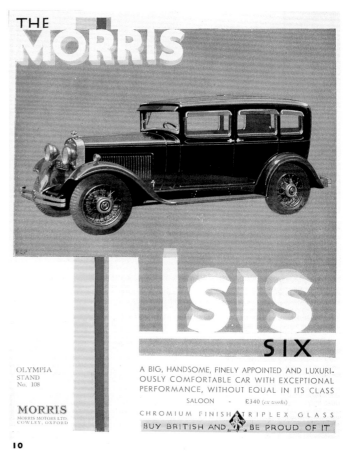

THE MORRIS

ISIS SIX

OLYMPIA STAND No. 108

MORRIS
MORRIS MOTORS LTD.,
COWLEY, OXFORD.

A BIG, HANDSOME, FINELY APPOINTED AND LUXURIOUSLY COMFORTABLE CAR WITH EXCEPTIONAL PERFORMANCE, WITHOUT EQUAL IN ITS CLASS

SALOON   -   £340 (*ex works*)

CHROMIUM FINISH   TRIPLEX GLASS

BUY BRITISH AND BE PROUD OF IT

10

1

CLIENT: SHELL-MEX & B.P.
LIMITED, UK

1 *LORRY BILL, 1931*

ARTIST: E. MCKNIGHT KAUFFER

2 *LORRY BILL, 1932*

ARTIST: DAVID LEWIS

3 *LORRY BILL, 1934*

ARTIST: BARNETT FREEDMAN

4 *LORRY BILL, 1935*

ARTIST: E. MCKNIGHT KAUFFER

5 *LORRY BILL, 1935*

ARTIST: E. MCKNIGHT KAUFFER

6 *LORRY BILL, 1932*

ARTIST: E. MCKNIGHT KAUFFER

The 1930s were the golden years of Shell advertising. Under the guidance of Advertising Manager, Jack Beddington, the company became a liberal patron of the arts — Graham Sutherland's first commercial work was for Shell and they frequently commissioned E. McKnight Kauffer, whose integration of typography and illustration has led many to regard him as one of the first 'graphic designers'.

2

3

4

5

6

YOU CAN BE SURE OF SHELL

MOTORISTS PREFER SHELL

1

TO VISIT BRITAIN'S LANDMARKS

HALDON BELVEDERE NEAR EXETER   CAREL WEIGHT

YOU CAN BE SURE OF SHELL

2

TO VISIT BRITAIN'S LANDMARKS

"ROMAN" TOWER, TUTBURY, STAFFS.   L. H. ROSOMAN

YOU CAN BE SURE OF SHELL

3

TO VISIT BRITAIN'S LANDMARKS

JOHN KNOX MONUMENT, GLASGOW.   PAMELA DREW

YOU CAN BE SURE OF SHELL

4

TO VISIT BRITAIN'S LANDMARKS

BRIMHAM ROCK, YORKSHIRE   GRAHAM SUTHERLAND

YOU CAN BE SURE OF SHELL

5

PULLS like— SHELL!

6

PROGRESS

BP ETHYL

"BP" ETHYL
NOW LEADING

7

JUST OUT SUMMER SHELL

8

THESE MEN USE SHELL

JOURNALISTS · ZERO

YOU CAN BE SURE OF SHELL

9

THESE MEN USE SHELL

RACING MOTORISTS · R.GUYATT

YOU CAN BE SURE OF SHELL

10

ADOLF–DER ÜBERMENSCH

CLIENT: ANTI-NAZI PROPAGANDA

ARTIST: JOHN HARTFIELD

1 POSTER, GERMANY

HEADLINE: 'ADOLF THE SUPERMAN SWALLOWS GOLD AND TALKS TRASH'

2 POSTER, GERMANY

HEADLINE: 'OUT OF THE SWAMP'

3 POSTER, GERMANY

HEADLINE: 'HURRY, BUTTER IS EVERYTHING'

4 POSTER, GERMANY

HEADLINE: 'THAT'S SALVATION YOU'RE BRINGING'

Even before photography was commonplace in advertising, Hartfield had developed his extraordinary photo-montage techniques and used them to great effect in pre-war political satire.

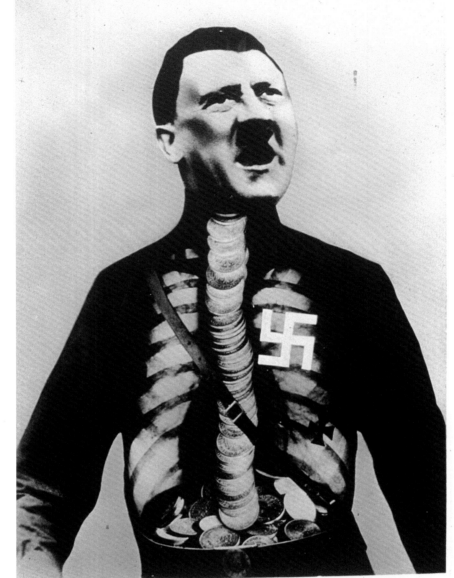

SCHLUCKT GOLD UND REDET BLECH

1

2

3

Das ist das Heil, das sie bringen!

4

1 *POSTER, 1936, SPAIN*

CLIENT: REPUBLICAN PARTY OF ESQUERRA

HEADLINE: 'ADVANCE! EVERYONE AS A SINGLE MAN'

ARTIST: COVES

2 *POSTER, 1935, SPAIN*

CLIENT: CATALAN GOVERNMENT

HEADLINE: 'CITIZEN! HAVE YOU ALREADY GOT AN ELECTORAL BALLOT, A GUARANTY OF YOUR VOTE?'

ARTIST: MORELL

3 *POSTER, 1937, SPAIN*

HEADLINE: 'THEY SHALL NOT PASS JULY 1936! JULY 1937 WE SHALL PASS!'

ARTIST: PUYOL

4 *POSTER, 1936, SPAIN*

CLIENT: CATALAN DEFENCE COUNCIL

HEADLINE: 'FIND OUT FROM THOSE FIGHTING AT THE FRONT'

ARTIST: UNKNOWN

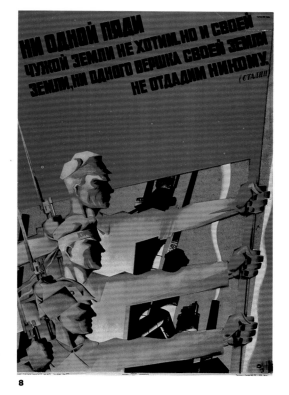

5/10 POSTERS, 1930s, USSR

These posters were part of a campaign by the Soviet Union to win support for its five-year industrialisation plan.

6 POSTER, 1930s, USSR

ARTIST: DAVID MOOR

7 POSTER, 1932, USSR

HEADLINE: 'GET READY FOR THE DEFENCE OF THE OCTOBER REVOLUTION'

ARTIST: UNKNOWN

8 POSTER, 1931, USSR

HEADLINE: 'WE DON'T WANT ANY FOREIGN LAND BUT WE'RE NOT GIVING UP ANY OF OUR LAND'

ARTIST: JANG

9 POSTER, 1931, USSR

HEADLINE: 'IN 1931 LETS GIVE 8 MILLION TONS OF IRON TO THE FIRST FOUNDATIONS OF SOCIALISM'

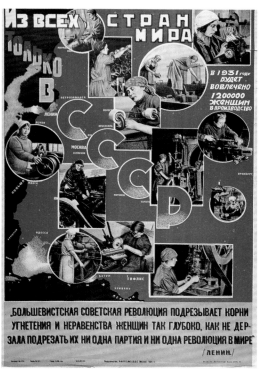

CHAPTER SEVEN

THE IMAGE OF a triumphant Neville Chamberlain waving his 'peace with honour' agreement was no more than a bitter memory by the time Great Britain reached the 1940s. The decade began with the country hunched in ill-prepared defence against the onslaught of the Third Reich. In the following year the war took an unexpected turn when Hitler, who had learned little from the experience of Napoleon Bonaparte, invaded the Soviet Union and the Japanese bombed Pearl Harbor. America, abandoning its role of quartermaster, joined the fighting.

Once again, in both Europe and the United States, advertising's style was cramped by war-torn economies. Utilitarian imagery replaced the glamour of the 1930s and the keynote of every campaign was patriotism. Many manufacturers continued to advertise even when their products were not available, just to maintain brand loyalty. Others, like the Ethyl Corporation, stressed that they had down-graded their products only in support of the war-effort and that normal standards would be resumed once the Allied Forces had prevailed.

It is hard not to question the integrity of some of these ads. While the tone is serious and sincere, the underlying commercial motivations appear crudely obvious. Others, however, managed to combine patri-otism and salesmanship with a lighter touch—the most notable example here being H.M. Bateman's hilarious cartoons for Guinness in Great Britain.

As in the Great War, governments relied on advertising agencies to produce propaganda—recruitment, war bonds and public information returned as the subjects on which advertising exercised its creative skills. Paper and ink shortages necessitated the use of smaller spaces and encouraged the development of spot colour and duotone—devices that remained popular after the war was over.

In 1945 Roosevelt was succeeded by Harry S. Truman and, when the Japanese refused to surrender, atom bombs were dropped on Hiroshima and Nagasaki—the light of those explosions casting the shadow of fear in which we live today.

With the return of peace there were radical social reforms both in Europe and America. Churchill was defeated in election and the Labour government built the welfare state—there was an immediate programme of nationalization and the creation of the National Health Service—and America invested heavily in the rebuilding of a democratic Europe, while making special provision, in the form of loans and subsidies, for the ten million returning war veterans. After five years of unprecedented turmoil and uncertainty the world at last celebrated to the crooning sounds of Frank Sinatra and Bing Crosby, went to the cinema and started a baby boom.

CLIENT: GENERAL TIRES

1-3 *PRESS ADS, 1945, USA*

4 *PRESS AD, 1943, USA*

5 *PRESS AD, 1944, USA*

6 *PRESS AD, 1947, USA*

7 *PRESS AD, 1945, USA*

General Tires were up against the problem that most people think that one tyre is very much the same as another. During the war years they played upon patriotism, stressing that their product was made of American rubber, and created the triplets device as a way of reminding people not to judge things by appearances.

YES! A NEW TIRE IS BORN

No wonder they're thrilled! Because it's built with American-Made rubber . . . bears the name GENERAL . . . and is the tire everyone knew American engineering ingenuity would produce.

In this new General Tire . . . from American-Made rubber . . . you see the result of the relentless effort by General's corps of research engineers to help solve America's rubber problem.

All the knowledge gained by General's production specialists in 25 years of building quality tires . . . all their methods for getting *the most* out of rubber . . . have contributed to the development of this new-day General.

It has General's famous Silent-Grip tread design. It has General's same extra strong cord body, as always. And, it has American-Made rubber processed by the same craftsmen who gave you General's quality in the past.

You are invited by your local General Tire dealer now to see this new General that someday, when the rubber crisis is over, will be available to all without restriction.

THE GENERAL TIRE & RUBBER COMPANY · AKRON, OHIO

The **GENERAL TIRE**

4

On hot desert roads
Test cars proved General's mileage
. . . with American-Made Rubber

● Over the tire-defying roads of the Mojave Desert went test cars . . . through noonday heat and the cold of desert nights . . . to learn for you the kind of *mileage* and *safety* you could expect from the new General Tire . . . with *American-Made* rubber.

The results are in. This General delivers the kind of *performance* that has made General, for 25 years, the leader in *Top-Quality.* Yes, if you are eligible to buy, you get *the most* from American-Made rubber . . . in today's General with its quick-stopping, slow-wearing Silent-Grip tread . . . and the same extra strong, blowout-resisting cords, as always.

Remember, however . . . tires are still very precious and will be for a long time to come. You *must* save those you have. For every tire need: Kraft System recapping, repairing or new tires, see your General Tire Dealer. *He is a tire expert.*

THE GENERAL TIRE & RUBBER COMPANY · AKRON, OHIO

The **GENERAL TIRE**

".. Now remember, Butch, it's a GENERAL!"

BUY MORE WAR BONDS

5

When it rains, it stops! The quick-stopping ability of *Action-Traction* on wet pavements is only one outstanding advantage of the General Squeegee Tire. It completes the peace of mind that comes from the blowout protection of extra carcass strength . . . longer, safer mileage from top-quality rubber . . . quieter running from straight, free-rolling ribs. These features make The General Squeegee cost a little more—*but worth much more.* It is truer than ever that *the least of the difference is the difference in price.*

COPYRIGHT 1947, THE GENERAL TIRE & RUBBER CO., AKRON, OHIO

Action-Traction
RUNS LIKE THIS · STOPS LIKE THIS

The **GENERAL SQUEEGEE TIRE**

6

WHAT HAS CAKE BAKING TO DO WITH *Synthetic Tires?*

Starting with the same ingredients, women will bake cakes of widely varying quality. Why? Because it takes more than just the ingredients for a prize-winning cake . . . you've got to have That Special "Knack".

GENERAL has a special "knack" too
. . . in compounding Synthetic Rubber for LONG MILEAGE

Today, when all tires are made from synthetic rubber, General's famous 30-year "knack" for mileage is more important to you than ever . . . because, it takes *extra skill* and careful control to build long mileage into synthetic tires. That is why there is actually more difference in tire mileage today than before. And, that is why General's special "knack" for getting the *most miles* out of rubber now brings you still greater long-mileage dividends. From start to finish, General uses its exclusive formula to build a synthetic tire that is a *Top-Quality* General in every way . . . a tire made under rigid quality controls by craftsmen who know only the best; a tire that is as far ahead of ordinary tires in mileage as Generals always have been.

The **GENERAL TIRE**

—goes a long way to make friends

7

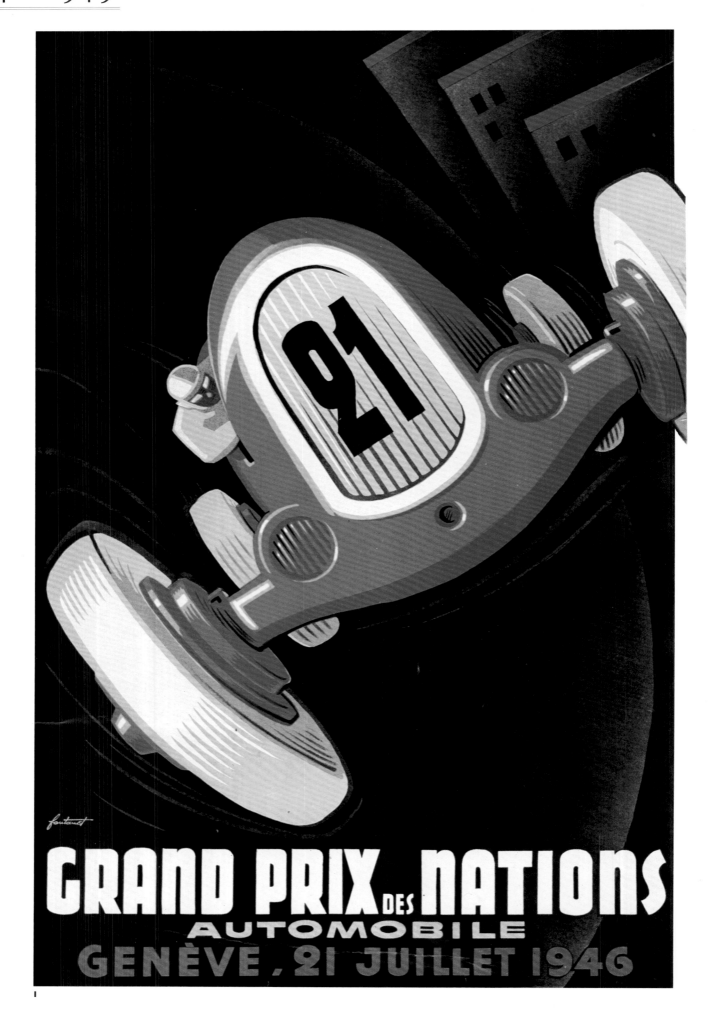

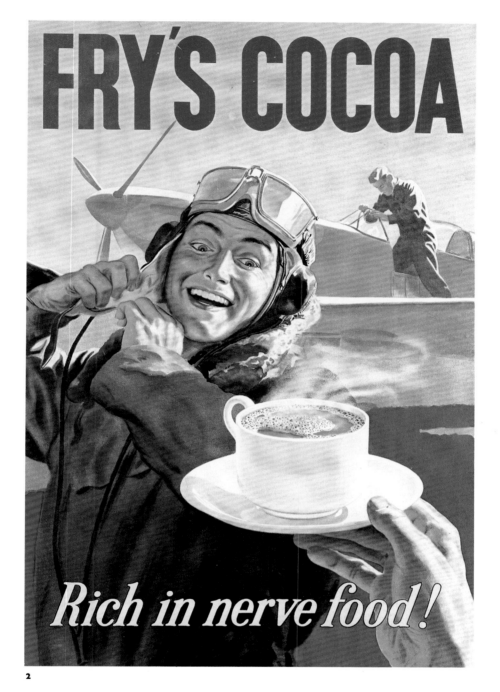

Rich in nerve food!

2

3

1 *POSTER, 1946, SWITZERLAND*
CLIENT: INTERNATIONAL GRAND
PRIX
ARTIST: NOEL FONTANET

2 *POSTER, 1940, UK*
CLIENT: FRY'S COCOA

3 *POSTER, 1942, UK*
CLIENT: OXO

Compliments of Motorist Jones!

Block-busters that crash Axis morale, screaming shells that blast his troops and ships, "ash cans" that sink his submarines . . . all contain the explosive TNT, now derived from petroleum which might have been made into gasoline for your car.

In a great new unit at one of The Texas Company's refineries, vast quantities of the essential *toluene* for the making of high-explosive TNT are now being made from a part of the raw material that in peacetime would be made into Fire-Chief and Sky Chief gasolines.

So from petroleum comes this added fighting strength for our cause, along with great quantities of 100-octane gasoline and other fighting fuels and lubricants now pouring from Texaco refineries in an ever increasing flood.

The gasoline which you, "Motorist Jones," are doing without is being turned into war products to speed our fighting forces to Victory.

THE TEXAS COMPANY

TEXACO FIRE-CHIEF AND SKY CHIEF GASOLINES • HAVOLINE AND TEXACO MOTOR OILS

HEIL . . . !

They salute you, Fuehrer . . . your dead warriors.

They died . . . for what? Not Victory, for today the legions of decency are growing ever stronger.

Here in America, millions of peace-loving citizens are willingly skimping on food . . . going without gasoline . . . working and investing their savings to defeat you.

Our vast industrial plants are pouring out munitions in ever greater quantity.

From The Texas Company's refineries alone are coming millions of gallons of powerful 100-octane aviation gasoline . . . toluene for making "block-busting" bombs and shells . . . vast quantities of other war fuels and lubricants.

Our armies have just begun to show their real strength. Our civilians are setting new records of production. To put an end to your militarism and murder. To restore the right to *live* in peace and freedom.

THE TEXAS COMPANY

TEXACO FIRE-CHIEF & SKY CHIEF GASOLINES • HAVOLINE & TEXACO MOTOR OILS

Report to the Emperor

"Sacred One. Son of Heaven.

"I report a great change in the temper of our American enemies.

"Our ruthlessness has only made them more angry—more aroused.

"Their soldiers fight with redoubled fury.

"Their people work harder—and sacrifice more.

"Sublime Majesty, we fight a determined foe. Remind us again that we are unconquerable."

Our enemies are realists. Don't think it doesn't bother them to see us buying war bonds; to watch us conserve clothes, food and gasoline. Don't think Tokio doesn't know, and curse, the new thousands pouring into industry—the vast quantities of war material pouring out.

And even now, Tokio, our slogan is *more*. At The Texas Company that means *more* of the powerful 100-octane gasoline for our planes and PT boats . . . *more* toluene for making deadly block-busting TNT and *more* butadiene for synthetic rubber.

America *is* a determined foe. Determined to be victorious.

THE TEXAS COMPANY

TEXACO FIRE CHIEF & SKY CHIEF GASOLINES • HAVOLINE & TEXACO MOTOR OILS

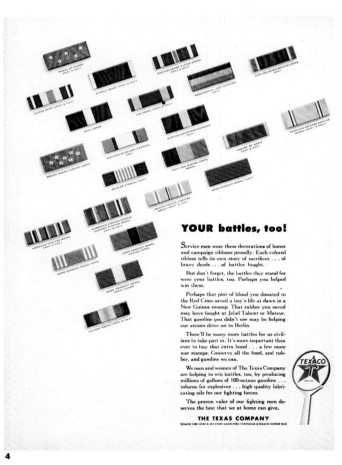

YOUR battles, too!

Service men wear these decorations of honor and campaign ribbons proudly. Each colored ribbon tells its own story of sacrifices . . . of brave deeds . . . of battles fought.

But don't forget, the battles they stand for were your battles, too. Perhaps you helped win them.

Perhaps that pint of blood you donated to the Red Cross saved a boy's life at dawn in a New Guinea swamp. That rubber you saved may have fought at Jebel Tahent or Mateur. That gasoline *you* didn't use may be helping our armies drive on to Berlin.

There'll be many more battles for us civilians to take part in. It's more important than ever to buy that extra bond . . . a few more war stamps. Conserve all the food, and rubber, and gasoline we can.

We men and women of The Texas Company are helping to win battles, too, by producing millions of gallons of 100-octane gasoline . . . toluene for explosives . . . high quality lubricating oils for our fighting forces.

The proven valor of our fighting men deserves the best that we at home can give.

THE TEXAS COMPANY

TEXACO FIRE CHIEF & SKY CHIEF GASOLINES • HAVOLINE & TEXACO MOTOR OILS

U. S. AIRCRAFT CARRIERS not only carry *more* gasoline than any service station ashore, but they also carry *better* gasoline.

Every drop of gasoline used by our fighting carrier planes is the highest octane fuel made by oil companies in America. All of these companies use Ethyl fluid to improve their aviation gasoline.

Since the Army and Navy must have millions of gallons of this 100 octane fuel, government agencies have had to place limits on the quantity and quality of gasoline for civilian use. But—when the fighting is over you'll get better gasoline than ever before.

ETHYL CORPORATION
Chrysler Building
New York 17, N. Y.

COPYRIGHT 1944, ETHYL CORPORATION

1-4 *PRESS CAMPAIGN, 1943, USA*
CLIENT: TEXACO OIL

5-7 *PRESS CAMPAIGN, 1944, USA*
CLIENT: ETHYL CORPORATION

Petrol is a vital resource in wartime. Texaco advertised their military applications — aviation fuel, explosives, synthetic rubber and lubricants. The Ethyl Corporation stressed that they were sending their high-grade fuel to the war and that with the return of peace their 'knock-free' formula would once again be available to the public.

5

6

7

1

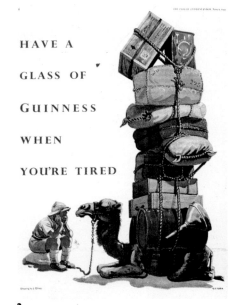

2

3

4

5

6

7

8

"My Goodness — My Guinness"

9

"My Goodness — My Guinness"

11

"My Goodness — My Guinness"

12

GUINNESS for STRENGTH

13

My Goodness — My GUINNESS

14

CLIENT: ARTHUR GUINNESS SON
AND COMPANY

AGENCY: S. H. BENSON, LONDON

1 *POSTER, 1947, UK*

ARTIST: JOHN GILROY

2-3/13 *PRESS ADS, 1945, UK*

ARTIST: JOHN GILROY

4 *PRESS AD, 1949, UK*

ARTIST: JOHN GILROY

5 *PRESS AD, 1944, UK*

ARTIST: J. HART

6 *POSTER, 1947, UK*

ARTIST: JOHN GILROY

7 *PRESS AD, 1943, UK*

ARTIST: JOHN GILROY

8 *PRESS AD, 1942, UK*

ARTIST: JOHN GILROY

9 *PRESS AD, 1944, UK*

ARTIST: H. M. BATEMAN

10 *PRESS AD, 1943, UK*

ARTIST: H. M. BATEMAN

11 *PRESS AD, 1943, UK·*

ARTIST: H. M. BATEMAN

12 *PRESS AD, 1940, UK*

ARTIST: H. M. BATEMAN

14 *PRESS AD, 1941, UK*

ARTIST: JOHN GILROY

*Even during the war Guinness never lost its
sense of humour and was quick to make use
of military imagery with such headlines as
'Today, more than ever, what you need is a
Guinness'. So keen was the company to
maintain an advertising presence, that
during the paper shortage it printed new
posters on the back of old ones — hence the
occasional dark background to cover up
print through.*

2

3

4

5

PRESS ADS, 1949, USA

CLIENT: STETSON HATS

ARTIST: S. UNDERHILL

This forties campaign used a sort of double endorsement — not only did it feature the testimony of famous stars, it cast them in their roles from famous films. Today, it would be unusual to find a celebrity endorsement that was drawn and not photographed.

Four ads with classic forties styling promise elegance despite the wartime restrictions on materials available for tailoring.

It becomes hard to imagine a product that can't be sold on the strength of its value to the war effort.

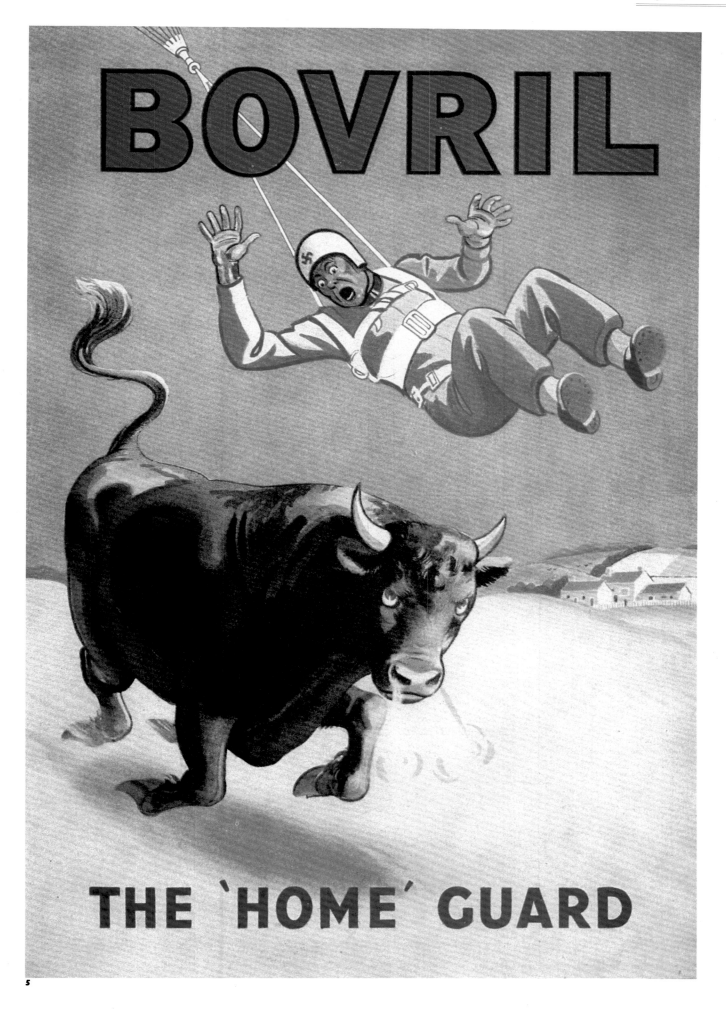

1

2

3

Now . . . He Shoots For Freedom

Life began at ten for Bill, strutting out with his first Winchester and a pocketful of Western Super-X long range .22's! Sure those two big leaping jackrabbits caught him "flat-footed", but it didn't matter! He'd do better next time—and he did.

Today, instead of shooting for fun, Bill is shooting for Freedom—and doing a great job of it. Out on the training ranges, and in the front lines getting the range of the enemy, millions of men like Bill are making good use of the military cartridges Western is producing for them.

They know how Western ammunition shoots and are looking forward to the days when they can hunt game in peaceful fields and woods at home, with Western Super-X and Xpert ammunition . . . Western Cartridge Company East Alton, Illinois.

Performance Made These Names Famous: Super-X — Xpert — Silvertip

The fame won by Super-X, Xpert and Silvertip ammunition was earned by outstanding performance. Hunters long have recognized that these names stand for the highest developments in shot shells and cartridges. When sporting ammunition can again be manufactured, you can expect the same fine performance that made Western the World Champion Ammunition.

WORLD CHAMPION AMMUNITION

CARTRIDGES • SHOT SHELLS • TRAPS AND TARGETS

Relying upon Winchester is an Old American Custom

Down from the skies come U. S. Paratroops. A new American fighting force in this war, it is natural they should need a new firearm. And just as natural that it should be *originated, engineered and designed by Winchester!*

This Winchester Carbine, officially called the U. S. Carbine Caliber .30, M1, weighs little more than one-half as much as the standard service rifle. It's greater in fire power, longer in range, faster in action and more deadly in accuracy than the automatic pistol.

Reliance upon Winchester gun-making craftsmanship is natural to Americans. For perhaps nothing which has ever been made in America has been so much a part of our nation's history as Winchester guns and ammunition.

Look at the record: In 1866, the Winchester Model 66, the world's first commercially successful repeating rifle, was born. Men swore and lived by it. In Mexico, it helped Juarez break the despotic yoke of Maximilian. A few years later, the Model 73 became as renowned as the heroes of the Western plains who lived by it.

In the Spanish American War and World War 1, Winchester fought for America. And today, Winchester is on every battle front.

All America today knows the history of the U. S. M1 Garand rifle that won its spurs at Bataan and Wake Island. Here at Winchester, we are producing Garand rifles in ever increasing quantities. Better yet, our 76 years of gun-making craftsmanship made it possible for us to cut their unit cost to Uncle Sam . . . *to one-half their original contract price!*

Such outstanding gun-making achievements as these are the reasons for the unquestioned reliance that America reposes in Winchester—in both war and peace.

WINCHESTER REPEATING ARMS CO., New Haven, Conn.
Division of WESTERN CARTRIDGE COMPANY

WINCHESTER
"On Guard for America Since 1866"

RIFLES • SHOTGUNS • CARTRIDGES • SHOTSHELLS • FLASHLIGHTS • BATTERIES

Wherever America Fights . . .
Western Is Fighting, Too!

"Americans are the best-equipped soldiers in the world"
Maj. Gen. Levin H. Campbell, Jr.
Chief of Ordnance

AMMUNITION

More than 5 billion rounds of rifle and machine gun ammunition, in .30 and .50 caliber, and many other types, have been produced by Western-operated plants at East Alton, Ill., New Haven, Conn., and the St. Louis Ordnance Plant, operated by The United States Cartridge Company, a Western subsidiary. The latter is producing more small arms ammunition than was turned out by all American factories during World War I.

GARANDS

Winchester is manufacturing, in great quantities, the famous Garand semi-automatic rifle, which won its spurs at Wake Island and Bataan. Winchester was the first commercial arms company to make it—and, due to manufacturing economies, has reduced the cost to the government to less than one half of the original contract price.

CARBINES

Thousands of Winchester carbines are being produced by Western's Winchester division, which originated and developed this new, speedy, deadly efficient semi-automatic arm-weapon. Adopted by the Ordnance Department as the U. S. Carbine, Caliber .30, M1, it greatly increases offensive fire-power of combat units.

METALS

As leading producers of cartridge brass for our own and other ammunition plants, and of critical metals for many other uses, vastly enlarged brass mills at East Alton, Ill. and New Haven, Conn. are greatly aiding the war effort . . . In fact, too, Western is helping Uncle Sam saving millions of pounds of brass. Tons of vital aluminum are being produced by an affiliated organization. Heat exchangers and tubes of seamless copper radiator tubes, both developed and produced by Winchester, are used in airplanes, tanks and landing barges.

On land and sea, and in the sky wherever America is fighting—products of the Western Cartridge Company, its divisions and affiliates, are contributing to the crushing offensive power of the United Nations.

Torrents of retribution for the Axis are pouring from Western-operated plants and factories, manned by more than 50,000 production soldiers. Accuracy and reliability of rifles and carbines, high efficiency of shells and cartridges, including strength of metals, devastating force of military explosives—all these, and many more, are Western contributions to freedom.

From the manufacture of sporting arms and ammunition and related products in the metals and explosives fields, Western has diverted a half-century of peace-time experience to producing weapons of war. The basic

"know-how" of Western's own technicians, acquired through years of research, has been multiplied over and over through the expansion of our facilities and by the extension of Western management to government-owned plants.

Today, the Western organization measures its production in billions of units, each representing the highest skills known to American precision manufacture. Many parts of cartridges and primers once produce must be held within tolerances finer than those of a jeweler's watch. Most Western explosives require split-second perfection in manufacture as in performance. Winchester rifles and carbines are now, as ever, among the most precisely built products on earth. But with it all, Western's vast production reaches out to equip and hearten Allied fighting men beyond all the seven seas.

EXPLOSIVES

Western loads the 20 mm. shell, highly effective against dive bomber attacks on our ships—and we are making betryl, used in the shell's bursting charge, by an improved, Western-developed process . . . Smokeless ball powder, another Western development, produced 5 times faster than other smokeless powders, was put into quantity production rapidly when speed was vital . . . Among other products for war, we are making detonators and primers for naval shells and other projectiles; igniters for incendiary bombs—and great quantities of black powder, dynamite and other explosives.

SHOTGUNS-SHELLS

Aerial gunners, in training, are using Winchester shotguns and shot shells. Western shot shells, target-throwing equipment and "clay" targets are the peacetime choice of sportsmen everywhere.

Western
CARTRIDGE COMPANY
EAST ALTON, ILLINOIS

WINCHESTER REPEATING ARMS COMPANY
New Haven, Conn.
THE UNITED STATES CARTRIDGE COMPANY
St. Louis, Mo.
BOND ELECTRIC CORPORATION
New Haven, Conn.
OLIN CORPORATION
Aluminum Division
Tacoma, Wash.
And Other Divisions and Affiliates

FLASHLIGHTS

Thousands of flashlights and batteries, made by Winchester and by Bond Electric Corporation, New Haven, Conn., another Western division, are providing dependable, portable light in war plants.

Look to the Sky. . . .

There's plenty of excitement in this anti-aircraft gunner's job, "dishing it out" to enemy planes and taking it in return. But the thrills he longs for, just as you do, are those that only a duck marsh can provide.

How well you know those thrills . . . the nerve-tingling whir-r of wings knifing through morning mist . . . an unforgettable sunrise . . . the excitement of having a great flock streak over you. After picking up two you barely reach your blind before three

more swerve in over the decoys—then twelve—then twenty! High? Yes, but all the more thrilling when you're shooting powerful long-range Super-X with its effective short shot string.

With liberty made secure and ammunition for war no longer needed, unlimited quantities of Western Super-X and Xpert shot shells and cartridges will again be available for sportsmen. . . . Western Cartridge Company, East Alton, Illinois.

Powerful Super-X Pulls Down High Flyers

There are extra thrills in the extra range of Super-X. Ducks and geese that are beyond the reach of ordinary shells are brought down clean by the greater power, high velocity and short shot string of Super-X. Daily bag limits come easier. When ammunition for hunting is again plentiful, shoot this famous Western load—long range Super-X.

WORLD CHAMPION AMMUNITION

SHOT SHELLS . . . CARTRIDGES . . . TRAPS AND TARGETS

CLIENT: USSR ARMY

1 POSTER, 1941, USSR

HEADLINE: 'FORWARD, VICTORY IS
AT HAND'

2 POSTER, 1941, USSR

ARTIST: VKUMASHIN

3 POSTER, 1943, USSR

HEADLINE: 'ALL OUR HOPE LIES
WITH YOU, RED WARRIORS'

4 POSTER, 1942, USSR

5 POSTER, 1944, USSR

ARTIST: VICTOR DENI

HEADLINE: 'DESPATCHES FROM
THE FRONT'

6 POSTER, 1942, USSR

ARTIST: VDENIA DOLGORUKOV

HEADLINE: 'STALINGRAD'

Aesthetically, these posters owe a great deal
to the Revolution Art of 1919. It is
interesting to see that, in the absence of
voluntary service, there is none of the guilt
imagery that one finds in European posters
for the 1914-18 war — here the tone is one of
exhortation.

196

4

5

6

1 *POSTER, 1940, UK*

CLIENT: NATIONAL SAFETY FIRST
ASSOCIATION

ARTIST: MORRIS

2/5 *POSTERS, 1940, UK*

CLIENT: NATIONAL SAFETY FIRST
ASSOCIATION

1RTIST: PAT KEEL

3 *POSTER, UK*

CLIENT: MINISTRY OF
EMPLOYMENT

4/6 *POSTERS, UK*

CLIENT: MINISTRY OF HOME
SECURITY

7-10 *POSTERS, UK*

CLIENT: MINISTRY OF
AGRICULTURE AND FISHERIES

11-15 *POSTERS, UK*

CLIENT: NATIONAL SAVINGS
COMMITTEE

*During the war the British Government
encouraged the public to buy National
Savings Certificates to help finance the war
effort. As soon as peace was declared, it
issued posters encouraging people not to cash
them in but to continue saving for the
nation's prosperity.*

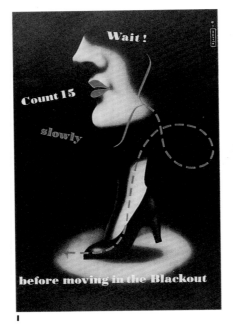

1

2

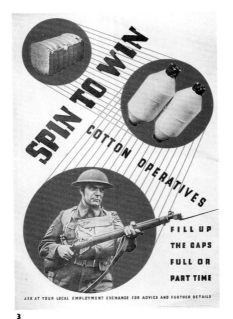

3

4

5

6

7

8

9

10

11

12

13

14

15

Another Zero Nearer that *Happiest* New Year!

If you think Zeros don't add up, better revise your pre-Pearl Harbor mathematics . . . and *ask the man who downs one!*

The fighter pilot who has just chalked up his third victory is three long steps nearer the front porch of his home—nearer the girl who's waiting—nearer the happiest New Year a war-tired world may ever know. Every American worthy of the name will back that Zero-eradicator to the limit, with bonds, with bombs, with better fighting planes and equipment.

Greyhound's share in bringing our fighters back to the land they love consists of carrying manpower and womanpower by the millions—supplying the vital transportation that is life-blood to war production. Today, with more than 4,000 Greyhound employees in the fighting forces, another 17,000 are helping carry the war load here at home.

And when this war is over and won, Greyhound will bring 'em back home from seaports and airports and training camps by the hundreds of thousands—to the very doorsteps of the homes they left behind.

After that, look ahead with Greyhound to luxurious, scenic travel on a brand new scale—marked by the economy that made Greyhound famous—made to measure for a new and better world!

Will you give 45 minutes to save a fighter's life?

About 45 minutes after you walk into Red Cross Blood Donor headquarters, you walk out with a glow of pride that won't ever come off . . . *for you've given a pint of blood that may save an American fighter's life on some far battlefield.* It means so much—yet it's surprisingly easy to do. Write or phone your nearest Red Cross headquarters for an appointment.

GREYHOUND

1

Shaping up NOW

—for the day when "Highways are Happy Ways" again!

GREYHOUND

2

"I drove a Greyhound
. . I'll drive one again!"

5180

GREYHOUND

3

DEATH CAR...

ONLY A CHILD'S TOY on an unlighted stairway. Yet as lethal as a speeding truck for killing or crippling. For causing heartbreak and tragedy in someone's home.

Accidents . . . in the home . . . on the highways . . . in factories and offices . . . cost this nation 102,500 lives last year. This tragic toll, preventable to a great extent, was augmented by the permanent disabling of 350,000 other people . . . by 9,000,000 lesser casualties.

Production-wise, America's war effort lost heavily. In all, 480 *million* man days were lost forever. Enough to have built a total of 20 battleships, 100 destroyers, 9,000 bombers, and 40,000 tanks! Money-wise, the loss was almost 4 *billion* dollars!

Where did these accidents happen? Two-thirds of them happened outside of industry. In the home, where workers take chances they would not dream of taking on the job. They happened in darkened hallways . . . in bath tubs . . . in garages and basements. They happened in industry where someone gambled with safety.

No matter what you do, your life is precious to this nation. Don't take chances with it. Guard it for America . . . at day . . . and at night. Fight carelessness, the Master Saboteur! Join the anti-accident crusade! Help save a life!

The perfection of the famous "Eveready" fresh DATED flashlight battery called for coordination between various Units of Union Carbide and Carbon Corporation. The exact grade of graphite necessary for the "mix" was developed by the Acheson Graphite Corporation. Special alloy for protecting molds and machinery was produced by the Haynes Stellite Company, and Carbide and Carbon Chemicals Corporation provided a specially prepared paint made of "Vinylite" resins for the spun metal cap.

"EVEREADY" FLASHLIGHTS AND BATTERIES

NATIONAL CARBON COMPANY, INC.
30 EAST 42ND STREET · New York, N. Y.
Unit of Union Carbide and Carbon Corporation

The words "Eveready" and "Vinylite" are registered trade-marks.

4

5

6

PRESS CAMPAIGN, USA

CLIENT: FARNSWORTH

1 ARTIST: SERGE SONDEIKINE

2 ARTIST: JULIO DE DIEGO

3 ARTIST: FRED NAGLER

4 ARTIST: ROBERT RIGGS

This campaign for radiograms is a triumph of what is now called 'borrowed interest'. The agency forged a relationship between Farnsworth and the idea of superb musical reproduction by commissioning artists to illustrate moments from popular classical masterpieces — the choice of music helping to define the target market.

The carnival scene from Stravinsky's "Petrouchka," painted for the Capehart Collection by Serge Soudeikine. The canvas depicts the puppet show characters ... Petrouchka, The Ballerina, The Blackamoor, and The Showman ... in the colorful animation of the entire carnival. Portfolios of reproductions of paintings in the Capehart Collection may be secured at nominal cost from your Capehart dealer, or you may write direct to Fort Wayne 1, Indiana.

Puppets and People

Puppets are endeared to all ages of men. And they are the more beloved when, as in "Petrouchka," their stories are synchronized with great music. For music lends enchantment ... especially if its color and meaning are provided in full measure by the Capehart or the Farnsworth.

Those who have made music part of their most intimate lives look with pride ... and listen with pleasure ... to these sublime instruments. Their delight will be shared tomorrow by many others when the Farnsworth Television & Radio Corporation turns from making war-vital Radar and electronic instruments.

Then, all may have the new Capehart or Farnsworth so eagerly awaited now ... radios and phonograph-radios which will include far-reaching advances in faithful reception and round, true tone.

Perhaps your ultimate choice may be a radio with glorious FM ... perhaps a phonograph-radio with the time-proved Capehart record-changer that turns the records over. Eventually, you may decide upon a television model, bringing the world into your living-room. In a variety of cabinet styles and sizes, each will be built by Capehart and Farnsworth engineers to be the best in its price field! Farnsworth Television & Radio Corporation, Fort Wayne 1, Ind.

INVEST IN VICTORY — BUY WAR BONDS

THE CAPEHART   THE FARNSWORTH
Television · Radio · Phonographs
FARNSWORTH TELEVISION & RADIO CORPORATION

N. W. AYER & SON

1

Folly and Fiesta

2

On a Far Hill

3

Village Festival

An interpretation of Liszt's "Hungarian Rhapsody No. 1," painted by Robert Riggs for the Capehart Collection. Merrymaking villagers are celebrating the harvest with a whirling "Czardas." Mr. Riggs, a noted American artist, is represented in many of the leading museums.

Fast-falling shadow . . . and fast-twirling figures of the village dance. Festive laughter fills the twilight, and, through it all, the singing rhapsody of the music!

How fortunate are those to whom the blessing of good music is a familiar experience. That good fortune is a double felicity when the Capehart or the Farnsworth is music's medium . . . for theirs is a supreme interpretation of the full richness of the world's great compositions.

War's needs now demand vital Radar and electronic instruments produced by the Farnsworth Television & Radio Corporation. With the return of peace, however, you will welcome a new Capehart or new Farnsworth into your own home.

Many of these matchless radios and phonograph-radios will bring the glorious reception to be found with FM. And one day, with television, others will open windows to a whole new world.

Your choice can range tomorrow across a wide array of cabinet styles and sizes. And you may be confident that in each field your Capehart or Farnsworth will express a quality finest at its cost. Farnsworth Television & Radio Corporation, Fort Wayne 1, Indiana.

Portfolios of reproductions of paintings in the Capehart Collection may be secured at nominal cost from your Capehart dealer, or you may write direct to Capehart Division, Fort Wayne 1, Indiana.

INVEST IN VICTORY—BUY WAR BONDS

THE CAPEHART

THE FARNSWORTH

Television · Radio · Phonographs

FARNSWORTH TELEVISION & RADIO CORPORATION

N. W. AYER & SON

4

1 *POSTER, 1941, SWITZERLAND*

CLIENT: CIBA

PRODUCT: BI ORO SUNTAN LOTION

ARTIST: NIKLAUS STOECKLIN

2 *POSTER, 1945, SWITZERLAND*

CLIENT: LUX SOAP

HEADLINE: 'LUX SOAP PROTECTS
AGAINST WRINKLES'

3 *POSTER, 1942, SWITZERLAND*

CLIENT: MAHALLA CIGARETTES

ARTIST: VICTOR RUTZ

1

2

CHAPTER EIGHT

IN THE FIFTIES society wrestled with a new kind of problem—abundance. Economies as well as babies were booming and the population explosion led to a new urban phenomenon, the 'suburban sprawl'. In America, vast grid systems of bungalows were built to accommodate the rapidly increasing number of young families. And into these box-like structures came another box—the television set. The roofs bristled with antennae as a house-bound generation consumed its daily diet of quiz shows, sports events and comedy adventures. Cinema, which had survived the advent of radio unscathed, was suddenly struggling. Audiences dwindled and hundreds of movie houses closed down at the very time that Hollywood was offering the glories of colour and a new wide screen. Fortunately, box-office stars such as Bogart, Bergman, Brando and Monroe had the pulling-power to keep the industry alive. But the moguls sealed their own fate when they started selling old movies to the TV stations. Even book publishers were running scared. Fearful of losing their readership, they boosted sales and profits with the introduction of the paperback.

Advertising, on the other hand, stood only to gain from the arrival of a new medium. And the promise of a 'captive audience' made television an extremely attractive proposition to manufacturers who invested heavily as programme sponsors. However, television had a more profound effect on advertising than simply extending its range. As well as creating a new area of expertise, it forced agencies to focus their thinking and to develop themes within campaigns. This then became evident in press and poster work, where the same proposition was restated through different ideas, but within the same graphic format. Admittedly, this trend had started in the previous decade; but in the fifties consistency became the order of the day.

Television also encouraged the development of 'lifestyle' advertising. Confronted as it was by the crescent arrangement of a three-piece suite, it held up a false mirror to society, presenting an idealized view of happy families living healthy lives, an 'image world' that advertising was quick to colonise.

These were the years in which American culture led the world. Its artefacts were synonymous with progress and prosperity. Conspicuous waste, as in the gas-guzzling, tail-finned motor car, celebrated the denial of scarcity. To Europeans, America represented the future for which they had to wait only a little longer.

And then lightning flashed across a cloudless sky. A new character entered the stage—the angry young man, epitomised by Dean and Brando. Angry, it seemed, at the numb insensitivity of middle-aged forbears who had wallowed for ten years in comfort and complacency. On the West Coast, dope-smoking beatniks snapped their fingers in applause at readings of Ginsberg's poetry and took their lead from the novels of Jack Kerouac. On the East Coast, Miles Davis turned jazz upside down with modulation and in the South Elvis Presley dethroned Bill Haley as the King of Rock 'n Roll and attacked traditional family values with that most potent of weapons—sex appeal.

The sixties were coming.

1

2

3

4

5

6

"Oh, Boy! It's Pop with a new PLYMOUTH!"

1

THIS "TWELVE" IS DIFFERENT, YES... BUT WHY?

Lincoln-Zephyr V12

THE STYLE LEADER

2

Look! all the glamor of a hardtop!

Look Again! all the comfort of a 4-door!

OLDSMOBILE'S

ENTIRELY NEW

Holiday Sedan

3

Of course it's a Lincoln!

You *can't* mistake it

1949

Lincoln makes America's Most Distinctive Cars

4

"Kansas City Bows

TO THE

Spirit of Youth!"

BE HAPPY *Buy Chrysler!*

5

Never have so many
bought so much for so little

Thrill of the year is Buick

6

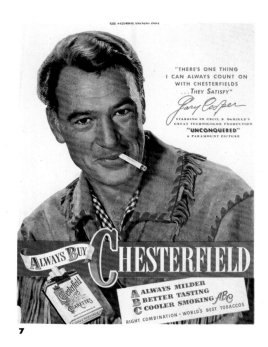

7

8

Remember how great cigarettes used to taste?
LUCKIES STILL DO

L.S./M.F.T. – Lucky Strike Means Fine Tobacco
TOBACCO AND TASTE TOO FINE TO FILTER

9

10

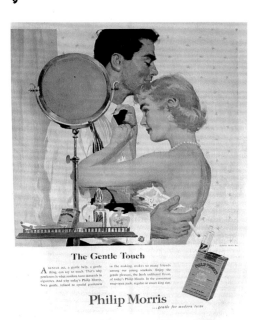

11

12

1

2

3

4

5

6

7

8

9

10

11

12

POSTERS, 1950s, UK

1-2/6 *CLIENT:* MG

3/5 *CLIENT:* RILEY

4/7/8 *CLIENT:* WOLSELEY

In the UK in the fifties it was quite common to see cars illustrated and not photographed for advertisements but rarely with the distortions and elongations so often found in American car ads of the same period.

9 *PRESS AD, 1954, UK*

10 *PRESS AD, 1955, UK*

11 *PRESS AD, 1956, UK*

12 *PRESS AD, 1954, UK*

CLIENT: BLACK MAGIC
CHOCOLATE

The device of using hand-written letters or diaries to attract the reader's attention is now quite common. Thirty years ago, Black Magic used it to show how grateful a woman would be to receive a box of their chocolates.

1-5 *PRESS ADS, 1951, UK*
CLIENT: ROWNTREE'S FRUIT GUMS

*Long before Rowntree started their famous
'Don't forget the fruit gums, Mum'
campaign, they positioned themselves as an
adult, refreshing sweet with these
sophisticated, life-style duo-tones.*

6-9 *PRESS ADS, 1955, UK*
CLIENT: PERSIL

*In the last three decades the Persil
advertising strategy has barely changed.
Back in the fifties it was still 'washing
whiter' and they were using a comparison
device called 'The Look Test'.*

Someone's doing the LOOK test!

1st LOOK Make sure you pass the look test! Wash your whites in Persil and see how much whiter they are! A clean, true WHITE white! Persil white!

2nd LOOK See how Persil copes with stains—it even shifts blackcurrant juice. And that's one of THE TOUGHEST WHITENESS TESTS OF ALL!

3rd LOOK See how bright Persil washes your coloureds, how it keeps woollens soft, fine things fresh and clean.

4th LOOK Your hands! Persil is so much kinder to hands and nails— you can feel it in

YES, BOIL OR NO BOIL, PERSIL BEATS THE LOT!

BEST IN YOUR WASHING MACHINE, TOO!

PERSIL washes whiter!
—and that means cleaner!

Persil washes whiter

6

Someone's Mum doesn't know about this LOOK test!

1st LOOK Look for whiteness! Wash your whites in Persil and see how much whiter they are! A *clean,* true WHITE white! Persil white!

2nd LOOK See how Persil copes with stains —it even shifts blackcurrant juice. And that's one of THE TOUGHEST WHITE-NESS TESTS OF ALL!

3rd LOOK See how bright Persil washes your coloureds; how it keeps woollens soft, fine things fresh and clean.

4th LOOK Your hands! Persil is so much kinder to hands and nails—you can feel it is.

Persil washes whiter —that means cleaner!

PERSIL washes whiter!
—and that means cleaner!

7

Ooh, Look!

A message to Someone's Mum!

Once you wash your whites in Persil you'll see why far more women buy Persil than any other washing powder. It washes so much *whiter.*

Whatever the whites — grubby shirts, towels, sheets, hankies, even badly-stained table-cloths — every scrap of dirt disappears when Persil's special oxygen bubbles get going! You can *see* Persil washes whiter. That means cleaner!

Yes, cleaner—that's why Persil-washed coloureds stay bright as new! And Persil is gentle, too—keeps woollies soft and cosy, fine things fresh and pretty.

YES, BOIL OR NO BOIL, PERSIL BEATS THE LOT!
BEST IN YOUR WASHING MACHINE, TOO!

Persil washes whiter —that means cleaner!

PERSIL washes whiter!
—and that means cleaner!

8

A surprise for Someone's Mum!

Someone's Mum took one look at those two youngsters dressed up in newly washed shirts —and saw for herself why far more women use Persil than any other washing powder! It washes whiter—and that means cleaner. Persil's special oxygen bubbles roll out the dirt from *all* your whites — grubby shirts, towels, hankies, even badly stained table-cloths. Persil is kinder to hands, too.

...And kinder to washing machines! Persil won't degrease the bearings, won't harm the rollers or metal container.

Coloureds, woollens, too
Coloured things come up bright and clean when they're washed in Persil. And because Persil is so gentle it's perfect for woollies and fine things, too.

Persil washes whiter —that means cleaner!

PERSIL washes whiter!
—and that means CLEANER!

9

All buttoned up

"WHY is a gaiter like a bottle of Guinness?" the Mad Hatter asked suddenly.

"You ought to know there's nothing like a Guinness," Alice said severely. "You shouldn't ask riddles that have no possible answer."

"But there *is* an answer," said the March Hare. "You use a button-hook on both."

"Dear me!" Alice exclaimed. "It must be very difficult to open a bottle of Guinness with a button-hook."

"It is," said the Hatter. *"Very difficult."*

"You have to be very strong," said the March Hare.

"And we can't be strong till we've had the Guinness, you know," the Hatter concluded. "Can you wonder we're mad?"

GUINNESS IS GOOD FOR YOU

Copies of this page may be obtained from Arthur Guinness, Son & Co. (Park Royal) Ltd., Advertising Dept., London, N.W.10

1

Bottle and Jug
(A passage which, by some oversight, Lewis Carroll never wrote.)

"Hatta's only just out of prison," said Haigha.

"What was he in for?" Alice ventured to ask.

"A month," said the King.

"I mean," said Alice patiently, "what crime had he committed?"

"He's going to take someone else's Guinness," replied the King nervously. "But does he go to prison *before* he takes the Guinness?" asked Alice.

"Of course," said the King. "That's how we do it in Looking-Glass Land. It's much better that way. Then when he does take it no-one will mind."

"Except me," said Haigha, stretching out his hand, just too late. "Will you have the goodness to return my Guinness," he cried to Hatta.

"I can't have the Goodness if I return the Guinness," said Hatta. "My Goodness, your Guinness," he added politely.

GUINNESS IS GOOD FOR YOU
(By arrangement with Macmillan & Co. Ltd.)

Copies of this page may be obtained from Arthur Guinness, Son & Co. (Park Royal) Ltd., Advertising Dept., London, N.W.10

2

My Goodness—
My GUINNESS

3

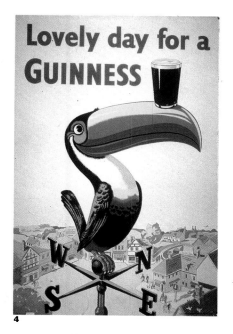

4

5

6

7

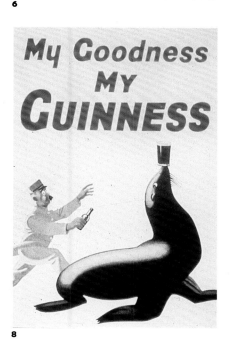

8

9

CLIENT: ARTHUR GUINNESS SON
AND COMPANY

AGENCY: S. H. BENSON, LONDON

1 *PRESS AD, 1953, UK*

ARTIST: ANTHONY GROVES RAINES

2 *PRESS AD, 1954, UK*

ARTIST: ANTHONY GROVES RAINES

3 *POSTER, 1956, UK*

ARTIST: JOHN GILROY

4 *POSTER, 1955, UK*

ARTIST: JOHN GILROY

5 *POSTER, 1957, UK*

ARTIST: JOHN GILROY

6 *POSTER, 1951, UK*

ARTIST: JOHN GILROY

7 *POSTER, 1957, UK*

ARTIST: JOHN GILROY

8 *POSTER, 1954, UK*

ARTIST: JOHN GILROY

9 *POSTER, UK*

ARTIST: JOHN GILROY

*During the early fifties, S. H. Benson
broadened the scope of Guinness advertising
with the subtler humour of the Alice in
Wonderland campaign. At the same time,
Gilroy developed his usual themes and
continued to appear, in caricature, as the
harassed zoo keeper.*

Schweppshire shows the Way
1 CONVERSATION PIECE

This glimpse at the Conversation Room of a typical home in Schweppshire shows how we try to embody the future in the present while retaining at the same time a lingering look at the past. Schweppaiev, our leading architect, has long ago dispensed with roof and walls in his buildings and these are now confined to out-of-door settings. Freedom from what has been called the carpet terminal is ensured by the elevation of seats above it, and a swing of the knee, easily practised, will bring talkers face to face or back to back as desired. A lifted finger, and the intercepted electronic eye swings the cocktail table into place. A compact gesture machine which ranges from the meditative stroke of the back of the head to the angrily pointed forefinger, enables speakers to obtain complete rest and relaxation while talking. Note the return to nature in the airy interplay of the communing figures reminiscent of the arboreal life of our remote ancestors.

Professor Schweppaiev tells us that in a few years furniture will be done away with altogether, and, trained in the exercises of the New Schwyogi, adaptable Schweppsians will achieve the supra-furniture state and be their own tables, footrests, pianos, or, as here, rocking chairs.

SELF ROCKER

Designed by Lewitt-Him, written by Stephen Potter.

SCHWEPPERVESCENCE LASTS THE WHOLE DRINK THROUGH

The Schweppshire Way of Life
5. CARE OF THE ATHLETE AND INFIRM

SCHWEPPERVESCENCE LASTS THE WHOLE DRINK THROUGH

2

Schweppshire shows the Way—2
THE TECHNIQUE OF SLUMBERCRAM
(SLEEP WHILE YOU LEARN)

SCHWEPPERVESCENCE LASTS THE WHOLE DRINK THROUGH

3

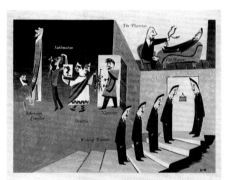

RE-INHIBITATING CENTRE
Schweppshire shows the Way—5

SCHWEPPERVESCENCE LASTS THE WHOLE DRINK THROUGH

4

SCHWEPPSYLVANIA
the motocracy

SCHWEPPERVESCENCE LASTS THE WHOLE DRINK THROUGH

5

Schweppshire shows the Way—3
Chlorophyll Fashions
THE MODERN BIO-ELEGANCE

SCHWEPPERVESCENCE LASTS THE WHOLE DRINK THROUGH

6

Schweppshire Shows the Way
6. GASWORKS REVIVAL

SCHWEPPERVESCENCE LASTS THE WHOLE DRINK THROUGH

7

CLIENT: SCHWEPPES' TONIC
WATER

1 *PRESS AD, 1954, UK*
DESIGNER: LEWITT HIM
WRITER: STEPHEN POTTER

2/3/4/6/7 *PRESS AD, 1953, UK*
DESIGNER: LEWITT HIM
WRITER: STEPHEN POTTER

5 *PRESS AD, 1955, UK*
DESIGNER: LOUDON SANTHILL
WRITER: STEPHEN POTTER

This classic campaign appeared in the early 1950s in the British humorous magazine, Punch. Except in the endline, the ads made no direct reference to tonic water but instead described the weird and wonderful events in the mythical county of Schweppeshire and, in so doing, gave the product the 'added values' of humour and imagination.

1

2

3

4

5

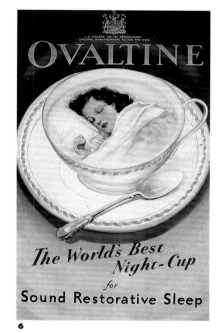

6

7

8

9

10

1/2 *POSTERS*
*CLIENT:*JAFFA ORANGES, UK

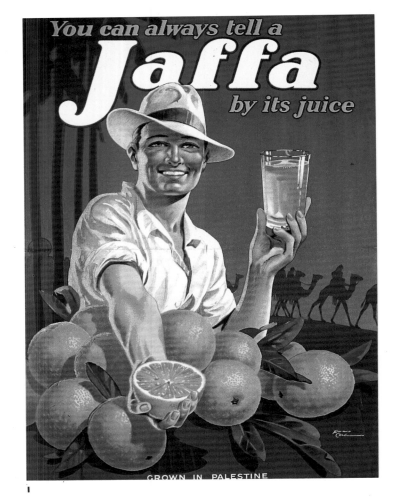

1

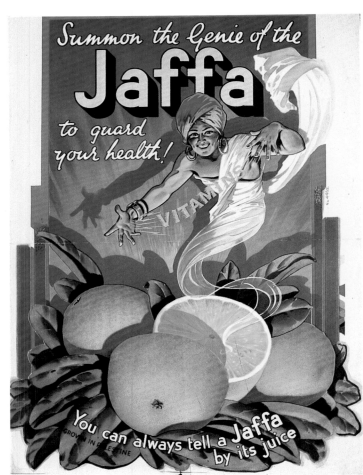

2

Le Roy Soleil

Schiaparelli

schiaparelli's new perfume . . . made and packaged in france

3

3/4 *PRESS ADS, USA*

CLIENT: SCHIAPARELLI PERFUMES

5 *PRESS AD, USA*

CLIENT: BOURJOIS PERFUME

Eau de Cologne

SNUFF

Schiaparelli

the all-male favorites — Snuff cologne-perfume-lotion-powder-soap

4

mais Oui

a frankly flirtatious perfume by

BOURJOIS

5

MAKES COOKING SO EASY

1

IT'S AN ODD HOUSE

WHERE THERE'S NO

OXO

2

3

4

The best "drop" on Earth!

5

1-2 *PRESS ADS, UK*	
CLIENT: OXO	
3-4 *PRESS ADS, UK*	
CLIENT: DOUBLE DIAMOND BEER	
5-6 *PRESS ADS, UK*	
CLIENT: DEWAR'S SCOTCH WHISKY	
ARTIST: MICHAELSON	

"Among the distinguished passengers"...

6

1

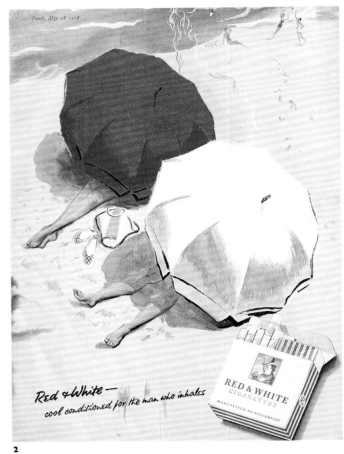

2

3

4

The Rolls-Royce Silver Cloud—$13,550.

"At 60 miles an hour the loudest noise in this new Rolls-Royce comes from the electric clock"

*What <u>makes</u> Rolls-Royce the best car in the world? "There is really no magic about it—
it is merely patient attention to detail," says an eminent Rolls-Royce engineer.*

1. "At 60 miles an hour the loudest noise comes from the electric clock," reports the Technical Editor of THE MOTOR. The silence of the engine is uncanny. Three mufflers tune out sound frequencies – acoustically.

2. Every Rolls-Royce engine is run for seven hours at full throttle before installation, and each car is test-driven for hundreds of miles over varying road surfaces.

3. The Rolls-Royce is designed as an owner-driven car. It is eighteen inches shorter than the largest domestic cars.

4. The car has power steering, power brakes and automatic gear-shift. It is very easy to drive and to park. No chauffeur required.

5. There is no metal-to-metal contact between the body of the car and the chassis frame—except for the speedometer drive. The entire body is insulated and under-sealed.

6. The finished car spends a week in the final test shop, being fine-tuned. Here it is subjected to ninety-eight separate ordeals. For example, the engineers use a stethoscope to listen for axle-whine.

7. The Rolls-Royce is guaranteed for three years. With a new network of dealers and parts-depots from Coast to Coast, service is no longer any problem.

8. The famous Rolls-Royce radiator has never been changed, except that when Sir Henry Royce died in 1933 the monogram RR was changed from red to black.

9. The coachwork is given five coats of primer paint, and hand rubbed between each coat, before fourteen coats of finishing paint go on.

10. By moving a switch on the steering column, you can adjust the shock-absorbers to suit road conditions. (The lack of fatigue in driving this car is remarkable.)

11. Another switch defrosts the rear window, by heating a network of 1360 invisible wires in the glass. There are two separate ventilating systems, so that you can ride in comfort with all the windows closed. Air conditioning is optional.

12. The seats are upholstered with eight hides of English leather—enough to make 128 pairs of soft shoes.

13. A picnic table, veneered in French walnut, slides out from under the dash. Two more swing out behind the front seats.

14. You can get such optional extras as an Espresso coffee-making machine, a dictating machine, a bed, hot and cold water for washing, an electric razor.

15. You can lubricate the entire chassis by simply pushing a pedal from the driver's seat. A gauge on the dash shows the level of oil in the crankcase.

16. Gasoline consumption is remarkably low and there is no need to use premium gas; a happy economy.

17. There are two separate systems of power brakes, hydraulic and mechanical. The Rolls-Royce is a very safe car—and also a very lively car. It cruises serenely at eighty-five. Top speed is in excess of 100 m.p.h.

18. Rolls-Royce engineers make periodic visits to inspect owners' motor cars and advise on service.

ROLLS-ROYCE AND BENTLEY

19. The Bentley is made by Rolls-Royce. Except for the radiators, they are identical motor cars, manufactured by the same engineers in the same works. The Bentley costs $300 less, because its radiator is simpler to make. People who feel diffident about driving a Rolls-Royce can buy a Bentley.

PRICE. The car illustrated in this advertisement—f.o.b. principal port of entry—costs $13,550. If you would like the rewarding experience of driving a Rolls-Royce or Bentley, get in touch with our dealer. His name is on the bottom of this page. Rolls-Royce Inc., 10 Rockefeller Plaza, New York, N.Y.

JET ENGINES AND THE FUTURE

Certain airlines have chosen Rolls-Royce turbo-jets for their Boeing 707's and Douglas DC8's. Rolls-Royce prop-jets are in the Vickers Viscount, the Fairchild F-27 and the Grumman Gulfstream.

Rolls-Royce engines power more than half the turbo-jet and prop-jet airliners supplied to or on order for world airlines.

Rolls-Royce now employs 42,000 people and the company's engineering experience does not stop at motor cars and jet engines. There are Rolls-Royce diesel and gasoline engines for many other applications.

The huge research and development resources of the company are now at work in many projects for the future, including nuclear and rocket propulsion.

David Ogilvy turned this simple observation into one of the most famous ads of all time. Later, when discussing the idea at the factory, a Rolls Royce engineer said to him quite seriously, 'Yes, we must do something about that clock'.

CLIENT: CONTAINER
CORPORATION OF AMERICA

1 *PRESS AD, 1958, USA*

ARTIST: MILTON GLASER

2 *PRESS AD, 1956, USA*

ARTIST: ARTHUR WILLIAMS

3 *PRESS AD, 1957, USA*

ARTISTS: SEYMOUR MEDNICK AND
DON MADDEN

4 *PRESS AD, 1956, USA*

ARTIST: WALTER ALLNER

5 *PRESS AD, 1957, USA*

ARTIST: FELIKS TOPOLSKI

*This campaign was a series of illustrations
that ran under the headline 'Great Ideas of
Western Man'. Each one was an
interpretation of a great thinker and by
association bestowed the quality of genius
upon the Container Corporation of America.*

Great Ideas of Western Man...
ONE OF A SERIES

Artist: Milton Glaser

Dr. Johnson on the human horizon

*Everything that enlarges the sphere of human powers, that shows man he can do what
he thought he could not do, is valuable.* (James Boswell, *Life of Samuel Johnson*, 1791)

CONTAINER CORPORATION OF AMERICA

1

2

3

4

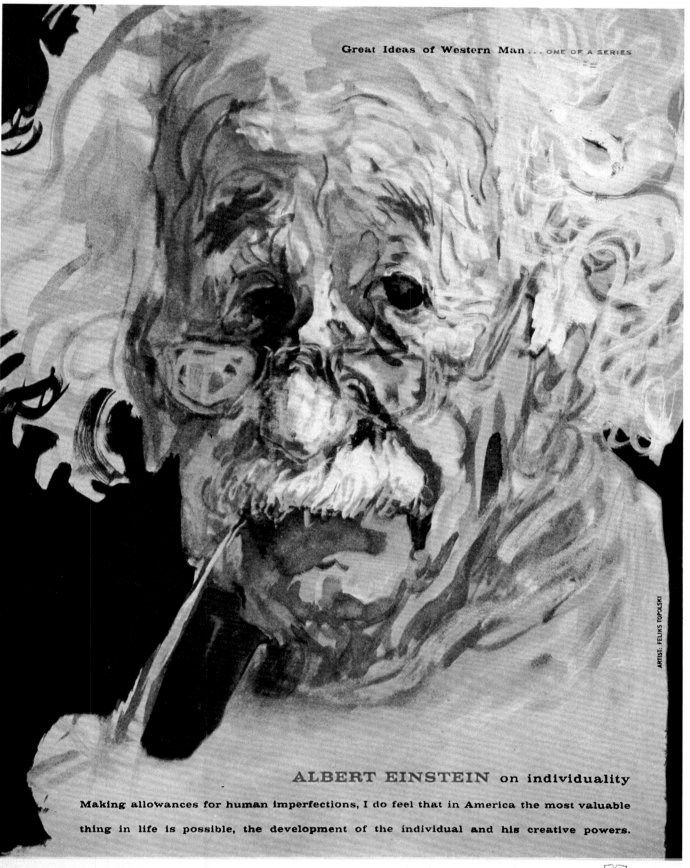

Great Ideas of Western Man... ONE OF A SERIES

ARTIST: FELIKS TOPOLSKI

ALBERT EINSTEIN on individuality

Making allowances for human imperfections, I do feel that in America the most valuable

thing in life is possible, the development of the individual and his creative powers.

CONTAINER CORPORATION OF AMERICA

CLIENT: GILLETTE

PRESS CAMPAIGN, 1952-53, UK

This was an early and extreme example of negative sell. Gillette proposed that their razors were a new and modern invention with illustrations that portrayed the beard as an old and barbaric one.

At the races...

before Gillette made

the world clean-shaven!

Good mornings begin with Gillette

1

At a concert...

before Gillette made

the world clean-shaven!

Good mornings begin with Gillette

2

At the barbers...

before Gillette made

the world clean-shaven!

Good mornings begin with Gillette

3

An athletic meeting..

before Gillette made

the world clean-shaven!

Good mornings begin with Gillette

4

At a coronation...

before Gillette made

the world clean-shaven!

Good mornings begin with Gillette

5

At a curling match...

before Gillette made

the world clean-shaven!

Good mornings begin with Gillette

6

On the river . . .

before Gillette made

the world clean-shaven!

How strange that gentlemen could once appear like sea-lions struggling through seaweed without arousing comment; but how natural when removing the whiskers meant hard labour and danger. Indeed, when Gillette made shaving easy, safe and inexpensive, whiskers vanished almost overnight. Today millions of well-groomed men facing the world clean and unafraid prove that Gillette not only made, but *keeps* the world clean shaven. Leadership in research, maintenance of standards — in one word *quality* — ensure that the world's first easy shaving system remains incomparably the finest.

Gillette quality the same the world over.
Factories in U.S.A., Canada, Gt. Britain, Mexico,
France, Argentina, Switzerland, Brazil.

Good mornings begin with Gillette

7

YOU CAN BE HERE TOMORROW, watching the graceful hula, racing the waves on lovely Waikiki beach, enjoying the vacation of a lifetime! Hawaii is less than a day away from New York on United Air Lines!

CLIENT: UNITED AIRLINES

PRESS ADS, 1953, USA

This campaign is often remembered for the effectiveness of the advertising strategy — cheap Hawaiian holidays at the start of air tourism. However, we chose it for the classic fifties imagery and art direction and we particularly like the garland-of-flowers-style headline 'Hawaii'.

HAWAII

Closer, and costs less than you think on **United Air Lines**

YOUR HAWAIIAN HOLIDAY COSTS NO MORE than many Mainland vacations. Choose United's FIRST CLASS or AIR TOURIST service, to suit your budget. All flights pressurized, with seating limited to two abreast on each side of a wide aisle. Air-sea tours available; fly out, return by ship. For information, air and island hotel reservations, call United Air Lines or an Authorized Travel Agent.

FIRST CLASS, from New York: **$326.90** one way; $604.30 round trip. Go via San Francisco, return via Los Angeles (or vice versa) at no extra fare.

AIR TOURIST, from New York: **$224** one way; $423 round trip. Complete island vacations, $441 and up from New York. All fares plus tax.

United Air Lines serves 79 cities

UNITED AIR LINES

FIRST CLASS fare includes luxurious twin-deck Mainliner®. Stratocruiser service over the Pacific with delicious meals, refreshments, and spacious lower-deck Hawaiian Lounge (left). Reclining seats with leg rests, no extra charge. You may have a private stateroom at slight extra cost. Berths only $10 extra.

1

HAWAII

So near in time, and low as $125 (from California) on United Air Lines

2

United Air Lines to

HAWAII

takes less than a day—little as $224! (from New York)

3

232

HAWAII

by United Air Lines... Low as $224— (from New York) and less than a day away!

SWIFT UNITED AIR LINES' MAINLINERS® bring Hawaii as near as tomorrow, and there's a fare to fit any vacation budget! By DC-6 Tourist Mainliners, only $224 one way from New York. First Class, with luxurious twin-deck Mainliner Stratocruiser service over the Pacific, only $326.90 one way. If you wish, United will arrange your complete Hawaiian vacation, including hotel. Also, air-sea trips; fly out, return by ship. For information and reservations call United or an Authorized Travel Agent.

FIRST CLASS service is on Mainliner Stratocruisers with lower-deck lounge, delicious meals and refreshments included in your fare, a private stateroom at slight extra cost, or full-size berths $10 extra. AIR TOURIST service is on fast, 4-engine DC-6 Mainliners with seats only 2 abreast on each side of a wide aisle for walk-around spaciousness.

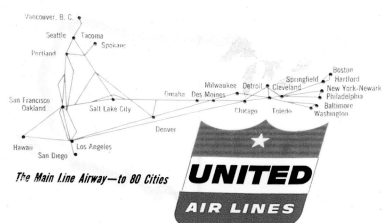

The Main Line Airway—to 80 Cities

UNITED AIR LINES

WIDE-AISLE, 2-ABREAST SEATING ON ALL FLIGHTS, AIR TOURIST AND FIRST CLASS

All fares plus tax

4

United Air Lines offers the fastest one-airline service from the East to Hawaii, and the most Air Tourist flights.

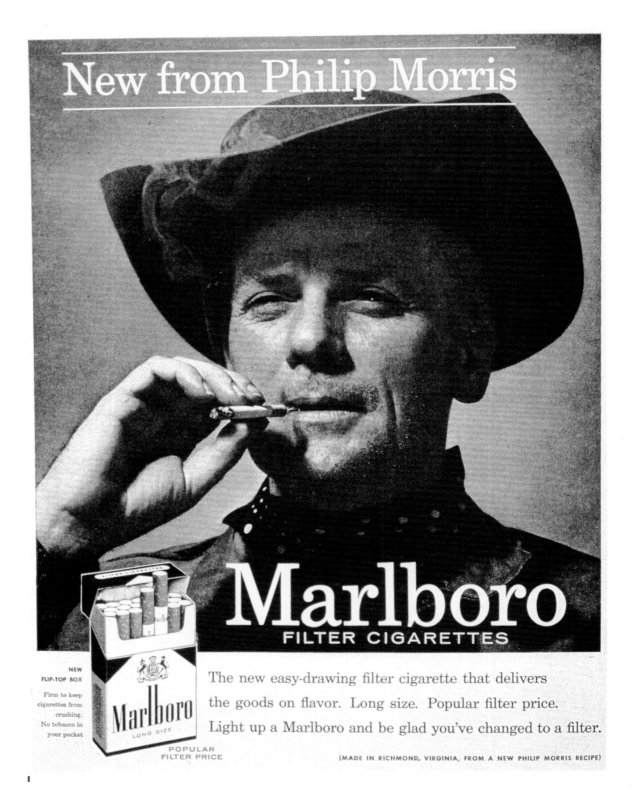

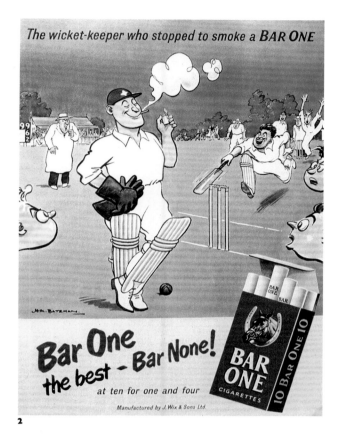

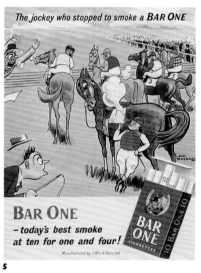

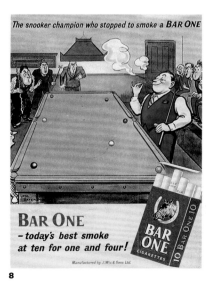

CHAPTER NINE

THE SWINGING SIXTIES—the century's most colourful decade—began in a blaze of optimism but soon revealed a darker side to its nature. England was widely criticized over Suez and the world shivered with fear as the Cold War deepened during the Cuban missile crisis. The space race, like the arms race, became a military contest. When Yuri Gagarin pipped Alan Shepard at the post, Kennedy bolstered the nation's spirits by promising an American on the moon before 1970 (Armstrong and Aldrin made it with only five months to spare). Kennedy did not live to see his promise made good—he was assassinated in 1963. His hopes for an end to segregation had been ill-founded. Peaceful civil-rights demonstrations led to racial violence that culminated, five years later, in the murder of Martin Luther King. The East Germans built a wall to keep communism in; America entered the Vietnam war to keep communism out.

In the midst of it all, four mop-topped musicians from Liverpool became 'more popular than Jesus Christ'. The arrival of the Beatles marked the beginning of an era in which music became the most eloquent voice of disaffected youth. The times really were a-changin'. The Angry Young Man was replaced by a Hippy, whose contemplative nature expressed itself in a more passive rejection of social mores. Dropping out— and 'dropping acid'. In San Francisco, 1967 was a time of psychedelia, free love and flower-power. The drug culture had a fantastic effect on the arts. Graphics were kaleidoscopic in their use of colour and a new age of the poster began with the artists Milton Glaser, Peter Max and Jacqui Morgan.

But while London was the centre of fashion and music, it was in New York that the revolution in advertising took place. The industry was facing a new problem—how to appeal to increasingly young and sceptical consumers who were busy rejecting the materialistic values that had developed during the post-war reconstruction of the 1950s.

The answer came from one man—Bill Bernbach, creative director of Doyle, Dane and Bernbach and architect of the 'Creative Revolution'. Under his guidance, art directors and copywriters discovered the synergy of working together in teams. Bernbach ignored the old-school-tie recruitment procedures of Madison Avenue and hired solely on the strength of talent. He looked for creative people who could generate strong, arresting ideas and who could reduce all the elements of an ad into a single, integrated and relevant proposition.

The style that emerged was witty, honest and simple. The cluttered illustrative styles of the 1940s and 1950s were almost totally replaced by photography, which gave Doyle Dane's work an immediately recognisable quality. The cornerstone of Bernbach's beliefs was that if you want to persuade people that your product is different, you need advertising that is different. And so he threw away the rule books and put his faith in the gods of inspiration.

The revolution was a success. Three decades later, the regime is still in power.

CLIENT: VOLKSWAGEN USA

AGENCY: DOYLE DANE AND BERNBACH, NEW YORK

PRESS ADS, 1960-62, USA

At its inception, this campaign was the work of art director, Helmut Krone, and copywriter, Julian Koenig. Together with Bill Bernbach and the VW client, they revolutionised car advertising. Out went the distorted air-brush illustrations, suave drivers and admiring females. In came realistic photography, intelligent and informative copy and humour. The result was a campaign that gained the involvement of the readers and was disarmingly honest. Not only was it the most talked-about campaign of its day, the sales figures proved it to be one of the most successful.

Old Volkswagen Station Wagons never die.

What if you only need part of a Volkswagen?

It's been replaced.

Repair 'em? I've got enough parts to build 'em!

The famous Italian designer suggested one change.

Don't laugh.

A new VW is cheaper at twice the price.

Think tall.

(1960)   (1961)

Can you see the 27 changes?

Cheap new.

Expensive used.

2 shapes known the world over.

1 - 6 *PRESS ADS, 1960s, USA*

CLIENT: VOLKSWAGEN

AGENCY: DOYLE, DANE AND
BERNBACH, NEW YORK

Lemon.

Will we ever kill the bug?

1

2

After we paint the car we paint the paint.

Is the economy trying to tell you something?

3

4

A Volkswagen, obviously.

Think small.

5

6

You don't have to be Jewish

to love Levy's

real Jewish Rye

7

7-9 *POSTERS AND PRESS ADS, 1962,
USA*

CLIENT: LEVY'S BAKERY

AGENCY: DOYLE DANE AND
BERNBACH, NEW YORK

*How do you take a product that belongs to
one ethnic community and market it to the
most cosmopolitan city in the world? This
campaign was the successful solution to the
problem and, in its simplicity, directness and
wit, epitomises the style of Bernbach's
creative revolution.*

You don't have to be Jewish

to love Levy's
real Jewish Rye

8

You don't have to be Jewish

to love Levy's
real Jewish Rye

9

Some people spell performance "hp." We spell it "Wildcat."

Even though there's a deep-breathing, big-muscled 325-hp Wildcat V-8 under the hood, there's more to Wildcat performance than just horsepower. You see, we remember you've got owners to turn. And bumpy roads to drive on. And traffic to fight. So we harnessed our husky Wildcat V-8 to a crisp-handling, smooth-riding, utterly responsive chassis. And then made available our Super Turbine automatic transmission—so silkily efficient you'd hardly suspect it's putting traffic lights behind you so quickly. But enough talk. Time for action. Go see your Buick dealer and whisper the magic word. Wildcat. Wouldn't you really rather have a Buick? A wild '65 Buick?

1

How to buy a new Buick.
(An easier lesson than you might expect.)

Not only is owning a new Buick pleasant, it's entirely possible. What you do is this—first, you just look. Long and hard. At the styling. At the interiors, with their rich fabrics and vinyls. Next, you drive. A LeSabre 400, say, like the one in our picture. Choose this one and you get a 250-hp Wildcat V-8 and that feather-smooth, Super Turbine automatic of ours. (Put your test route past your house and watch the neighbors eat their hearts out.) And finally, your price. That should be the start of a long and beautiful friendship. Visit your Buick dealer soon. Your friendly Buick dealer.

Wouldn't you really rather have a Buick?

2

A 360-hp Wildcat V-8 isn't all that's new with Riviera Gran Sport.
But what a start.

You can easily spend a party or two talking enthusiastically about the engine in Buick's new Riviera Gran Sport. A 425 cubic incher with 460 ft-lb of torque makes for considerable performance talk. (And, together with the Skylark GS, Car Magazine's 6th annual "Performance Cars of the Year" award.) But after your friends have heard all there is to hear, you can start in on some of the Gran Sport's extra added attractions. A limited-slip differential. Power steering and brakes. If you specified them, the heavy-duty springs, shocks and stabilizer bar. Better than talking, though, is driving. You can start that at your Buick dealer's. After all, wouldn't you really rather have a Buick?
One of the new Gran Sports from Buick
You need not be a professional driver to qualify.

3

Life was just one diaper after another until Sarah got her new Mustang. Somehow Mustang's sensationally sophisticated looks, its standard-equipment luxuries (bucket seats, full carpeting, vinyl interior, chiffon-smooth, floor-mounted transmission) made everyday cares fade far, far into the background. Suddenly there was a new gleam in her husband's eye. (For the car? For Sarah? Both?) Now Sarah knows for sure, Mustangers have more fun.

MUSTANG!
MUSTANG!
MUSTANG!

4

Wolfgang used to give harpsichord recitals for a few close friends. Then he bought a Mustang. Things looked livelier for Wolfgang, surrounded by bucket seats, vinyl interior, padded dash, wall-to-wall carpeting (all standard Mustang...and a big V-8 option that produces some of the most powerful notes this side of Beethoven. What happened? Sudden fame! Fortune! The adulation of millions! Being a Mustanger brought out the wolf in Wolfgang. What could it do for you?

MUSTANG!
MUSTANG!
MUSTANG!

5

Desmond was afraid to let the cat out...until he got his Mustang. Mustang! A car to make weak men strong, strong men invincible. Mustang! Equipped with bucket seats, floor shift, vinyl interior, padded dash, full carpeting, more. Mustang! A challenge to your imagination with options like front disc brakes, 4-on-the-floor, lively new V-8's, you name it. Desmond traded in his Persian kitten for an heiress. He had to. She followed him home. (It's inevitable...Mustangers have more fun.)

MUSTANG!
MUSTANG!
MUSTANG!

6

Land-Rover 109 Station Wagon with Hart Shield Roof.

"At 60 miles an hour the loudest noise in this new Land-Rover comes from the roar of the engine"

What makes Land-Rover the most conspicuous car in the world? "There is really no secret," says an eminent Land-Rover enthusiast.

1. "Except for rattles, I am against silence in a car," writes John Steinbeck, a Land-Rover enthusiast, "and I don't know a driver who doesn't want to hear his engine."

2. If this is so, then you may like the Land-Rover very much indeed.

3. Our 4-wheel drive (8 speeds forward, 2 in reverse) masterpiece is not mousey. Its throaty authority is assuring in times of stress; which nowadays is usually.

4. Nor is this claim true only at 60 miles an hour. A Land-Rover is more conspicuous even when it is standing still. With the ignition off.

5. The Land-Rover stands nearly seven feet tall. All its features tend to heroic proportion.

6. Therefore, when driving, you will simply loom over traffic which previously had seared the devil out of you.

7. This is not only safe and enjoyable, but you will exult to observe how other drivers, awe-inspired by the Land-Rover's casual might, yield in deference.

8. (Small wonder that women are enormously fond of driving Land-Rovers. The easy command of such massive, maneuverable masculinity is heady stuff.)

9. You may have read of tests where "imported cars" fared badly in collisions? It's a pity we weren't there to help out the side. The Land-Rover is built to resist the charge of a bull rhinoceros; or a bull Lincoln for that matter.

10. The Land-Rover's sturdiness of construction (the under-frame resembles a reinforced section of railway track) makes it ideal for truckless wastes, car pools of small children, wretched ordeals, etcetera.

11. There are perhaps 14 Land-Rover hardy perennials ranging from safari cars and campers to police vans and getaway cars. Our most popular passenger models are the 7-seater Model 88 and the 10-seater Model 109 Station Wagons.

11-A. An attractive feature of the '85 Land-Rover is that it is precisely as attractive as the '84.

12. Both of these have capacious rear doors for unloading bulk or people. The mathletic may use the fold-down step.

13. The after-compartment has farringests. This arrangement, although somewhat reminiscent of riding in a paddy-wagon, is extremely sociable. Late at night, it is hilarious.

14. The Land-Rover is available with a spare tire either mounted on the rear door or on top of the hood. The tires are identical in every respect save that it costs $7.40 more to have one on the hood.

LAND-ROVER WITH & WITHOUT TIRE ON HOOD

15. People who feel diffident about driving a Land-Rover with the spare tire on the hood can buy the conventional Land-Rover and save $7.40.

PRICE: The Model 109 Station Wagon illustrated in this advertisement costs **$3,906** on the Atlantic Coast, **$4,092** on the Pacific Coast; at places in between, it costs in between. The Model 88 Station Wagon (shorter by 1 door) costs about **$600** less.

If you would like to listen to the Land-Rover, or to the embarrassingly quiet Mark II Rover Sedan, or to the Rover 2000 Sports Sedan (which has "a little pasty mutter when idling that rises to a whispering roar in the lower gears," according to Mr. Steinbeck), please ask any dealer here listed.

(LR) signifies a Land-Rover dealer; (R), a Rover dealer; (R & LR), both.

Thank you.

AUTHORIZED ROVER and LAND-ROVER DEALERS:

7

If you need more reasons to buy a Jaguar...

2. double overhead camshaft engine
3. all synchromesh 4-speed gearbox, diaphragm clutch
4. Powr-Lok limited slip differential
5. aerodynamic styling, wind tunnel tested
6. lightweight all-steel monocoque body
7. torsion bar front suspension
8. quadri-coil independent rear suspension
9. wood-rimmed, racing-type telescopic steering wheel
10. positive, responsive rack-and-pinion steering
11. power-assisted, 4-wheel disc brakes
12. dual hydraulic braking systems
13. bucket seats, upholstered in finest leather
14. painstaking craftsmanship
15. the Jaguar racing heritage
16. There is a special feeling the Jaguar owner has for his own different breed of cat. He likes to be alone with it out on the road. He likes to run up the rev's and let the air with a throaty growl. He likes to downshift coming into a curve and power through the turns in complete control. He likes the feel of the butter-soft leather and he likes the way the seat holds him. He likes the way people look at him and he likes looking at his car.
There is nothing in the world to compare with the Jaguar feeling and there's only one way to get it. Buy one.

Jaguar: A different breed of cat. Roadster $5384, Coupe $5580 P.O.E. Money-saving overseas delivery can be arranged. See your dealer or write Jaguar Cars Inc. 32 East 57th Street, New York, N.Y. 10022.

8

The
tip
that's
setting
the
trend

9

THE TREND
IS TO
TIPPED

THE TIP IS BACHELOR

10

All of these ads, if you include the copy for Jaguar, are typical of life-style advertising for American motor cars. The exception is number 7 for Land Rover, an hilarious send-up of David Ogilvy's famous ad for Rolls Royce.

The penchant for silhouetted photographs spanned both sides of the Atlantic in this campaign for Bachelor cigarettes.

Avis is only No.2 in rent a cars. So why go with us?

We try harder.

(When you're not the biggest, you have to.)

We just can't afford dirty ash-trays. Or half-empty gas tanks. Or worn wipers. Or unwashed cars. Or low tires. Or anything less than seat-adjusters that adjust. Heaters that heat. Defrost-ers that defrost.

Obviously, the thing we try hardest for is just to be nice. To start you out right with a new car, like a lively, super-torque Ford, and a pleasant smile. To know, say, where you get a good pastrami sandwich in Duluth.

Why?

Because we can't afford to take you for granted.

Go with us next time.

The line at our counter is shorter.

Would you believe Avis is No.1½?

Avis.

Well, in a manner of speaking, we're still No.**2**.

But technically, we're No.**1**.5556. After four years of trying harder, we've cut No.**1**'s lead almost in half. (Based on the latest figures from 26 major airports.)

And do you know what happens when you get that close to the top? Your people try even harder.

Take Ernie Foote, for example.

A customer showed up with an expired out-of-state driver's license. So Ernie took him to the highway patrol for a driver's test. He passed. Got a Mississippi license. And was off in a shiny, new Plymouth.

Obviously, our people are keeping score.

And they can smell the pennant.

No. 2ism.
The Avis Manifesto.

We are in the rent a car business, playing second fiddle to a giant. Above all, we've had to learn how to stay alive.

In the struggle, we've also learned the basic difference between the No.**1**'s and No.**2**'s of the world.

The No.**1** attitude is: "Don't do the wrong thing. Don't make mistakes and you'll be O.K."

The No.**2** attitude is: "Do the right thing. Look for new ways. Try harder."

No.**2**ism is the Avis doctrine. And it works.

The Avis customer rents a clean, new Plymouth, with wipers wiping, ashtrays empty, gas tank full, from an Avis girl with smile firmly in place.

And Avis itself has come out of the red into the black.

Avis didn't invent No.**2**ism. Anyone is free to use it.

No.**2**'s of the world, arise!

The writer of this ad rented an Avis car recently. Here's what I found:

Cigarette butts. A whole ashtray full.

I write Avis ads for a living. But that doesn't make me a paid liar.

When I promise that the least you'll get from Avis is a clean Plymouth with everything in perfect order, I expect Avis to back me up.

I don't expect full ashtrays; it's not like them.

I know for a fact that everybody in that company, from the president down, tries harder.

"We try harder" was their idea; not mine.

And now they're stuck with it; not me.

So if I'm going to continue writing these ads, Avis had better live up to them. Or they can get themselves a new boy.

They'll probably never run this ad.

Avis is only No.2.
But we don't
want your sympathy.

It hasn't come to this.

Have we been crying too much? Have we overplayed the underdog?

We didn't think so till David Biener, 11 years old, sent us 35¢, saying, "It may help you buy another Plymouth."

That was an eye-opener.

So now we'd like to correct the false impression we've made.

We don't want you to rent Avis cars because you feel sorry for us. All we want is a chance to prove that a No.**2** can be just as good as a No.**1**. Or even better. Because we have to try harder.

Maybe we ought to eliminate the negative and accentuate the positive.

Instead of saying "We're only No.**2** in rent a cars," we could say "We're the second largest in the world!"

PRESS ADS, 1963, USA

CLIENT: AVIS CAR RENTALS

AGENCY: DOYLE DANE AND BERNBACH, NEW YORK

ART DIRECTOR: HELMUT KRONE

COPYWRITERS: PAULA GREEN AND GENE CASE

The Avis campaign is probably the most extreme example of Doyle Dane taking a product negative and turning it into a positive. Admitting that you are number 2 is not the obvious way of winning the hearts of a public which seldom favours the underdog. Many people thought the ads were doing a better job for Hertz. But Bernbach and his team proved them all wrong. The year that the campaign broke, Avis turned a $3 million loss into a $3 million profit and one research study revealed that the Hertz sales force were seriously demoralised.

CLIENT: HATHAWAY SHIRTS

PRESS ADS, 1960-62, USA

AGENCY: OGILVY AND MATHER,
NEW YORK

In a design sense these classic ads for Hathaway shirts follow David Ogilvy's rules for his agency — picture at the top, headline beneath it in upper and lower case and copy beneath that. However, Ogilvy had always distrusted humour in advertising and believed that no one bought anything from 'clowns'. And yet this campaign seems to be nothing but a sly joke. Who was Baron Wrangel? Why is he wearing an eye-patch? We never found out, but the intrigue generated a great deal of interest in Hathaway shirts.

Hathaway pays a penalty for making this drip-dry shirt

1

Hathaway discovers the India Madras print — very rare

2

This is Hathaway's Club shirt
(staunchly Ivy League — with several tidy little differences)

3

Hathaway announces the first summer-weight broadcloth

4

Hathaway strikes a blow for peace and quiet
— with a soft-spoken, all-cotton plaid that looks and feels uncannily like silk

5

Hathaway announces a totally new stripe: rather costly and very discreet

6

"Hathaway's India Madras shirts always fade — evidence that they are the genuine stuff," says Baron Wrangell as he strolls in the noonday sun.

How three trunks of India Madras
started Yale University

Heaven knows what Yale's name might have been if Elihu Yale hadn't shipped
India Madras to New England in 1718. Hathaway now imports the same hand-
woven, hand-dyed fabrics—and offers you genuine India Madras shirts for $10.

WHEN ELIHU YALE was governor of the province of Madras in southern India, he was struck by the unusual cotton fabrics that the Indian cottagers made. He collected a wealth of them.

Later he sent three large trunks of his most valuable Madras cottons to friends in New England—"*to be sold or otherwise improved for the Benefitt of the Collegiate School in New Haven*." The handsome stuff brought enough money to finish the buildings for the new college, which grateful trustees promptly named after Eli Yale.

If you were to visit Madras today, you would see Indian cottagers making their marvelous fabrics exactly as they did in Governor Yale's time.

These are the fabrics that Hathaway imports for genuine India Madras shirts.

"Guaranteed to fade" says Hathaway

Madras is hand-spun and hand-woven. It is also hand-dyed with natural dyestuffs that are never completely colorfast.

Hathaway guarantees that your shirt will fade in the wash and in the sun, and gradually take on the look of mellowed maturity that is one famous hallmark of genuine India Madras. Another hallmark:

the patterns seldom if ever repeat. This is because the weavers have only enough room in their cottages to make one short piece of fabric at a time, and they always like to change the pattern before they start a new one. So you will probably never see

---

Hathaway revives the brave and brilliant colors of old India

Unfathomably, some shirtmakers are persuading the Indians to tone down their Madras this year.

"Down with Milquetoasts!" says Hathaway. "Male plumage should be brave and brilliant—just as it has been since the beginning of time."

We've given our weavers the go-ahead to revive the uninhibited shades their ancestors used. Turkey red from the roots of madder plants. Indigo blue from the indigo plant itself. A lively yellow from turmeric, the gingery spice used in making curry powder.

These vivid primary colors are blended into a thousand and one different shades. And the astonishing thing is that they never clash. Your shirt may be bold—but it will never look garish.

---

another Madras shirt that looks exactly like yours.

$10 for solid colors and patterns

Madras traditionally comes in plaids and stripes. You can now also get genuine Madras solid-color shirts. And Madras prints that date back to the 18th century.

Now for some details of the tailoring. Hathaway uses single-needle stitching— with stitches so small that there are 22 to the inch. This makes the seams strong, flat, and almost invisible.

You also get cuffed short sleeves, which look more finished than the kind that just comes to an end. And Hathaway gives you plenty of room through the shoulders and chest and under the arms. Our India Madras shirts cost about $10.

Send for handy dictionary

If you found this advertisement interesting, you will enjoy *Hathaway's Handy Dictionary of Shirts and Shirtings*—a 16-page guide to comfort, collars, and curiosa.

We will also tell you which stores in your vicinity sell Hathaway shirts. Write to C. F. Hathaway, Waterville, Maine. Call OXford 7-5566 in New York.

7

[Or, The Eagle Also Rises]

THE STRIPES OF KILIMANJARO;
OR,
FOR WHOM THE PIPE BOWLS

*Kilimanjaro is a snow covered mountain 19,710 feet high
and it is said to be the most popular mountain in Africa.
Close to the western summit there is the striped and
button-downed carcass of an Eagle. No one has explained
what a shirt company was seeking at that altitude.*

AT THIS POINT it is necessary that you see a meerschaum pipe. Some
aficionados try to imagine one, but either the imagine-ing is not good
and true and honest or they imagine something else entirely, a calabash
perhaps, which is the wrong color.

Where the bowl sticks out did you notice that its color is that of the
oxford shirting, and that the inside is that of the stripes running up and
down vigorously? This is the why of Eagle's Meerschaum Tromblees.

A *Tromblee* is like this: buttoned-down at collar and cuff and at
pocket-flap too. Men find security where they can. It costs about $8.00.
It is true that some men who can't find security can't find Eagle shirts
either. So they write Revera Afflerbach, the Pennsylvanian, at the address below. It seems to work out, clearly.

What may not be clear to the reader, or *consumero*, is how Africa
comes in here as implied unless dragged by its heels. In this fashion,
Señor; do not the celebrated Amboseli Block Meerschaums, of which
this twenty dollar pipe is one, come from Lake Amboseli in the shadow
of Mount Kilimanjaro? A far-fetched tie-in, Bwana, but is it not
damned manly? And look at that shirt.

©1966, EAGLE SHIRTMAKERS, QUAKERTOWN, PENNSYLVANIA. 18951

1

[Another Eagle First: The Buttonless Button-Down]
IF YOU WANT TO LOOK AS SUAVE AS A
1935 BAND LEADER HERE'S YOUR CHANCE!

THE first major button break-through since the laundry! Yet it looks so simple. ∗ It's simple,
all right. All we did was take all the buttons off our beloved, button-down collar. You may
be asking why. Because the Buttonless Button-down in our Snuff stripes looks extremely well with
a collar pin; which in turn looks extremely well with the great, gatsbyesque, gabardine suit now
making its comeback in putty, clay, pearl, buck, and other good earth colors. ∗ The Snuff stripes
—here on George Scandals' White—also come on Lost Horizon Blue and Front Beige (really
Journalism Yellow); in Batiste Madras with short sleeves for about $7.00. If you don't know
where to find Eagle Shirts in your town, write Miss Afflerbach at the address below.
© 1965, EAGLE SHIRTMAKERS, QUAKERTOWN, PENNSYLVANIA

2

[Eagle Goes Along With The Law Of Gravity]
WINDOWPANE CZECHS

∗∗∗∗∗∗∗∗∗∗∗∗∗∗∗∗∗∗∗∗∗∗∗∗∗∗∗∗∗∗∗∗∗∗∗∗∗∗

EVERYBODY talks about the Defenestration of Prague but nobody
does anything about it. ∗ Therefore Eagle has decided to commem-
orate the 547th anniversary of the First Defenestration — or throwing
people out the window — in which both the people and the windows were
high up in City Hall. ∗ (The Second Defenestration, in 1618, was of Am-
bassadors from the Hradčany Palace, and started the Thirty Years War;
which is too long to go into here.) ∗ The lesson is clear: When in Prague
do as the Czechs do; and do it low down. ∗ Now, in addition to Blue
on Greenish, these checks also come Blue on Yellowish, and Yellow on
Bluish. The shirting is our very own Oxford Voile; the sleeves short; the
collar, Eagle's beloved, bulgy button-down. ∗ If you'd like to get in on
the ground floor, you may buy Windowpane Czechs for about $7.00
wherever Eagle shirts are sold. Please write Miss Afflerbach at the address
below if you aren't sure where that is in your town.
© 1960, EAGLE SHIRTMAKERS, QUAKERTOWN, PENNSYLVANIA

3

[Flavor-Of-The-Month at Howard Eagle's]

THE TUTTI-FRUTTI TROMBLEE!

THIS shirt is so nice we could have called it Max. ☆ However, since it is for summertime, when ice cream sells like hotcakes (and hotcakes sell like Max), it's Tutti-Frutti all the way. ☆ The colors are, hold on: Tutti-Frutti (shown here), Lemon on Pistachio, Burnt Almond on French Vanilla, and Dill Pickle on Blue, if you can imagine those last as ice cream flavors. The neo-Spumoni brick there will give you an idea of the other three. ☆ The fabric we call Oxfjord Voile, though a Viking would probably freeze to death in it. ☆ Like all Tromblees it has a button-down pocket and collar. It comes in short sleeves and goes for about eight dollars where Eagle Shirts are sold. If you don't know where that is write the Good Humor Lady, Miss Afflerbach, at the below.

© 1967, EAGLE SHIRTMAKERS ("We Churn Our Own Shirts"), QUAKERTOWN, PENNSYLVANIA 18951

4

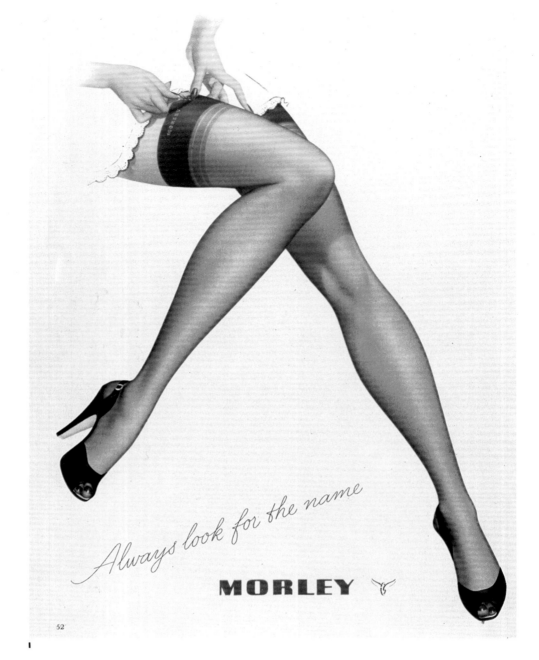

Always look for the name

MORLEY

52

1

1 *PRESS AD, UK*
CLIENT: WOLSEY

2 *PRESS AD. UK*
CLIENT: ANGEL FACE

3 *PRESS AD. UK*
CLIENT: MARY QUANT

Fashion and glamour models achieved real star status in the sixties — featured here are Twiggy and Penelope Tree.

tomorrow angel face dare you to be seen with **Nothing On**

angel face ... the face makers

2

TO THE NAKED EYE IT'S A NAKED FACE.

MARY QUANT

3

4

4 *PRESS AD, USA*

CLIENT: MITSOUKO

5-6 *PRESS ADS, USA*

CLIENT: GIVENCHY

Mitsouko by Guerlain

5

6

1-2 *PRESS ADS, 1968, UK*

CLIENT: DHOBI

AGENCY: DOYLE DANE AND
BERNBACH, LONDON

ART DIRECTOR: DOUG MAXWELL

COPYWRITER: JOHN WITHERS

ILLUSTRATOR: ROBERT OSBORN

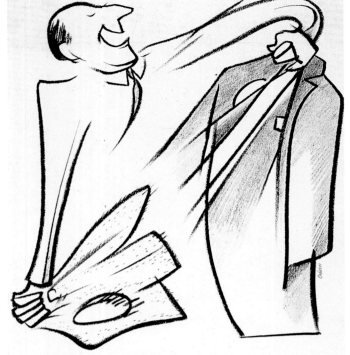

Black the Ripper.

Lionel Black is our Chairman, Managing Director and roughest customer.

He treats our raincoats and topcoats with the utmost brutality.

(After all, if our standards dwindle, he'll stand to lose more than the rest of us.)

Recently, he's taken to tearing out our linings.

Warm, furry linings of Orlon. Lighter and harder-wearing than anything animals have invented.

Lest you think we're at the mercy of a nut, we should explain that these linings are meant for tearing.

They're attached to our coats by Velcro tracks. Narrow nylon strips, with thousands of little loops and hooks. They're guaranteed for the life of the coat. So any lining-ripper can indulge himself ad nauseam.

Presumably we don't have to go on much about the virtues of tear-out linings in a climate as fickle as ours.

Instead, we suggest you visit your nearest Dhobi stockist and tear one out yourself.

See if you can beat Mr. Black's 0.8 of a second.

Of course, it takes him longer to stick the lining back in. A full eleven seconds.

But nobody's perfect.

Dhobi Raincoats and Topcoats with linings of Orlon.

1

If you don't like the Dhobi lining, tear it out.

The trouble with most linings is, they're there to stay. No matter how warm it gets.

So this year, we're providing many Dhobi raincoats and topcoats with tear-out linings. Made of Orlon. Red or grey. As furry and durable a fabric as you'll find.

They're attached to the coats by Velcro tracks. Narrow, nylon strips, with thousands of tiny hooks and loops.

Highly ingenious. And guaranteed for the life of the garment.

When you're heated enough to remove the lining, you literally tear the strips apart. Very satisfying. Gets rid of all kinds of aggressions. (We suggest you go to a nearby Dhobi stockist and let rip.)

Comes winter's icy grip, you just stick the lining back in. The Velcro tracks close at a touch. A lot less fussy than zips. And completely unjammable.

Dhobi raincoats with tear-out linings are made of Dacron and cotton, the best raincoat fabric to date. The topcoats come in a variety of excellent fabrics.

Naturally we'll continue to make coats without tear-out linings. And we'll be delighted if you choose one of them.

But if you buy a Dhobi coat with a tear-out lining, you really get two coats. A light one and a heavy one.

And if the weather's as unpredictable for you as it is for us, maybe we've said enough.

Dhobi Raincoats and Topcoats with linings of Orlon.

2

JAMAICA

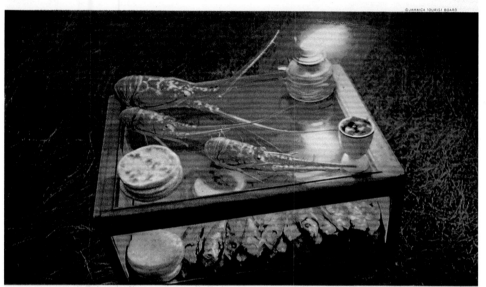

© JAMAICA TOURIST BOARD

3-5 *PRESS ADS, USA*

CLIENT: JAMAICA TOURIST BOARD

AGENCY: DOYLE, DANE AND
BERNBACH, NEW YORK

*This is one of Doyle Dane's great campaigns
of the sixties and it did an amazing job for
the Jamaican tourist board. The double-
page spread version of the ads ingeniously
used a full-page colour bleed opposite a black
and white page.*

*At Old Harbour's
lamplighted stands, fried fish,
cold lobster and spiced roti
bread costs about 70¢.
Because you can't bargain
like we do, you may
have to pay up to 90¢.*

You can eat yourself silly in Jamaica without even going indoors. (Some of our poshest restaurants don't have much use for a roof here.)

Of course, a restaurant gives you a table and chairs, while at a roadside stand, you stand. But try it. If your feet can take it, your palate and purse will be grateful.

Start your gastronomic tour at a fruit cart. Mango, naseberries or pawpaw washed down with a draught from a freshly lopped-off coconut. Then maybe a codfish fritter for a penny. Breakfast might cost 15¢.

For lunch, drive up in the mountains to Diablo, where some people feel full just from viewing the edible landscape. Get a hot (both meanings) meat patty from a baker's. It's

a crusty crescent with something magical inside. Then buy a bottle of cold Red Stripe beer from a grocer's. No; better buy two. Now hurry on to a roast corn stand.

Then stand in the shade of a cotton tree and eat your 45¢ lunch.

Oh, we almost forgot dessert. But don't you. For 3¢ at any snowball cart you get shaved ice all dripped over with lovely pink syrup. It tends to settle your lunch and make room for the excesses to follow.

Now move-along; southwesterly to change the scenery. And to get to Star Apple near Middle Quarters in time for the afternoon snack.

This is where you'll get the river shrimp. They're pink, tiny, and so delicate that we eat them shells and

all. Stop at the deserted crossroads and before you have time to remind yourself that a shilling equals 14¢, it isn't deserted any more.

Fishwives appear from all sides, flourishing basins of rosy shrimp sprinkled with fiery Scotch Bonnet peppers. A paper sack-full at 2 shillings is enough to stop a large appetite. And to start a small bonfire. Calm it down with a bite of bulla, a molasses-and-cinnamon cake. (1¢)

Ready for dinner? Better wait till later, don't you think? Besides, it'll taste even better by lamplight.

For facts on more conventional food (and lodgings, too) see your travel agent or Jamaica Tourist Board, in New York, Miami, Los Angeles, Chicago and San Francisco.

3

JAMAICA

To get to this crossroads, you can take a bus named *Romance*. Or you can hire a Buick named *Rover.* Operated by a man named *Vivian.*

If you miss Romance, you catch Confidence or Blue Danube or Lion of Judah. London's country buses all run by names instead of numbers.

But there's only one Vivian and forty the Buick. If they're busy, you go on foot or Hertz.

The names of our villages run to coy, abstract or British. You picture always. They can also be cheery. Buck-Up. Or vivid. Cut Throat Hill. Or plush coo-coo: Catadupa. Cookie Bar Point.

Jamaican women have funsnap-sounding names. Venice, Lionel, Carline. Men are named

Winston or Egbn or Chang. And sometimes Winston Chang.

We name hotels after pirates: Frenchman's Cove; Runaway Bay; Morgan's Harbour (Henry). Or after Boon. Boston Hill. Hibiscus Lodge. Or after the scenery: Bonnie View, Blue Mountain Inn.

As cocktails, we sip Brandy-Eyed Blackers or Rumbocrazies often made with a rum named Charley's or a rabbit-herd boiled Brittle Rage.

We dote on Dip-and-Fall-Back. (a curry stir time). And when a dish treats steaming, we douse it with Pickapeppa to pick up.

We call the poorhouse the Lord me-done-hand.

Sneakers are Hard-heels. And about any hot liquid is Tea (Coffee Tea, Cocoa Tea) except cough, which is Chaw-Water.

Our buses Red Stripe. It's tiring for policeman, too (red stripe on trousers). So when we say "more, you go careful de red stripe get you," we're calling your leg in two directions.

For more of Jamaica's fun and names, see your local travel agent or Jamaica Tourist Board in New York, Chicago, San Francisco, Miami, Los Angeles, Tmmm.

4

JAMAICA

This dhobie belongs to a girl. We smuggled him onto the island for a very important assignment: to sun our beach and tan.

He did a good job, too. And so did the Yankee members of our "vegetable gang" from the faculty of the School of Hotel Administration at Cornell University.

In proper scholarly fashion, they prepared a report that toted up a hotel for value (gives the relation to prices charged) in three categories: food, service and accommodations.

Of course, we coloured it up a bit for easy reading with starfish and other symbols. (They work like the stars in a movie guide.)

That it was a success from the very first day of publication is apparent by the high wind it created among Jamaican hotelkeepers.

In a way, we can't blame them.

One luxury-priced hotel, which prides itself on its food, received a lousy rating thus: a medium-priced hotel with a most modest menu. (According to our experts, the prices were too high—even for the best.)

And so it went—each hotel being rated strictly on what it gives for what it gets.

The result is that now things are changing in Jamaica.

One very fashionable hotel—with a railing lower than it considers acceptable—has completely redecorated, bright down, to new mattresses.

And another has imported the most expensive French chef ever to show up on the island.

You see, they never knew when our spies will be around to update their ratings. (Notices have decidedly we've promoted the identity of our spies in the picture above.)

Of course, some bookish tourists have made a thing of paradise around with a notebook and pencil in hopes of intimidating nervous hotel managers.

But, for the average, kind-hearted traveler, there's a much simpler way of getting one's money's worth in Jamaica.

Just ask for a copy of the Jamaica Value Guide from your travel agent or the Jamaica Tourist Board, in New York, Miami, Chicago, San Francisco.

5

Yes, it has been known to rain in Israel.

Once upon a time we had quite a lot of it. Forty days and forty nights by all accounts.

Since then, the weather seems to have cleared up quite a bit. The old millibars, isobars and anti-cyclones etc. are all in our favour.

Most of the country can rely on 9 months uninterrupted sunshine a year. And Eilat, a lush resort on the Red Sea, only gets 5 days rain out of 365.

If you want to bake gently till a golden brown you'll find plenty of beaches to do it on.

We have four seas (Med., Dead, Red and Galilee), scores of sandy beaches and modern resorts like Nathanya, Ashkelon and Herzlia.

When you get browned-off sunbathing there are plenty of other things to see and do.

There are three thousand years of history to browse through. Biblical place names to bring to life. Colourful street markets and fashionable shops. Classical concerts in Roman amphitheatres. Wining, dining and dancing in bars, bistros and discotheques.

And all this is only 4½ hours away from London by EL AL's non-stop Boeings. Any day of the week.

Talk to your local travel agent. He says the nicest things.

Like, 'Yes, sir. Of course you can afford it. Even after devaluation. There are special low cost holidays which include 14 days in a hotel as well as return air fare. Sign here.'

Sign there. And go.

And don't worry about the rain. If it ever happens again, every one will be in the same boat, anyway.

EL AL. The Airline of the People of Israel.

1

Just a few of the people who dropped in on us at one time or another.

Constantine arrived, built the Church of the Holy Sepulchre in Jerusalem, and started the Byzantine rule of Israel. They lasted for 300 years only to be pushed out of their place in the sun by the Persians.

At Appolonia, about a mile out of Herzlia, one of the modern resort towns, Richard Coeur de Lion defeated Saladin. You can still see the remains of the Crusaders' fortress, walls, moats and ancient harbour. In fact, pick almost any town along that coastline and you'll find remnants of the Crusaders' rule. When you get tired of knocking about the ruins, head for the bright lights of Nathanya, another resort town, close at hand.

Bonaparte—well, he didn't have much of a time here. He was all set to whizz through and extend his empire but he was stopped at Acre. He never came back. Perhaps if he'd got into Acre, he might have done. See it. You'll want to come back.

All over Israel the Romans left their mark. You can listen to concerts in the Roman amphitheatre at Caesarea and relieve your rheumatism in the sulphur spring baths at Tiberias. As well as building his famous wall, Hadrian was given the job of rebuilding Jerusalem as a Roman City (Aelia Capitolina). It didn't last very long but there are still bits for you to see.

Goliath's people, the Philistines, occupied most of the Mediterranean coast. One of their main centres was Ashkelon. Now, a flourishing resort town sets alongside the Old Town of the Philistines.

You can find out a lot more about our visitors and their handiworks from the *Israel Government Tourist Office, 59 St. James's Street, London S.W. 1*. They'll be glad to tell you about our own handiworks, too.

One thing all those guests had in common. They were all uninvited. We're inviting you. Take up the invitation at your local travel agents.

Tell him you want to visit Israel. He'll tell you how to go. How long it will take. And how much it will cost.

Any day of the week by EL AL. 4½ hours. There are low cost holidays which include 14 days in a hotel as well as return air fare.

Drop in and see us sometime. Soon.

EL AL. The Airline of the People of Israel.

3

The lowest night-spot on earth.

Is air conditioned. And very respectable.

It's a restaurant called Lot's Wife at Sodom.

(Don't let the name bother you, all that was a long time ago. Just go easy on the salt. You don't know who it's been.)

It's 1,292 feet below sea level, in the Dead Sea area.

Note for non-swimmers. While you're down there, take the plunge in the Dead Sea. Amaze your friends, as they say.

The rest of the country has plenty more night-life to offer.

'The End of the World' is at hand in Eilat.

'The Walls of Acre' resound nightly to the sound of wining, dining, dancing and cabaret.

You can add your little bit to the gaiety of nations by joining in a folk sing-up. And by tasting some Israeli dishes in a little bistro. (Or watching them in a sophisticated revue theatre).

And you can listen to the world-famous Israel Philharmonic Orchestra at the exciting new Frederic Mann Auditorium in Tel-Aviv.

During the day, if your crowded evening schedule is taking it out of you, you can soak up the sun on the beaches at our modern resorts. We've got four seas (Med., Red, Dead and Galilee) so there are plenty of beaches to choose from.

You can bring to life the biblical place names. Jericho, Jerusalem, Bethlehem, Hebron and Nazareth.

Then you can have a look round some of the souvenirs left by our previous visitors. Greeks, Romans, Crusaders, Phoenicians, Philistines, Babylonians.

It's taken us ages (roughly 3,000 years) to collect them. And they're on show everywhere.

Would you like to know more about what to look for? Get in touch with the *Israel Government Tourist Office, 59 St James's Street, London, S.W. 1.* They've got lots of handouts which they're just waiting to hand out.

But if you're looking for some action, pop along to your local travel agent.

Say 'I want to go to the lowest night-spot on earth. Can I afford it? Especially since you-know-what'.

He'll smile discreetly and say, 'Yes, sir. Even after devaluation. There are special low cost holidays in Israel which include 14 days' hotel accommodation as well as return air fare. An EL AL flight from London any day of the week will get you to Israel in 4½ hours'.

Press him for more details. Book up. And go.

Visit Lot's Wife.

You'll never look back.

EL AL. The Airline of the People of Israel.

2

It took 40 years for our first flight to get here. You can make it in 4½ hours.

Not surprising, really. The Children of Israel only had a handful of mules and perhaps the odd camel to carry them.

We've got 32,000 horses to help us along. (By courtesy of Rolls-Royce, Pratt & Whitney and The Boeing Corporation.)

We can promise you a more comfortable flight as well as a faster one. Air conditioning, comfortable seats and tasty meals.

No quails and manna, we're afraid. But with prices starting at £96 (from next March, including 14 days hotel accommodation as well as return air fare,) what do you expect?

When you get here you'll find a few things have changed since Moses first looked upon the land and saw that it was good.

We doubt whether The Children would recognise the modern hotels. Or the discotheques. Or the night life in general.

They might be surprised by the fashionable shops on Dizengoff Street in Tel Aviv. And some of the swimsuit styles on the beaches at Nathanya, Ashkelon and Herzlia, might cause a bit of a stir.

But things change in 3,000 odd years. That's life.

Some things haven't changed though.

Ashkelon, one of the holiday resorts, began its life 5,000 years ago as a Canaanite city. It's still the same Ashkelon that King Herod called 'The Bride of the East'.

Massada, where the Zealots held out against a long Roman siege, still stands. And it's now being excavated and restored.

Eilat, an exciting resort on the Red Sea, with 360 days of sunshine, plus water skiing, skin-diving, speed-boating and nightlife, is next to the harbour from which King Solomon's navy sailed to bring back the treasures of Ophir.

And King Solomon's Mines are in the Negev Desert near at hand.

Jerusalem is Jerusalem. Need we say more?

Some things have changed, some haven't. That's the fascination of Israel.

It's what makes a holiday here quite different. The sort of difference you'll remember when other holidays are just faded snapshots in an album.

Would you like to know a little more about how the Promised Land lives up to its promise? The *Israel Government Tourist Office, 59 St James's Street, London, S.W. 1,* can give you masses of information.

But if you're the direct action type, say to your local travel agent, 'I'd like to visit Israel'. Even if it still took 40 years it would be worth it.

EL AL. The Airline of the People of Israel.

4

To you, the label may not be the most important part of your baggage.

To us, it is.

We don't see any point in you arriving safe and sound somewhere, while your baggage is arriving safe and sound somewhere else.

We happen to think that wherever your baggage is going its label should tag along.

And we've gone to a fair bit of trouble to see that it does.

We experimented with all kinds of materials before we made our labels:

Paper. Cardboard. Plastic. Even cloth.

We tried string fasteners, rubber bands and gum.

And we saw samples from seven different label makers.

After two years, what we finally came up with was a label of specially treated paper bonded to a plastic stiffener.

One that clings to your case with the help of a strong rubber band.

We don't really expect to persuade you to travel with us just because of our baggage label.

But we'd like to think it means something to you that little things mean such a lot to us.

Lufthansa International
We'll do all we can.

If it doesn't get there, your baggage won't either.

5

Flying is easy, once you find the plane.

You know what it's like in a big international airport.

Everybody seems to know his way about except you.

You can't hear the announcements for listening.

You can't see the direction boards for looking.

At Lufthansa, we know how you feel. So we've tried to make life easier for you.

In every major airport, we've set up Redcaps. They're our ground stewardesses.

(They wear red caps so you can pick them out in the crowd.)

If you're the least bit unsure of yourself, buttonhole one the minute you arrive.

She can tell you when your plane goes. Which gate to go through.

She can tell you where to change your currency. Where the loo is.

She can help you with anything you want to know.

She'll do all this for sick people. For the disabled. The old. Or for children travelling alone.

And she'll do it for perfectly healthy passengers just because they don't speak the language.

The way we see it, no self-respecting airline should wait till take-off to get off the ground.

Lufthansa International
We'll do all we can.

Reprinted from Management Today, November 1969 issue.

6

CLIENT: EL AL

AGENCY: JOHN COLLINGS AND PARTNERS, LONDON

PRESS CAMPAIGN, 1968, UK

1 *ART DIRECTOR:* JOHN HEGARTY

COPYWRITER: LINDSAY DALE

ILLUSTRATOR: RON CARRUTHERS

2 *ART DIRECTOR:* JOHN HEGARTY

COPYWRITER: LINDSAY DALE

PHOTOGRAPHER: JULIAN COTTRELL

3 *ART DIRECTOR:* JOHN HEGARTY

COPYWRITER: LINDSAY DALE

4 *ART DIRECTOR:* JOHN HEGARTY

COPYWRITER: LINDSAY DALE

ILLUSTRATOR: ROY CARRUTHERS

CLIENT: LUFTHANSA

AGENCY: DOYLE, DANE AND BERNBACH, LONDON

5-6 *PRESS CAMPAIGN, 1970, UK*

ART DIRECTOR: NEIL GODFREY

COPYWRITER: DAWSON YEOMAN

PHOTOGRAPHER: TONY ELLIOT

18th Century French Provincial.

France is a time machine.

Slip into the provinces of France and you slip into the 18th century (or the 17th, or the 16th, or the Middle Ages; it's all there); it's a neat trick, and it works.

It can work for you, too.

Try Normandy, for example. Go into the country, where the big upland farms spread like a lush green quilt across the landscape. Out here heavy horses still draw the plows and wagons and the old Norman farmers still sow seed from flat-strapped baskets. (Not that they're anti-tractor; agriculture is big business in France. It's just that some farmers still like to do it the old way.)

Head on into town where the peasant women still wear their basic black (it's been basic for hundreds of years here) to market and the senior citizens still wear their berets and smocks as they sit in the shaded street cafés, sipping cider and talking crops. Join them at table and the chances are good they will tolerate your bad French and stand you to a glass of the local elixir: Calvados. This heady stuff hasn't changed for more generations than you could count; taste it and you'll see why.

Or try Brittany.

Make it into one of the tiny coastal villages, and make sure you're in town on one of the Holy Days. That's when all the folks (the kids, too) dress up in their centuries-old finery. The embroidered shirtbands, the rainbow sashes and the white lace coifs are too spectacular to be believed; you'll want to take slides. Watch them dancing on the town green to a wheezing band of Breton bagpipes.

While you're at it, try the Feast of the Great Pardon at the Shrine of Ste-Anne la Palud, out in Finistère. It's something like Brigadoon, only here it's real.

And while you're still in the neighborhood, try Pont-Aven. Watch the black-robed women lugging beige wicker baskets to market and watch them stocking up from the great straw vats of plump vegetables that line the quay. It's always been this way; why change?

(Note: Gauguin painted in Pont-Aven. Take one look at this incredibly picturesque provincial town and you'll see why. This is the kind of place you see only in paintings—unless you're there.)

Try the northeast pocket of France, a charming never-never land that nestles snug along the Rhine. On the feast days in these villages (start in Strasbourg and explore from there), the houses are strung with lights, flowers and thick green boughs, and draped with flags. The only difference between now and then is that some of the lights are electric, but there are still so many candles you won't know the difference.

And try Le Puy, in the heart of France, where whole constellations of candles float in flickering clusters up the side of a black volcano in the traditional pilgrimage processions to the 10th-century chapel of St-Michel-d'Aiguilhe.

Try the southwest corner of France, the foothills of the Pyrénées, where shepherds still watch over their sheep while standing on stilts.

Another custom to catch: the Dance of the Seven Jumps. If you find yourself wondering how these Basquemen can stay off the ground for such extended leaps, don't forget they've been doing this dance for the past thousand years.

Try Caen, back up in the northwest sector, during the annual tripe-eating contest, when the spectators heckle from the sidelines, as they always have.

Try Ribeauvillé during the annual procession of the cooks when huge floats of monster delicacies ride through the center of town.

Try France, where so much that was yesterday still stands intact today.

Try France, where you will see, in each face, the easy, open warmth of a people who have inherited (and welcome you to share) the traditions of centuries.

May we offer a suggestion?

If you've had it with 20th-century French provincial. The best way together? Take any road out of Paris and you're on your way.

(Another suggestion: Before you step into any time machines, step in to see a travel agent. Or write direct to: French Government Tourist Office, Dept. TE-5, 610 Fifth Avenue, New York, New York 10020.)

Jet travel had a dramatic effect on the development of tourism in the 1960s. In America it meant that even such far-flung places as India were accessible to the more adventurous holiday-makers. Naturally, there was a concurrent increase in travel advertising and all of the ads here are typical of the pioneering style that the creative New York agencies were developing at that time.

Think you've seen France? Think again.

2

IRELAND

3

When you come to Oslo, bring an open mind.

4

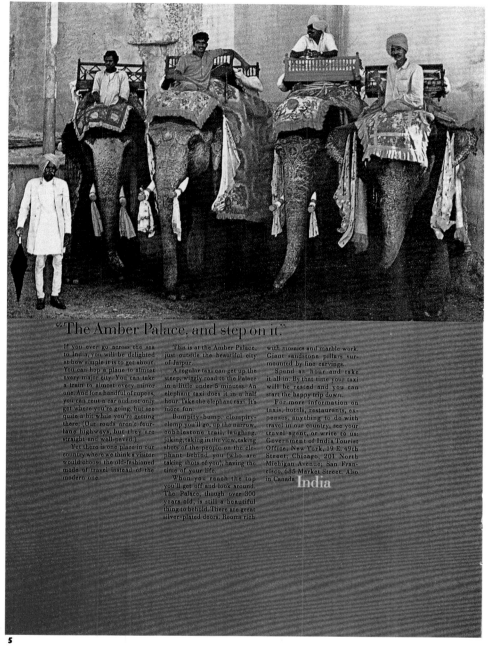

"The Amber Palace, and step on it."

If you ever go across the sea to India, you will be delighted at how simple it is to get about. You can hop a plane to almost every major city. You can take a train to almost every minor one. And for a handful of rupees, you can rent a car and not only get where you're going, but see quite a bit while you're getting there. (Our roads aren't four-lane highways, but they are straight and well-paved.)

Yet there is one place in our country where we think a visitor would choose the old-fashioned mode of travel instead of the modern one.

This is at the Amber Palace, just outside the beautiful city of Jaipur.

A regular taxi can get up the steep, wiggly road to the Palace in a little under 5 minutes. An elephant taxi does it in a half hour. Take the elephant taxi. It's more fun.

Bumpity-bump, clompity-clomp you'll go, up the narrow, cobblestone trail, laughing, joking, taking in the view, taking shots of the people on the elephant behind you (who are taking shots of you), having the time of your life.

When you reach the top you'll get off and look around. The Palace, though over 300 years old, is still a beautiful thing to behold. There are great silver-plated doors. Rooms rich

with mosaics and marble work. Giant sandstone pillars surmounted by fine carvings.

Spend an hour and take it all in. By that time your taxi will be rested and you can start the happy trip down.

For more information on taxis, hotels, restaurants, expenses, anything to do with travel in our country, see your travel agent, or write to us: Government of India Tourist Office; New York, 19 E. 49th Street; Chicago, 201 North Michigan Avenue; San Francisco, 685 Market Street. Also in Canada.

India

5

A message to anyone who's been to Europe.

6

No wonder there's a Taj Mahal.

7

1

2

3

兵民是胜利之本

4

一定要解放台湾

We are determined to liberate Taiwan!
Nous libérerons Taïwan!
Wir werden Taiwan unbedingt befreien!

5

CLIENT: JOSEPH E. SEAGRAM AND SONS

AGENCY: DOYLE, DANE AND BERNBACH, NEW YORK

As with VW and Avis, this is one of the great Doyle Dane campaigns of the sixties in which, with great wit and flair, they took a product negative, in this case price, and turned it into a positive — exclusivity.

And he calls himself a Chivas drinker.

If you count every dram of Chivas Regal, you're probably not having a very good time.

Buying our Scotch, and drinking it, should be an expensive gesture.

Expensive?

Rather. Chivas Regal costs $2 more than most other Scotches. But you can't pay less and get whisky like ours. Strathisla-Glenlivet, aged 12 long years.

To real Chivas drinkers this is a condition of life. So they don't count drams. They count their blessings.

12-YEAR-OLD BLENDED SCOTCH WHISKY 86 PROOF. GENERAL WINE & SPIRITS CO., N.Y.

1

Kiss it goodbye.

You know what's going to happen. It's hail and farewell. It happened last time at your house. It happened last time at his house.

Open a bottle of Chivas and there are more Scotch drinkers in the crowd than you'd ever have guessed.

Be brave. Don't cry. Don't think how much extra this 12 year old miracle costs you—remember how much more it does for you.

It makes you a superb host. It gives you the happiest guests in town.

It's a wonderful bottle of wonderful Scotch—wasn't it?

2

For people who are afraid to say it out loud.

Some people are afraid to buy a Cadillac.

They know it's a great car, and they'd like to have it.

But they're afraid it will look as if they're trying to prove something.

Some people don't buy Chivas for the same reason. This card is for people like that.

Just show it to the man who's pouring.

It'll get you the best Scotch in the world without saying a word.

It will prove something: that the only person you have to please is yourself.

We know Chivas is that good.

Let Cadillac look out for itself.

Chivas Regal please

The cards are for real.

General Wine & Spirits Company, 375 Park Avenue, Bot M, New York, N.Y. 10022.

3

Do you order Chivas Regal even when nobody's around?

"Chivas Regal, please."

We don't deny the fact that many people say it simply to turn a few heads. On the contrary, we're quite proud of it.

Chivas Regal has earned a reputation as the finest 12-year-old Scotch in the world.

The real Chivas drinker knows this reputation is deserved. And sooner or later the name-dropper will know it, too.

12 YEAR-OLD BLENDED SCOTCH WHISKY · 86 PROOF GENERAL WINE & SPIRITS CO., NEW YORK, N Y

CLIENT: JOSEPH E. SEAGRAM AND
SONS

AGENCY: DOYLE, DANE AND
BERNBACH, LONDON

PRESS CAMPAIGN, 1969, UK

ART DIRECTOR: MARTYN WALSH

COPYWRITER: TONY BRIGNULL

PHOTOGRAPHER: ELBOT BUDIN

Britain followed America in this campaign and positioned Chivas Regal as the most expensive and therefore the most precious of whiskies. Even the tone and graphics were consistent with the US.

That'll teach you to show off in company.

Try not to tell your guests that Chivas Regal is three times older than other Scotches.

Feign ignorance of the fact that it's softened by more Glen-livet whiskies than most other Scotches.

Refrain from answering the unspoken question: that it costs £1 more than other Scotches. Or you may find that while they're drinking your Chivas, you'll wish you'd eaten your words.

Go one better than the usual bottle of Scotch: a half bottle of Chivas Regal.

Taste isn't everything, you also need money.

Chivas Regal's clan-size jar holds five bottles-worth. And saves you 7/6.

We don't pretend it's the bargain of the year. But Chivas Regal isn't that sort of Scotch.

We blend up to twice as much prize Glenlivet whiskies as the cut-price boys.

And mature them for three times longer. A full twelve years.

This means twelve years warehousing, twelve years evaporation (a quarter of our stock goes out the window).

Then, we let the whiskies marry for a whole year to add the final touch of softness.

In view of all this, you might not think you're doing right by Chivas, buying it on the cheap.

Perhaps you'd prefer the expensive way: miniature bottles at 5/6.

Chivas Regal on the cheap. £17.0.0.

CLIENT: REMINGTON

AGENCY: DOYLE, DANE AND
BERNBACH, LONDON

PRESS CAMPAIGN, 1965

1 *ART DIRECTOR:* NEIL GODFREY

COPYWRITER: JOHN WITHERS

PHOTOGRAPHER: DUFFY

2-5 *ART DIRECTOR:* RICK LEVINE

COPYWRITER: JOHN WITHERS

PHOTOGRAPHER: RUDY LEGUAME

We sell a cordless shaver with a cord.
Maybe we should have our head examined.

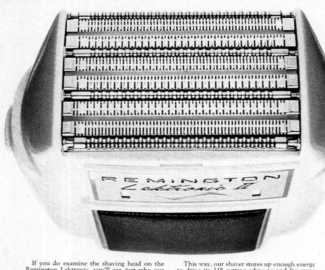

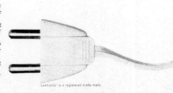

If you do examine the shaving head on the Remington Lektronic, you'll see just why our cordless shaver needs a cord.

It has the biggest shaving head there is. With 348 cutting edges. And more cutting actions than anybody else's shaver, cordless or plug-in.

To drive it, we've developed a very powerful motor. Too powerful, in fact, to operate on the ordinary dry-cell batteries that satisfy other cordless shavers.

So inside the Lektronic we put two rechargeable cells. And we give you the cord so you can charge them from the mains.

This way, our shaver stores up enough energy to drive its 348 cutting edges to and fro more than 8,000 times a minute.

And it can go full strength for ten days shaving on one charge. (Ordinary batteries grow weaker and weaker from the first shave on.)

A Remington Lektronic is really two shavers in one. You get the freedom of a cordless shaver and the power of a plug-in.

Which are two pretty good reasons for rushing you £15.

We'd have liked to shave the price. But your face comes first.

Lektronic is a registered trade mark.

1

If your kid buys you a Remington 25 for Christmas, he's getting altogether too much pocket money.

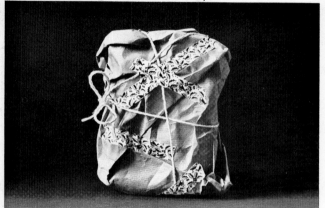

A few coins clutched in a grubby palm don't go far towards any electric shaver.

But the Remington 25 requires a special affluence, which is seldom achieved during childhood.

It costs ten quid. (About thirty shillings more than the other best-seller.)

Why should anybody, however well-heeled, fork out so much?

Glad you asked.

The Remington 25 has the largest shaving head you can get. And it stands to common sense that the larger the area a shaver shaves, the faster it will do the job.

Into the head we tuck 348 cutting edges.

They're driven by the most powerful motor there is. A cool 8,000 times a minute.

The Remington 25 is the only shaver with adjustable Roller-Combs.

When they're up, our shaver is gentle. For the tender spots. When they're down, it ploughs smartly through the thickets.

Now the only way you're going to own a shaver this grand is by getting a neat and dear one to part with ten pounds.

If that's too much to hope for, we have a more modest proposal:

The Remington Rollershave, which costs £5.19.6.

It has a smaller head and a less powerful motor. So it takes a bit longer to shift the stubble.

But it's a lot quicker to save up for.

And time is running out.

We don't want to skin you. So we charge a little more.

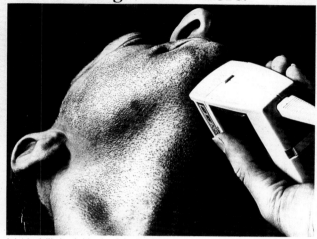

It takes guts to charge £10 for a shaver.

Spend an extra 30/- on his shaver. It's your face as well as his.

CHAPTER TEN

UNTIL 1973 MOST young people were still living in the 1960s. Fashion, music and attitudes had barely changed. The Woodstock generation clung to a Utopian dream and their commitment was fired by events on the American political stage. In 1968 Nixon had sneaked past Hubert Humphrey into the White House. Repeatedly stating his desire to secure peace, he intensified the war in Vietnam and began the secret bombing of Cambodia. However, in 1972, his career was destroyed by the revelations of Watergate and two years later he resigned in order to escape impeachment for the Watergate 'cover-up'.

But while the counter-culture was celebrating his demise, they were experiencing leadership problems of a different kind. The Beatles had disbanded and other key figures of the music scene were dead—Janis Joplin, Jim Morrison, Brian Jones and Jimi Hendrix had all burned out like shooting stars. Those that survived were holed up in mansions, growing flaccid on the proceeds of their former protest.

It was time for a new revolution and the return of the Angry Young Men. Only this time they were not just angry. They were crazy, spiky-haired 'mohicans'

whose ears, nostrils and cheeks were perforated with safety pins and who pogoed with frenzied and nihilistic abandon as they trashed the icons of a hollow culture. As well as a manic energy, the Punks brought with them an anti-aestheticism that was quickly appropriated and sanitised by the mainstream of commercial art. But their real problem was that they were unable to fill the void they had created. Andy Warhol, one of their more celebrated progenitors, summed it up succinctly when he described the seventies as crammed 'full of nothingness'.

From advertising's point of view this was a decade of consolidation. During the 1950s Rosser Reeves, in his book, *Reality in Advertising,* had introduced the concept of the 'Unique Selling Proposition'. In the 1960s Bill Bernbach had developed this idea with a lateral approach to the problems of persuasion. In the 1970s the advertising industry learned to put these creative principles into practice.

Bernbach had always eschewed formulae in the belief that they inhibited creativity. But his many observations provided criteria for judging an ad and throughout the seventies these thoughts evolved into creative philosophies such as the 'Relevant Unexpected'—a neat summation of advertising's two essential components, pertinence and surprise.

You could learn a lot from Mr. Statter.

1

All for the price of an Austin 1100.

2

It'll cruise all day at 60 mph.

3

It makes your tyres go farther.

4

£274.

5

In 1953, it was the Volkswagen that looked funny.

6

It was no accident that nobody died.

Crumple zone.   Rigid steel passenger safety cell.   Crumple zone.

Polo.

7

It's possible.

As far as we know, nobody has ever bought a Volkswagen because of its speed.

Its virtues have always been of the more homely kind.

An air-cooled engine that can't boil or freeze.

A paintwork job that can stay out all night and never show it.

A shape that doesn't go out of style every year, leaving the owner out of pocket.

As a result, the VW has a great image as a practical car.

And practically no image as a performance car.

And we do have a story.

The new 1500 c.c. VW does 78 mph. Fast enough to get copped for speeding on any road in the country.

In fact, in the long run, the VW can prove

faster than many faster cars.

Its engine is so low-revving, it's virtually impossible to over-work it. So its top speed is also its cruising speed.

It'll go flat out, all day. From the very day you drive it out of the showroom.

Volkswagens don't need running-in.

Though the police have been known to disagree.

VOLKSWAGEN MOTORS LIMITED VOLKSWAGEN HOUSE, PURLEY SURREY. TELEPHONE 01-668 4100

8

269

CLIENT: HEDGES AND BUTLER

AGENCY: J. WALTER THOMPSON, LONDON

PRESS CAMPAIGN, 1978, UK

1 *ART DIRECTOR:* TONY MURANKA

COPYWRITER: KEN MULLEN

ILLUSTRATOR: PAULINE ELLINSON

2 *ART DIRECTOR:* TONY MURANKA

COPYWRITER: KEN MULLEN

ILLUSTRATOR: LARRY LEARMART

3 *ART DIRECTOR:* TONY MURANKA

COPYWRITER: KEN MULLEN

ILLUSTRATOR: PETER LE VASSEUR

4 *ART DIRECTOR:* TONY MURANKA

COPYWRITER: KEN MULLEN

ILLUSTRATOR: BARRY CRADDOCK

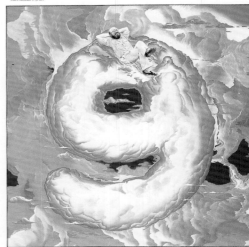

IT'S ABOUT AS LIKELY AS A DUFF BOTTLE OF HIRONDELLE.

1

2

IT'S ABOUT AS LIKELY AS A DUFF BOTTLE OF HIRONDELLE.

In 1973, in a comprehensive survey of the less expensive wines, *The Sunday Times* found that Hirondelle was "excellent value for money."

In fact, of more than 350 wines tasted, Hirondelle came top in two of its three categories (medium-dry white and rosé wines) and a close second in the third (vin ordinaire).

In 1975, the *Daily Express* also described Hirondelle as "excellent," and, in a survey conducted last year, placed it first in the 1½-litre category of red table wines.

These surveys only serve to reflect the public's view of Hirondelle over the years: a wine that's not only good, but one that's consistently so.

Hirondelle is selected and shipped by Hedges & Butler, wine merchants since 1667. It is available in red, sweet white, medium-dry white and rosé.

Hirondelle.
Every bottle is guaranteed.

3

IT'S ABOUT AS LIKELY AS A DUFF BOTTLE OF HIRONDELLE.

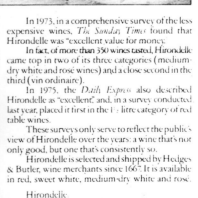

In 1973, in a comprehensive survey of the less expensive wines, *The Sunday Times* found that Hirondelle was "excellent value for money."

In fact, of more than 350 wines tasted, Hirondelle came top in two of its three categories (medium-dry white and rosé wines) and a close second in the third (vin ordinaire).

In 1975, the *Daily Express* also described Hirondelle as "excellent", and, in a survey conducted last year, placed it first in the 1½ litre category of red table wines.

These surveys only serve to reflect the public's view of Hirondelle over the years: a wine that's not only good, but one that's consistently so.

Hirondelle is selected and shipped by Hedges & Butler, wine merchants since 1667. It is available in red, sweet white, medium-dry white and rosé.

Hirondelle.
Every bottle is guaranteed.

69

4

CUT THINGS DOWN TO SIZE.

SURFORM®

1

THE BEST TOOLS
YOU CAN LAY HANDS ON.

STANLEY

2

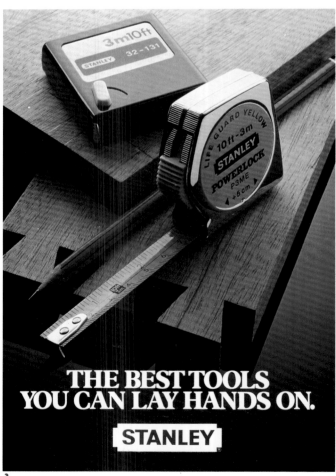

THE BEST TOOLS
YOU CAN LAY HANDS ON.

STANLEY

3

THE BEST TOOLS
YOU CAN LAY HANDS ON.

STANLEY

4

The art of pouring Chivas Regal for somebody else.

Take a tumbler.

Chock it full of ice: Leaving precious little room for anything else.

Then, bearing in mind you paid a pound more than for run-of-the-still scotch, carefully filter

in Chivas Regal, allowing the 12 year old blend of prize Glenlivet whiskies to form a small deposit in the bottom of the glass.

Generosity to such a fault brings with it obvious advantages: your Chivas Regal will live to

see another day.

It also brings its snags:

When you're in somebody else's house, you're not likely to be the one who's pouring.

Life is full of problems.

5

PRESS CAMPAIGN, 1977, UK

CLIENT: STANLEY TOOLS

AGENCY: ROW DOWNTON, LONDON

1-4 *ART DIRECTOR:* CATHY HENG

COPYWRITER: CATHY HENG

PHOTOGRAPHER: DAVID THORPE

CLIENT: SEAGRAMS

AGENCY: DOYLE DANE AND BERNBACH, LONDON

5 *PRESS AD, 1971, UK*

ART DIRECTOR: BRIAN BYFIELD

COPYWRITER: DAWSON YEOMAN

PHOTOGRAPHER: LYNN ST. JOHN

6 *PRESS AD, 1970, UK*

ART DIRECTOR: MARTYN WALSH

COPYWRITER: TONY BRIGNULL

PHOTOGRAPHER: ELBOT BUDIN

7 *PRESS AD, 1971, UK*

ART DIRECTOR: BRIAN BYFIELD

COPYWRITER: DAWSON YEOMAN

PHOTOGRAPHER: LESTER BOOKBINDER

Are your friends living beyond your means?

When you pay a good deal more for Chivas Regal than for ordinary scotch, exposing it to friends can be an extravagant gesture.

You see, once off, the caps on Chivas bottles are notoriously

difficult to put back on.

This may have something to do with the great age of our Scotch. 12 years.

Or its unique blend of prize Glenlivet malt whiskies.

Or both.

As it is, we have only one consolation to offer.

Once your friends have acquired the taste, they'll probably acquire some Chivas.

At which time, the more friends you have the better.

6

Do you only drink it after you've been abroad?

Judging by the amount we sell duty free, it seems our twelve year old whisky softens the blow of coming home.

This doesn't surprise us.

If there's one thing more gratifying than sipping prize Glenlivet whiskies, it's sipping prize Glenlivet whiskies you haven't paid the full 28/- a bottle for.

What we can't understand, though, is how you manage when the Chivas is ended but the memory lingers on.

Do you wait another year to renew the acquaintance?

Come now.

The extra pound you pay for Chivas Regal is really only 6d or so more a tot.

And far cheaper than the alternative: a winter sports holiday.

7

CLIENT: GALLAHER AND COMPANY

AGENCY: COLLETT, DICKENSON
AND PEARCE, LONDON

POSTER, 1977, UK

ART DIRECTOR: GRAHAM WATSON

PHOTOGRAPHER: ADRIAN
FLOWERS

*This poster was about the fourth in what
has now become the definitive British
cigarette campaign. At a time when
government controls were making it
increasingly difficult to use any imagery that
related to success, health, fame or sex, Collett
sidestepped the whole issue and took B&H
into the abstract. The ads appeared on
hoardings and in the press and the quality of
imagination and photography made the
territory of surrealism entirely theirs.*

MIDD
EVERY PACKET CARRIE

R As defined by H.M.Government

OVERNMENT HEALTH WARNING

CLIENT: GALLAHER AND COMPANY

PRODUCT: BENSON AND HEDGES CIGARETTES

AGENCY: COLLET, DICKENSON AND PEARCE, LONDON

1 POSTER, 1978, UK

ART DIRECTOR: GRAHAM WATSON

PHOTOGRAPHER: BRIAN DUFFY

2 POSTER, 1978, UK

ART DIRECTOR: GRAHAM WATSON

PHOTOGRAPHER: BRIAN DUFFY

3 POSTER, 1978, UK

ART DIRECTOR: GRAHAM WATSON

PHOTOGRAPHER: DAVID MONTGOMERY

4 POSTER, 1978, UK

ART DIRECTOR: ALAN WALDIE

PHOTOGRAPHER: BRIAN DUFFY

5 POSTER, 1979, UK

ART DIRECTOR: ALAN WALDIE

PHOTOGRAPHER: JIMMY WORMSER

6 POSTER, 1979, UK

ART DIRECTOR: NEIL GODFREY

PHOTOGRAPHER: JIMMY WORMSER

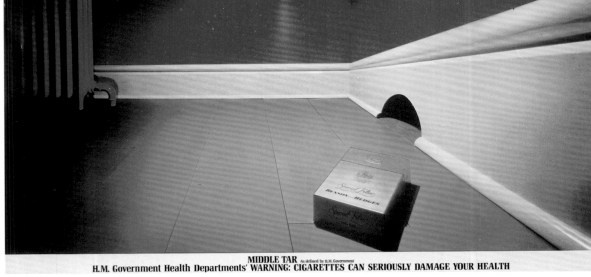

MIDDLE TAR As defined by H.M. Government
H.M. Government Health Departments' WARNING: CIGARETTES CAN SERIOUSLY DAMAGE YOUR HEALTH

1

MIDDLE TAR As defined by H.M. Government
EVERY PACKET CARRIES A GOVERNMENT HEALTH WARNING

2

MIDDLE TAR As defined by H.M. Government
EVERY PACKET CARRIES A GOVERNMENT HEALTH WARNING

3

MIDDLE TAR As defined by H.M. Government
H.M. Government Health Departments' WARNING: CIGARETTES CAN SERIOUSLY DAMAGE YOUR HEALTH

4

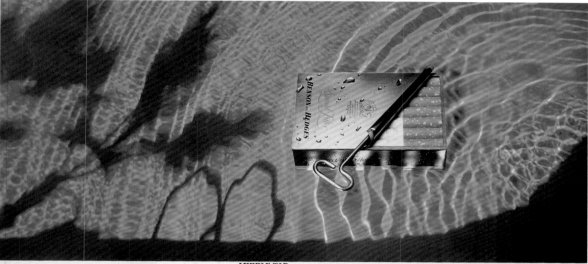

MIDDLE TAR As defined by H.M. Government
H.M. Government Health Departments' WARNING: CIGARETTES CAN SERIOUSLY DAMAGE YOUR HEALTH

5

MIDDLE TAR As defined by H.M. Government
H.M. Government Health Departments' WARNING: CIGARETTES CAN SERIOUSLY DAMAGE YOUR HEALTH

6

Have you ever wished you were better informed?

THE TIMES

1

POSTER AND PRESS CAMPAIGN,
1978-79, UK

CLIENT: TIMES NEWSPAPERS

AGENCY: LEO BURNETT, LONDON

1 *POSTER AND PRESS AD, 1978*

ART DIRECTOR: ROGER STANNIER

COPYWRITER: ROGER STANNIER

2 *POSTER AND PRESS AD, 1979*

ART DIRECTOR: MICHAELA DAY

COPYWRITER: NICK SOUTER

ILLUSTRATOR: BARRY CRADDOCK

3-4 *POSTER AND PRESS AD, 1978*

ART DIRECTOR: ROGER STANNIER

COPYWRITER: ROGER STANNIER

5 *PRSS AD, 1978, UK*

CLIENT: NEWSWEEK

AGENCY: TBWA, LONDON

ART DIRECTOR: JOHN HEGARTY

COPYWRITER: NEIL PATTERSON

ILLUSTRATOR: GUY GLADWELL

TYPOGRAPHER: BRIAN HILL

Have you ever wished you were better informed?

THE TIMES

2

Have you ever wished you were better informed?

THE TIMES

DANGER QUICK SAND 20 YDS.

3

Have you ever wished you were better informed?

THE TIMES

4

How is China managing without Mao?

Shortly after the death of Chairman Mao Tse-tung, Henry Kissinger commented: "I don't think even the Chinese know what the impact of the death of such a tremendous figure will be for them."

Can anyone ever hope to fill the vacuum left by China's legendary leader?

How much of a blow is the emergence of the seemingly moderate Hua to Mao's cherished concept that China should sustain a perpetual revolution?

How will the internal upheavals affect Peking's relations with Washington and Moscow? And US detente with the Soviet Union?

Along with examining the week's news and varied opinions from around the world, Newsweek analyses the build-up and history behind important events—for example, the death of Mao—fixing them firmly in perspective.

As the news ripples around the globe, Newsweek also traces the implications such events have on various countries and assesses their bearing on the future.

All of this plus regular Asian coverage makes Newsweek invaluable for the people who need to rely on an objective evaluation of what's happening in the world.

People in government, business, the professions or the arts. People who are active leaders in their community.

Whose actions week by week help contribute to the history of the world we live in.

Newsweek
THE INTERNATIONAL NEWSMAGAZINE
History in the making.

In the end it's the simple ideas that win through.

NATR Toy of the Year Award second year running.
Toys International Top Toy Award for 1975.
And if that wasn't enough, 1975 sales up 50% on the year before.
It's going to be hard work beating that in '76. Not that
that's anything new to us.

The world's most popular toy.

©1976 BRITISH LEGO LTD. LEGO® is a registered trademark.

1

2

3

Parker's Law.

At Parker we have a laboratory where scientists delight in torturing our pens.

It would be unfair to call them sadists but they do seem to have a vindictive streak.

"What if we take a brand new pen," they say with mounting glee, "put it in a bag of old nuts and bolts and keys and twirl it round for twenty-four hours?"

Applause. Only one dissenting voice comes from the back. "Let's make them *new* nuts and bolts. They're *sharper*."

Agreed. The experiment becomes part of Parker's Law.

Now every new Parker is put through this test in the lab, or how could it pass the real test in your briefcase or handbag?

The question "what if?" seems to be the button that turns these men on. For example:

1. What if a pen is flung forward suddenly, as when a car stops abruptly or your baggage is thrown across a counter?

To find out, they strap our pens to pendulums and crash them against walls. No more than a smidgin of ink must show on the nib if the pen is ever to get into your pocket.

2. What if the owner is, say, a Traffic Warden and takes her pen out of her pocket umpteen times a day, can the clip take it?

They invented a machine that simulates this movement monotonously 10,000 times. To pass it a Parker clip must not lose its grip.

3. What if someone leaves the cap off one of our fibre-tip pens overnight?

In the laboratory pens stand in rows capless like soldiers at a court-martial. Next morning they must write first time, or else.

4. What happens if a man has a nervous twitch as in the Caine Mutiny and clicks his ball-pen all day long? They made a machine that drives everyone nuts by doing just that. But at least you know that a Parker clicker will always click and return to its rightful place, not stay infuriatingly depressed.

5. Here's a crazy one. What if some space-age traveller should suddenly rocket from ground level to 7,000 feet (unpressurised)? Or from 60°F to 90°F?

You might say he deserves all he gets. But one thing he won't get is a pocketful of ink.

Reassuring if you climb mountains or visit hot countries.

6. What if you want to write a novel on greasy paper? The answer is, don't. You'll never make War and Peace. But a Parker ball-pen will get you out of a greasy spot.

We test them on greasy paper by writing the numbers one to ten. Each one must reach number nine.

The tests go on and on remorselessly. When will a pen crack under the strain? Never, we hope.

The metals are scrutinised under microscopes for flaws.

How do we know the cap won't stick on or slip off after a year or so?

We know because we have another machine that takes them on and off 10,000 times.

At what temperature will a Parker ball-pen make your fingers inky? (Answer, if it ever does, double bad luck, you will have melted yourself.)

There is just one more "What if" we must tell you about.

What if you lose your Parker?

The answer is we will replace it. We now have a free insurance scheme on our more expensive models.

We think this makes us the only pen manufacturer who guarantees that your pen will write and go on writing even if you lose it.

◊ PARKER

Hopefully a Parker Cirrus will last a lifetime. It takes long enough to make.

◊ PARKER

Not all imitations are cheap.

A £9.90 copy of a 12p throwaway pen? Have we taken leave of our senses? Before you label us insane, let us point out a few differences.

The main one being that our pen isn't finished when the ink is.

We make refills in blue, black, red and green, each comes complete with a new tip.

And it's a different tip to the Japanese original of 15 years ago.

It's made from compressed nylon fibres that won't lose their shape no matter how many angry letters you write to the taxman.

Another difference is the ink itself.

We researched 64 inks from 6 countries before finding one that won't dry up if you leave the top off overnight.

Something else distinguishes our pen from the original. The casing won't crack or splinter.

Instead of a tube of plastic we use a shell of bronze, with a generous coating of brushed rolled gold.

We have done everything we can to ensure our pen, the Cirrus fibre tip, will last many, many years.

This seems perfectly sensible to us.

The foolish thing, surely, is making a pen that will only last a few days. ◊ PARKER

Cheap original. Expensive copy.

Even when we've sold a pen we still like to look after it.

◊ PARKER

The attraction of some gold pens soon wears off.

Parker believe that if you buy a gold pen it shouldn't turn into a brass one.

Not a year later. Not 10 years later.

To ensure this never happens with a Parker pen we roll the gold on, in a layer thick enough not to wear off.

In fact, there is as much gold on the Parker Insignia at the bottom of the page, as there is on 10 of the plated pens at the top.

Admittedly, our pen does cost more. But nowhere near 10 times more.

The plated gold pen sells for £4.95, the Parker Insignia for £8.90.

If that is a little more than you intended to pay, ask yourself, in the end what kind of pen do you really want?

A brass one or a rolled gold one?

◊ PARKER

IN 4 WEEKS TIME WE TAKE ON GOLIATH.

In four weeks time we're launching a completely new kind of upright vacuum cleaner. The McDonald Electric 250.

It'll clash head-on with the really big names and come out on top. Because it breaks all the outdated rules on vacuum cleaners.

At only 8½ lbs it's half the the weight of more traditional models. Yet it's just as powerful. And far more efficient.

Its motor fits comfortably into a case only 4½" high. (Making it easy to get under low furniture.)

It easily sucks up fluff, crumbs, even grit through its hollow handle. And empties it into a disposable bag from the top. Instead of forcing it up from the bottom.

Which explains why the McDonald Electric works at full efficiency until the bag is completely full.

It's so simple that customers can do almost all the servicing themselves. And best of all the McDonald Electric costs about £20.

It's an impressive story. And we're going to tell it in an impressive way. With whole pages in the Express, Mirror and Sun. And colour pages in the Observer Magazine.

So get some McDonald Electrics and get on the winning side. You know what happened to Goliath last time.

The McDonald Electric 250.
The end of the traditional vacuum cleaner.

1

IN 3 WEEKS TIME A SMALL VACUUM CLEANER WILL BECOME A VERY BIG VACUUM CLEANER.

Weighing in at only 8½lb the McDonald Electric 250 is the smallest, lightest upright vacuum cleaner ever made.

Yet it's just as powerful as more traditional models. And far more efficient.

Its motor fits comfortably into a case only 4½" at the highest point. (Which makes it very easy to get under low furniture.)

It easily sucks up fluff, crumbs, even grit through its hollow handle. And empties it into a disposable bag from the top.

So, unlike other uprights, it doesn't try to force today's dirt through yesterday's dirt.

Because the McDonald Electric is so simple, your customers can do most of the servicing themselves.

But the really big incentive to buy a McDonald Electric is the fact that it retails for around £20.

All of which will help turn our small vacuum cleaner into a very big vacuum cleaner. Especially as far as sales are concerned.

To make sure, we're launching it in a very big way. With whole pages in the Express, Mirror and Sun. And colour pages in the Observer Magazine.

As you can see, the McDonald Electric has all the ingredients to make it very big.

Stock enough McDonald Electrics and you'll have all the ingredients to make it big as well.

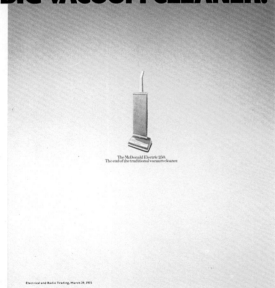

The McDonald Electric 250.
The end of the traditional vacuum cleaner.

2

IN 2 WEEKS TIME IT WILL BE A HOUSEHOLD NAME.

Right now no-one knows that the McDonald Electric 250 is a revolutionary new kind of upright vacuum cleaner.

No-one knows that it weighs only 8½lb yet is just as powerful as more traditional models and far more efficient.

No-one knows that its motor fits comfortably into a case only 4½" at the highest point. (Which makes it very easy to get under low furniture.)

No-one knows that it easily sucks up fluff, crumbs, even grit through its hollow handle. And empties it into a disposable bag from the top.

No-one knows that the McDonald Electric is so simple that customers can do most of their own servicing.

And no-one knows that even with all these features the McDonald Electric retails for about £20.

But in two weeks time everyone will know.

That's when we launch the McDonald Electric with whole pages. Colour and black and white. In the Express, Mirror, Sun, and the Observer Magazine.

That's when the McDonald Electric becomes a household name.

That's also when you can cash in on that name. Provided, that is, you've been farsighted enough to lay in sufficient stocks of the cleaner that carries it.

3

NEXT WEEK WE'RE ON THE MOVE. ARE YOU READY FOR US?

By now you may be sick of reading about McDonald Electric 250.

But we think it's only fair to remind you that in just seven short days we're launching it.

As you've probably gathered by now the McDonald Electric is a revolutionary new kind of vacuum cleaner.

It's been designed to needs and not traditions. So it's only about half the weight of ordinary models, but more powerful.

Yet it comes to your customers for about £20. If that isn't good news we don't know what is.

And in just a week's time we'll be on the move. In full pages (colour and black and white). In the Express, Mirror, Sun, and the Observer Magazine.

So you've still got a week to get a nice collection of McDonald Electrics in stock.

Because when we move, we'll move fast.

The McDonald Electric 250.
The end of the traditional vacuum cleaner.

4

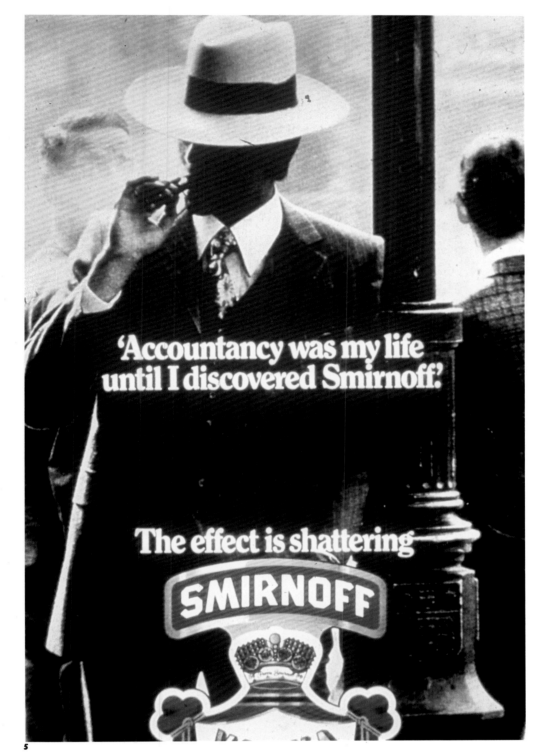

5

6

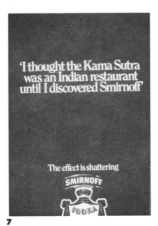

7

8

1-4 *PRESS CAMPAIGN, 1973, UK*

CLIENT: MCDONALD ELECTRIC

AGENCY: COGENT ELLIOT,
LONDON

ART DIRECTOR: GRAHAM LINCOLN

COPYWRITER: MIKE BELGROVE

PHOTOGRAPHER: JULIEN
COTTRELL

*This was a four-week trade campaign to
announce the introduction of a new vacuum
cleaner.*

5-8 *PRESS AND POSTER CAMPAIGN,
UK*

CLIENT: SMIRNOFF VODKA

AGENCY: YOUNG AND RUBICAM,
LONDON

*This was one of the most popular alcohol
campaigns ever to run in the UK. The theme
was also used in the cinema, but a change in
the laws concerning alcohol advertising
would make it unacceptable today.*

1-3 *PRESS ADS, 1979, UK*

CLIENT: KIMBERLY-CLARKE

AGENCY: FLETCHER SHELTON
DELANEY, LONDON

ART DIRECTOR: PAUL FONTEYNE

DESIGNER: BRUCE GILL

COPYWRITER: DAVID BROWN

1 *PHOTOGRAPHER:* GRAHAM FORD

2-3 *PHOTOGRAPHER:* DEREK
COUTTS

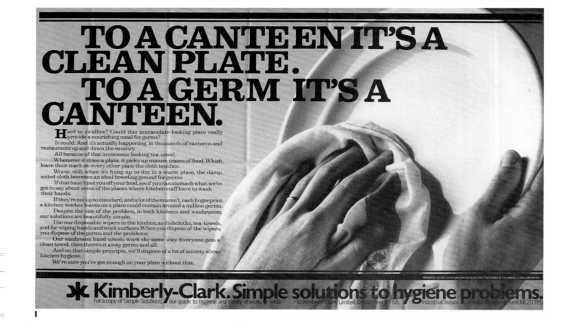

4

CLIENT: INTERNATIONAL
DISTILLERS AND VINTNERS
PRODUCT: HENNESSY
AGENCY: FLETCHER SHELTON
DELANEY, LONDON

4-6 *PRESS ADS, UK*
ART DIRECTOR: BRUCE GILL

5

6

CLIENT: COMMERCIAL UNION
ASSURANCE

AGENCY: DOYLE, DANE AND
BERNBACH, LONDON

PRESS CAMPAIGN, 1979, UK

ART DIRECTOR: BILL THOMPSON

COPYWRITER: SUZIE HENRY

PHOTOGRAPHER: MAX FORSYTH

TYPOGRAPHER: SIMON
PEMBERTON

These press ads ran at the same time as a television campaign that told some of the same stories. Its sympathetic tone and credibility, derived from real case histories, have made it one of the most successful and enduring insurance campaigns. So much so that when the creative team left to set up their own agency, they took the business with them.

To stem the flood from the attic, all our man had to do was turn off a tap.

On December 31st last year, when most of the country was in the grip of a severe blizzard, one of our policy holders, Mrs Dean, had a problem of another kind.

She was in the grip of a severe flood.

Caused, not by the elements. But by a pipe that had sprung a leak in a section leading from the cold storage tank.

The ceiling in one of the upstairs rooms of her sixteenth century cottage had collapsed, and cold water was pouring through onto the bed.

To add to her problems, Mr Dean was 5500 miles away at the time. On a business trip to Riyadh.

With great presence of mind, Mrs Dean decided there wasn't much point in phoning her husband.

Instead, she phoned her local Commercial Union District Sales Manager who lived but three miles away.

Having worked for Commercial Union for a good number of years, our man can tell a crisis a mile away (or, in this case, a little further).

More than that, though, he's a dab hand at knowing what to do in such nerve-wracking circumstances.

So, instead of getting into his car and setting off to the New Year's Eve party to which he had been invited, our quick thinking District Sales Manager got into his car and set off through the blizzard to Mrs Dean's house.

To cut a long story short, when he arrived, he first organised buckets to catch the water coming through the ceiling.

Then, he tracked down the main stopcock to a point in the front garden that was by now under several inches of snow.

Having turned that off, he turned his mind to getting hold of a qualified plumber.

Needless to say, by the time all this had been taken care of, he was more than a trifle late for his New Year's Eve celebrations.

But our story doesn't stop here.

The next day, our knight in shining gumboots was back.

This time, to disperse an air-lock that the plumber had inadvertently overlooked.

To be perfectly honest, it's not every day of the week that we can quote you such examples of devotion to duty.

And indeed, neither would we want to.

Since we'd much rather you looked upon us as a highly efficient insurance company.

And not a highly efficient plumbing service.

We won't make a drama out of a crisis.

When Mrs Marion Gibson first planned the evening's meal, nothing could have been further from her mind than hot-plate flambé.

In fact, the family dinner that night had started life as steak and chips.

But, by 6.20, there had been a dramatic change in the menu.

Moments earlier, the oil in the chip pan had been bubbling away quite merrily; so it was with every confidence that Mrs Gibson turned her back to lay the table.

It was then that the oil reached boiling point and instantly caught light.

Within seconds the entire cooker was ablaze.

Thankfully though, the fire brigade arrived in time to drown the kitchen, before the flames had a chance to take hold in the rest of the house.

The following morning, with the gloomy prospect of weeks of Chinese takeaways ahead of them, the Gibsons took little comfort from the fact they were insured.

After all, as everyone knows, it takes more than a completed claims form to restore life to some sort of normality after a serious fire.

At Commercial Union, we pride ourselves in the knowledge that we have these sort of people working in our midst. As the Gibsons were soon to discover for themselves.

The following day, we gave Mrs Gibson another chance to burn the dinner.

It takes people who are prepared to put themselves out.

Barely an hour after reporting the fire to our local branch office, Mr Gibson found himself opening his front door to one of our claims inspectors.

No sooner had he assessed the damage, than he agreed to a settlement. On the spot.

That afternoon a second surprise appeared on the Gibson's doorstep.

Quite simply, a brand new cooker. Identical in every way to their original.

Courtesy of Commercial Union.

In the normal course of events, we would replace a cooker with a cheque. Not a cooker.

But then, there are always exceptions to the rule.

Being down to earth insurance folk, we wouldn't never claim to work miracles.

Though Mrs Gibson would doubtless disagree with us.

We won't make a drama out of a crisis.

While others were assessing the damage, we were paying for it.

On the morning of January 11th 1978, you might have been forgiven for mistaking the streets of Sheerness for Amsterdam or Venice.

After a night of near hurricane force winds and waves as high as houses, the East Kent coastline was, quite simply, blown to bits.

In the light of this thirty mile trail of devastation, it became clear to us at Commercial Union that there was only one way we could be of real help.

Not with tea and sympathy. Or vague promises of compensation.

But rather, by agreeing to claims immediately. On the spot.

Now, it's not every day you'll find us popping in on policy holders, with a view to popping in a cheque in the past.

After all, like any other insurance company, every claim we deal with involves certain formalities.

There are details to be noted down. Policies to be checked out. Assessments to be made. And so on.

A process that can take anything from five minutes to five months. Or even longer.

Speaking for ourselves, we prefer to simplify the paperwork, for the sake of a speedy settlement.

Which is precisely how we coped with the mopping up of East Kent.

On January 12th, with the storm damage barely a day old, we set up an emergency claims centre in Canterbury.

Within two working days we had our own team of claims inspectors out and about on the waterways, personally totting up the cost of repairs.

In all, we paid out £115,000 from just one branch, to more than 400 policy holders.

So they could start rebuilding their lives, while others were still getting estimates.

We won't make a drama out of a crisis.

Seven days later, we bought a brand new red Volkswagen for the man who'd just bought a brand new red Volkswagen.

On 2nd April 1975, the morning weather forecast happened to mention there would be gusty showers around the South East.

For once, the clairvoyants at the Met Office were right.

But while other people were simply getting blown about, one man was getting more than he bargained for from the elements.

Though modesty prevents him from lending his name to our story, we can reveal that he was a school teacher in Guildford at the time. And the proud owner of a new Volkswagen Beetle.

No sooner had he parked it, locked it and turned his back on it than a ton and a half of tree trunk crashed down onto the bonnet.

With the result that his new red Volkswagen was effectively a new red write-off.

The teacher called his local branch of Commercial Union.

As his insurance company, we of course needed to see the damage for ourselves.

By late morning we had the claim form signed, sealed and on its way to head office for final approval.

This was received within two days, on 4th April.

Then came the tricky part.

We told the teacher that we'd be happy to replace his Volkswagen immediately with a new one, whereupon he told us he had this thing about red.

Then red it is, we said. But it may take a little time.

As it turned out, very little time indeed. On 9th April, just 7 days (not to mention scores of phone calls) later, our learned friend took delivery of a brand new Volkswagen.

And, we're happy to say, the colour was such you'd be hard put to spot a ripe tomato on the bonnet.

Of course, we can't always promise to deal with every claim with such speed and so little fuss. But we'll do our level best.

Whether you suddenly find yourself without a car or a colour television, your home or your health armed with the right policy, you'll find us more than willing to help.

And if that means a cheque within days, rather than weeks, we'll be the first with a first class stamp.

We won't make a drama out of a crisis.

Financial Times

Few people need reminding of the fact that last winter was the bleakest, most treacherous in years.

It was the winter of the burst pipe, the disappearing 'B' road, and everyone's discontent.

In the North of England, the conditions were nothing short of Arctic, when Clare Tapsfield, a local vet, set out on her daily calls.

It was the afternoon of 30th December.

The roads were more suited to a one-horse open sleigh than a 66 brake horse-power saloon.

As the good lady was soon to discover, when her car skidded on a patch of ice and disappeared into a drift.

Fortunately, Miss Tapsfield walked away without so much as a bruise.

Her car, however, had more than the odd dent to show for the experience.

In fact, the damage to the bodywork was such that it simply wouldn't budge.

With the result that the gallant 'Thorpes' of Thurgoland (the nearest garage for miles) were called upon to tow it away.

Once it was safely in their care, Miss Tapsfield promptly put in a claim to us, at Commercial Union.

Whereupon, we arranged to assess the damage personally, ourselves.

On the Tuesday after the New Year's holiday, our man muffled up, and set off on the rugged road to Thurgoland.

But before he could report his findings, he first had to find the car.

To help him in this simple task, the garage kindly suggested he use a shovel, and pointed him in the direction of a six foot snowdrift.

When he eventually dug Miss Tapsfield's car out of cold storage, he decided that it was past saving.

And we immediately agreed to settle in full.

C U ASSURANCE

Then all our man had to do was dig a path to the salvage truck.

A mere 20-feet away.

We won't make a drama out of a crisis.

Waiting for the thaw would have meant freezing the payment for Miss Tapsfield's new car.

Is it fair to force your baby to smoke cigarettes?

This is what happens if you smoke when you're pregnant.

Every time you inhale you fill your lungs with nicotine and carbon monoxide.

Your blood carries these impurities through the umbilical cord into your baby's bloodstream.

Smoking can restrict your baby's normal growth inside the womb.

It can make him underdeveloped and underweight at birth.

Which, in turn, can make him vulnerable to illness in the first delicate weeks of his life.

It can even kill him.

In just one year, in Britain alone, over 1,500 babies might not have died if their mothers had given up smoking when they were pregnant.

If you give up smoking when you're pregnant your baby will be as healthy as if you'd never smoked.

The Health Education Council

1

How to tell if he's becoming an alcoholic.

2

IS YOUR BODY COMING BETWEEN YOU AND THE OPPOSITE SEX?

There are times when you just can't hide it.

You're fat! Or overweight – or plump – or cuddly – or tubby...

But whatever you like to call it, it's not very attractive.

Most women prefer slender men as much as most men prefer slim women.

And what about the clothes that never quite fit, the puffing and sweating if you run for a bus.

Overeating and overdrinking are a major cause of heart disease (smoking and lack of exercise are two more) as well as a string of other illnesses.

But cheer up. You don't have to stop enjoying food and drink to start enjoying life.

Just cut down a bit, all round. One lump instead of two, two pints instead of three. Eat more lean meats,

fresh fruit and vegetables, liver, fish, and wholemeal bread.

And less cream, lard, butter, fried foods, sugar, sweets.

You'll feel better with every pound you lose, and you'll look a whole lot more attractive.

Send this coupon to the Health Education Council. We'll send you a package to help you look after yourself properly – a booklet on healthy eating and exercise, an exercise wall chart, a height/weight sticker and something for the kids.

The Health Education Council
18-19 Cramscott Street, London SE1 5TS.

LOOK AFTER YOURSELF!
Health Education Council. Helping you to better health.

3

"I never drank on Sundays so I thought I couldn't be an alcoholic."

George McCosker

4

WHY DO YOU THINK
EVERY PACKET CARRIES A GOVERNMENT HEALTH WARNING?

Issued by the Scottish Health Education Unit

5

CLIENT: HEALTH EDUCATION
COUNCIL

AGENCY: SAATCHI AND SAATCHI,
LONDON

1 *PRESS AD, 1975, UK*

ART DIRECTOR: RON MATHER

COPYWRITER: ANDREW
RUTHERFORD

PHOTOGRAPHER: JOHN THORNTON

2 *PRESS AD, 1979, UK*

ART DIRECTOR: RON MATHER

COPYWRITER: ANDREW
RUTHERFORD

PHOTOGRAPHER: BARNEY
EDWARDS

AGENCY: HALLS, EDINBURGH

3 *PRESS AD, 1978, UK*

ART DIRECTOR: JIM DOWNIE

COPYWRITER: PETER BARRY

4 *PRESS AD, 1978, UK*

ART DIRECTOR: JIM DOWNIE

COPYWRITER: PETER BARRY

PHOTOGRAPHER: MIKE McQUEEN

5 *POSTER, 1979, UK*

ART DIRECTOR: JIM DOWNIE

COPYWRITER: TONY COX

PHOTOGRAPHER: TONY MAY

POSTER CAMPAIGN, 1977, UK

CLIENT: HEINEKEN

AGENCY: COLLETT, DICKENSON AND PEARCE, LONDON

ART DIRECTOR: ALAN WALDIE

COPYWRITER: MIKE COZENS

1 *ILLUSTRATOR:* MIKE TERRY

2 *ILLUSTRATOR:* PAUL DAVIS

3 *ILLUSTRATOR:* BARRY CRADDOCK

4 *POSTER, 1979, UK*

CLIENT: PLANTERS PEANUTS

AGENCY: CHERRY HEDGER AND SEYMOUR, LONDON

ART DIRECTOR: TONY MURANKA

COPYWRITER: GEOFFREY SEYMOUR

ILLUSTRATOR: WARREN MADILL

TYPOGRAPHER: KEITH MACKENZIE

TEMPTATION BEYOND ENDURANCE.

4

CHAPTER ELEVEN

THE DECADE BEGAN with Ronald Reagan's election to the White House—a Hollywood dream come true. (Bob Hope was heard to quip, 'It's nice to see actors working again'.) In the previous year Margaret Thatcher had become the first woman prime minister of Great Britain, a position she was to retain in two subsequent general elections. Both leaders stand accused of having elevated economic and military strategies above the welfare needs of their societies and of ushering in an age of greed and acquisitiveness.

The eighties will probably be remembered as the decade of the Yuppy. But the first glimmer of a volte-face within the youth movement clearly predated both Reaganomics and Thatcherism and could be seen in the aftermath of Punk. It was then that a new mood of self-serving introspection emerged that was parodied and celebrated in Woody Allen's *Manhattan* and *Annie Hall.* It was a time that Tom Wolfe described as belonging to the 'Me Generation'.

This self-absorption has brought with it a whiff of cultural stagnation in the West—a statement that cannot be made at the moment about Russia or China.

Fine artists seem to have moved out of the public eye, unlike in the sixties when Warhol, Pollock and Hockney were household names. Nothing new is happening in the world of popular music. Rock 'n Roll has strengthened its political voice, as we have seen with Live Aid and Artists Against Apartheid. But the sounds are still rooted in the sixties.

In advertising we find the same inertia. During the 1970s London became the Mecca of the industry's creative world. There, in an environment mercifully free of unnecessary over-research, the agencies faithfully espoused Bernbach's doctrines and produced a decade of brilliant advertising. In the eighties, the principles remain largely unchallenged and unchanged. A language of advertising has developed that is rich in nuance—.the public is now described as 'adliterate'.

The future, however, is encouragingly uncertain. The combination of an economically united Europe in 1992 and the world-wide craze for satellite TV is going to turn McLuhan's global village into a global living room. Already Russia and China are experimenting with advertising. And as markets are developed internationally the cross-pollination of cultures should prove fertile for change.

WE SEE OPPORTUNITIES WHERE SOME SEE ONLY RISKS.

At 3i we're firm believers in the grass being greener on the other side.

Sometimes.

The assessment of risk versus opportunity is a fine judgement. A judgement at which we excel. Because, as well as being financial experts, we're business experts. And, being a private sector company, we don't employ any stuffed shirts. Or tolerate any red tape.

So when we see an opportunity, we can go for it.

In all modesty, we could hardly be better equipped to do so. Within 3i, we deal with large projects and are prepared to back any one company with up to £35m or more; we have ICFC, whose understanding of small companies' problems is unique; and our Ventures Division who specialise in high-technology businesses.

To date, we have enjoyed long-standing relationships with over 8,000 businesses.

If we hadn't been able to recognise greener grass, we wouldn't have been able to back half that number.

THE CREATIVE USE OF MONEY

1

HOW MANY INVESTORS IN BUSINESS INVEST IN THEIR OWN BUSINESS BRAINS?

At most investment companies, there is never a shortage of financial brains. Whereas business brains may often be very thin on the ground – if there are any at all.

At 3i, on the other hand, you'll meet both. But you won't meet a single stuffed shirt.

We're a private sector company and our attitude is both creative and innovative. And, because we're businessmen, we're quick to recognise a good business challenge.

Equally, and in all modesty, we are well equipped to act on our decisions.

Within 3i, we deal with large projects and are prepared to back any one company with up to £35m or more; we have ICFC, whose understanding of small companies' problems is unique; and our Ventures Division who specialise in high-technology businesses.

Up to now, we have enjoyed long-term relationships with over 8,000 businesses. But we're always looking for fresh opportunities.

Thank goodness we've got the brains to recognise them when they arise.

THE CREATIVE USE OF MONEY

2

UNLESS WE CAN MAKE A TEAM, WE'D RATHER NOT MAKE THE INVESTMENT.

Too often, no sooner has an investment company completed a deal, than it's good luck.

And goodbye.

But our attitude is just the opposite. We want to contribute to your success for years to come. For this reason, our financial brains must also be business experts. It is a policy which works.

Witness the 8,000 businesses with whom we have enjoyed long-term relationships.

We're well equipped to add to that number.

Within 3i, we deal with large projects and are prepared to back any one company with up to £35m or more; and through ICFC we have a unique understanding of small and medium-sized companies' needs. So we're ready for all comers.

But there has to be a proviso. Namely that, like us, they believe in something very important. The team spirit.

THE CREATIVE USE OF MONEY

3

SOMETIMES YOU NEED A FUND OF IMAGINATION, AS WELL AS FUNDS.

There are many sources of investment finance. But how many of them are also a source of inspiration? At 3i we can, in all modesty, claim to be both. Which is why a meeting with us is invariably a creative, as well as financial, experience.

As a private sector company, there isn't a stuffed shirt among us. As businessmen, we know business backwards. And as financiers, we're always looking forwards. So it's hardly surprising that we love a good challenge. And why not?

Within 3i, we deal with large projects and are prepared to back any one company with up to £35m or more; we have ICFC, whose understanding of small companies' problems is unique; and our Ventures Division who specialise in high-technology businesses.

To date we have successfully supported over 8,000 businesses, from small-scale family to major multinational companies.

Together we couldn't go wrong. Because they used their imagination. And we used ours.

THE CREATIVE USE OF MONEY

4

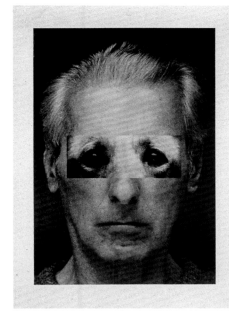

NO SURGEON IN THE WORLD CAN HELP
THIS BLIND MAN SEE. BUT A DOG CAN.

Try going blind.

Walk to the corner of the street with your
eyes closed.

Post a letter with your eyes closed.

Buy a loaf of bread with your eyes closed.

Discover how the simplest tasks become
a nightmare with your eyes closed.

Now walk to the corner of the street and
post a cheque with your eyes wide open.

THE GUIDE DOGS FOR THE BLIND ASSOCIATION
Department 3; 9 Park Street, Windsor, Berkshire SL4 1JR.

5

~~Congratulations~~
Mr. Smith,
you're the ~~proud~~
father of an
~~8lb~~ 3lb baby boy
with a hole in
his heart.

6

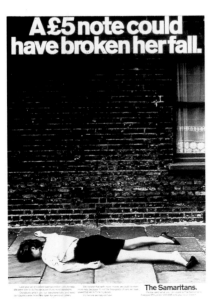

A £5 note could
have broken her fall.

The Samaritans.

7

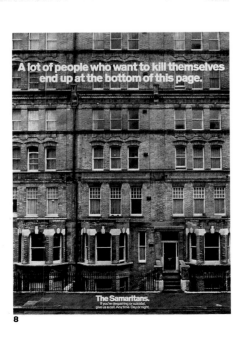

A lot of people who want to kill themselves
end up at the bottom of this page.

The Samaritans.
If you're desperate or suicidal,
give us a call. Any time. Day or night.

8

1-4 *PRESS CAMPAIGN, 1985, UK*

CLIENT: 31

AGENCY: DOYLE DANE AND
BERNBACH, LONDON

*This campaign ran in both black and white
and colour in the national daily press. We
included it here because aesthetically it is
such a radical departure from the style of
advertising one usually finds in the business
and financial categories.*

ART DIRECTOR: JOHN DODSON

COPYWRITER: PETER NEEVES

ILLUSTRATOR: JEFF FISHER

TYPOGRAPHER: JEFF JESSOP

5 *PRESS AD, 1986, UK*

CLIENT: ROYAL NATIONAL
INSTITUTE FOR THE BLIND

AGENCY: SAATCHI AND SAATCHI,
LONDON

*This appeal was one of many ads
commissioned by Reader's Digest Magazine
as part of their 'Open Space' programme. All
the agencies and artists contributed their
time and talents freely to the various
charities involved.*

ART DIRECTOR: MIKE SHAFFRON

COPYWRITER: JEFF STARK

PHOTOGRAPHER: PETER LAVERY

6 *PRESS AD, 1987, UK*

CLIENT: GREAT ORMOND STREET
HOSPITAL

AGENCY: COLLET DICKENSON AND
PEARCE

ART DIRECTOR: NEIL GODFREY

COPYWRITER: TONY BRIGNULL

7-8 *PRESS CAMPAIGN, 1986, UK*

CLIENT: THE SAMARITANS

AGENCY: SAATCHI AND SAATCHI,
LONDON

ART DIRECTOR: FERGUS FLEMING

COPYWRITER: SIMON PICKETTS

PHOTOGRAPHER: JOHN LONDEI

1-5 *PRESS CAMPAIGN, 1987, JAPAN*

CLIENT: ROH DOH BANK

AGENCY: KOH KOKU-SHA, TOKYO

ART DIRECTOR: TSUTOMU SO AND HIROYASU ITOH

ILLUSTRATOR: TSUTOMU SO

6 *PRESS AD, 1987, USA*

CLIENT: FIRST TENNESSEE

AGENCY: FALLON McELLIGOTT, NEW YORK

ART DIRECTOR: DEAN HANSON

COPYWRITER: JARL OLSON

PHOTOGRAPHER: MARJORIE NUGENT

1

2

3

4

5

296

See The Great Oils At The Memphis Brooks Museum.

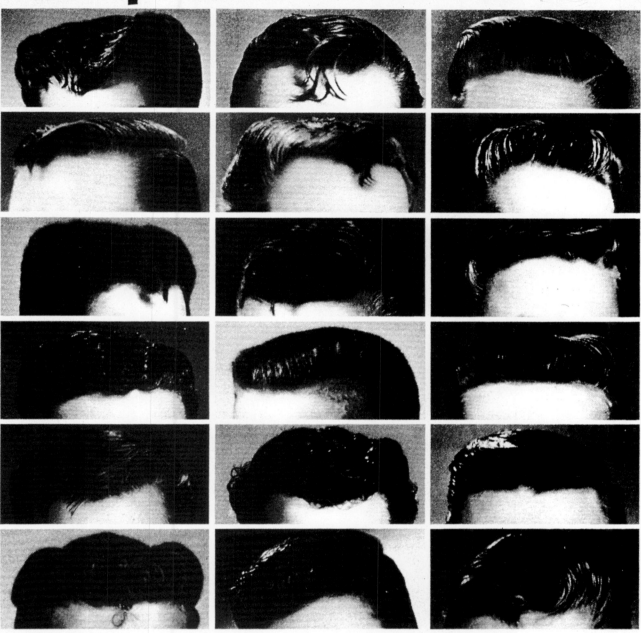

Return to a time when artists worked in Brylcreem. See Memphis 1948-1958, an exhibition of postwar photography, art, and popular culture at Memphis Brooks until January 11. Museum hours are Monday through Friday 10-5, and Sunday from 1-5. Open an IRA, CD, Premier Visa or All-in-One Account at First Tennessee and get two free tickets to the show or a commemorative poster when you bring in this ad. **1ST FIRST TENNESSEE**

6

Ceux qui sont tout noir ou tout blanc, sont-ils vraiment de bons vivants? Black & White Scotch Whisky.

1

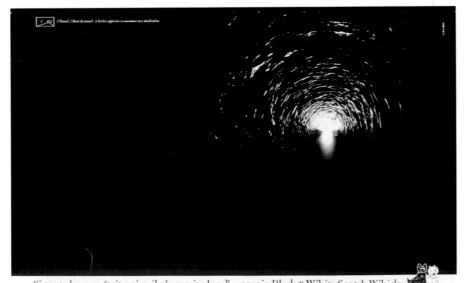

Si toute la page était noire, il n'y aurait plus d' espoir. Black & White Scotch Whisky.

2

&

Scotch Whisky.

3

FANTASMES DE COLLECTION.   SCÈNE 8. LA FEMME   CHARLES JOURDAN

Chaussures Farandole 780 F. Veste David 6 900 F. Jodhpur Dres 5 500 F. Chemisier Delta 900 F. Boucles d'oreilles Perles 345 F.

4

FANTASMES DE COLLECTION.   SCÈNE 3. L'HOMME   CHARLES JOURDAN monsieur

Chaussures Bardai 990 F. Blouson Bosnie 5 100 F. Pull Futuna 1 400 F. Chemise Oderic 455 F. Pantalon Chopin 595 F.

5

299

"I'll have a Perrier and water, please."

Quite how the barman at New York's Algonquin Hotel reacted to this young lady's order we shall never know.

We reacted with some horror, however. Perrier with Scotch, certainly. Perrier with dinner, of course. Perrier on its own, naturally. But Perrier with water?

However, when we thought a little deeper about her predicament – a smart hotel, a special evening, perhaps a desire to impress her companion by ordering a drink with style – we decided that never again should Perrier be a cause of such embarrassment.

So, for aficionados and the uninitiated alike:

"Everything you always wanted to know about Perrier but never dared to ask."

At Vergèze, between the somnolent volcanoes of the Auvergne and the Mediterranean, lies a mineral water spring which was bubbling long before Hannibal and his thirsty elephants crossed the Alps and rested there.

Source Perrier.

The Romans built baths there, the French added a spa and hôtel, and, in 1863 Napoleon III decreed that the naturally sparkling spring water be bottled "for the good of France." (Clearly it didn't do him much harm.)

It's rather ironic, however, that it took an Englishman – and a car crash – to put Perrier where it is today.

St. John Harmsworth had bought the spa, spring and all, in 1903.

So, when he crashed his car in England

three years later, where better to recuperate than his own sleepy spa in the South of France?

But, like Archimedes in the bath two thousand years before, the presence of so much water was to inspire him.

It occurred to him that, if people would come to Vergèze to take the waters, think how many would enjoy it if he took it to them? – Eureka!

Harmsworth promptly forgot the spa, and concentrated on giving Perrier the distinctive French livery by which it is recognised all over the world today.

The name. The classical logo. The unique Perrier bottle (based on the Indian clubs which he used for remedial exercise).

The water itself he left alone. For Man can add nothing to the natural sparkle which Nature has already provided.

Except a bottle to make sure it will travel well, and arrive as fresh as it left the source.

Which has made Perrier the ideal choice of bon viveurs, the perfect complement to good spirits, and the international hallmark of taste and good company.

No wonder our unfortunate lady was so eager to order it.

We hope the faux pas didn't ruin her evening.

And whether you're eating, drinking, trying not to drink, playing sport or staying at the Algonquin Hotel, we hope Perrier will add to yours.

A votre santé!

1

2

3

4

Eauasis.

CLIENT: AQUALAC

AGENCY: LEO BURNETT, LONDON

POSTER CAMPAIGN, 1980, UK

1 ART DIRECTOR: ROB KITCHEN

COPYWRITER: RICHARD WARREN

2 ART DIRECTOR: MIKE TRUMBLE

COPYWRITER: COLIN CAMPBELL

PHOTOGRAPHER: JOHN TURNER

3 ART DIRECTOR: MALCOLM GASKIN

COPYWRITER: DAVID O'CONNOR THOMPSON

PHOTOGRAPHER: JOHN TURNER

4 ART DIRECTOR: DOUGIE BUNTROCK

COPYWRITER: COLIN CAMPBELL

PHOTOGRAPHER: JOHN TURNER

5 ART DIRECTOR: PATRICK TOFTS

COPYWRITER: COLIN CAMPBELL

PHOTOGRAPHER: JOHN CLARIDGE

Over the last ten years, Perrier's Eau device has managed to combine style and wit within the format of a packshot campaign. If you look at a graph of the company's sales figures it would suggest that you can push water up hill—in the UK in 1978, Perrier sold 7 million bottles, but last year the figure was over 100 million.

5

Who knows better than Sainsbury's how dryness can age the skin?

The 'J' skin care range. Exclusive to Sainsbury's.

Sainsbury's have a peach of an idea for Parma ham. But it isn't peach.

Good food costs less at Sainsbury's.

Sainsbury's announce sandwich courses in Dutch, Hungarian, Polish, Belgian, French, Italian, Greek, German and Danish.

Dutch smoked sausage.   Italian mortadella with peppers.

Danish salami.   Belgian liver sausage.

Good food costs less at Sainsbury's.

The Côtes du Rhône boasts several Goliaths amongst its red wines. (Can Sainsbury's claim at least one David?)

Good wine costs less at Sainsbury's.

A good Stilton from Sainsbury's will make your mouth water. (Not your eyes.)

Good food costs less at Sainsbury's.

Just when you thought you understood Brie, Sainsbury's create delicious confusion.

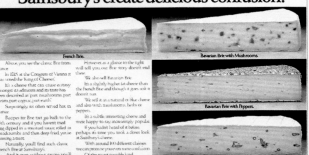

French Brie.   Bavarian Brie with Mushrooms.
Bavarian Brie with Peppers.
Bavarian Blue Brie.

Good food costs less at Sainsbury's.

Eat the same pasta they eat on the Via Veneto. (Via Sainsbury's).

Egg Tagliatelle.   Egg and Spinach Tagliatelle.
Tagliatelle Verde.   Egg Vermicelli.

Good food costs less at Sainsbury's.

What on earth are Sainsbury's up to?

Tomatoes as big as apples.
Lettuce as firm as cabbage.
Mushrooms like saucers.

Good food costs less at Sainsbury's.

9

10

11

1-8 *PRESS CAMPAIGN, 1982-5, UK*

CLIENT: SAINSBURY'S
FOODSTORES

AGENCY: ABBOT MEADE VICKERS,
LONDON

ART DIRECTOR: RON BROWN

COPYWRITER: DAVID ABBOT

TYPOGRAPHER: JOE HOZA

PHOTOGRAPHER: MARTIN
THOMPSON

*Every element of this campaign hits the
correct tone for the target audience — the
photography, typography, witty headlines
and straightforward endline combine to
create a reassurance that embraces both
quality and value for money.*

9-11 *POSTER CAMPAIGN, 1983, UK*

CLIENT: ARALDITE

AGENCY: FCO UNIVAS, LONDON

ART DIRECTORS: ROB KITCHEN, IAN
POTTER

COPYWRITER: ROB JANOWSKI

*Few people living in London at the time did
not either see or hear about these posters.
Using Araldite glue, FCO actually stuck a
Ford Cortina to a 48-sheet poster hoarding
in the Cromwell Road — one of the main
arterial roads into the city. As an encore they
stuck two Cortinas to the poster, making
advertising history and starting a craze for
three-dimensional posters.*

1

2

3

Sarah Moon on
Nikon lenses:

"

"

Nikon
We take the world's
greatest pictures.

4

Pete Turner on
Nikon lenses:

"

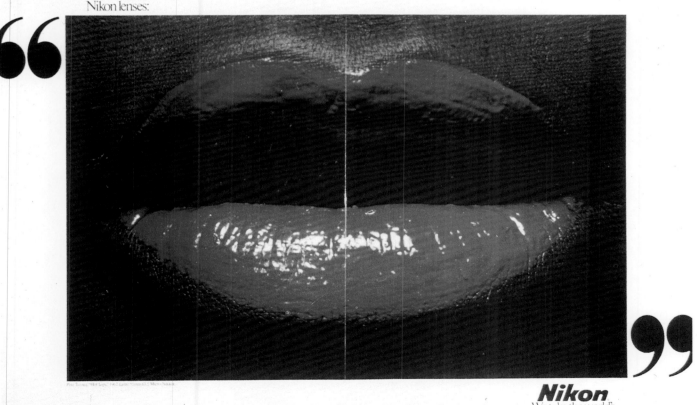

"

Nikon
We take the world's
greatest pictures.

5

1

2

3

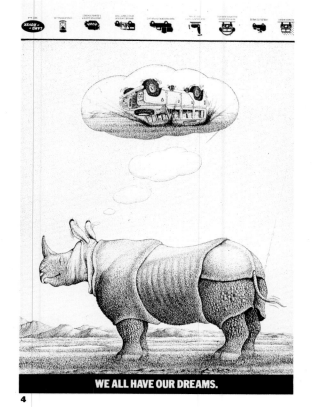

WE ALL HAVE OUR DREAMS.

4

" . . . 108 . . . 109 . . . 110 . . . "

5

**PROVIDE FOR THE FUTURE.
INVEST IN A LAND ROVER.**

6

THIS LAND ROVER IS IN REVERSE GEAR.

THIS LAND ROVER IS IN FORWARD GEAR.

7

1-3 *POSTER CAMPAIGN, 1986, UK*

CLIENT: SWAN VESTAS

AGENCY: DOYLE DANE AND
BERNBACH, LONDON

ART DIRECTOR: WARREN BROWN

COPYWRITER: BRUCE CROUCH

PHOTOGRAPHER: JAMES COTIER

4/7 *PRESS CAMPAIGN, UK*

CLIENT: LAND ROVER

AGENCY: TBWA, LONDON

4 *ART DIRECTOR:* MIKE HANNET

COPYWRITER: KEN MULLEN

ILLUSTRATOR: BERT KITCHEN

5 *ART DIRECTOR:* MALCOLM
GASKIN

COPYWRITER: KEN MULLEN

ILLUSTRATOR: BILL SANDERSON

6 *ART DIRECTOR:* MALCOLM
GASKIN

COPYWRITER: NEIL PATTERSON

PHOTOGRAPHER: GEOFF SENIOR

7 *ART DIRECTOR:* NEIL PATTERSON

PHOTOGRAPHER: IVOR LEWIS

1-5 *PRESS CAMPAIGN, 1987, JAPAN*

CLIENT: TAKEO, TOKYO

AGENCY: NIPPON DESIGN CENTRE

ART DIRECTOR: KAZUMASA NAGAI

These were magazine ads for the Takeo Company Limited, who are paper wholesalers. Each of the ads was printed on one of the company's paper qualities, ie, Komon, Sable, Filare, Dia-White and NT Rasha.

6 *POSTER, 1987, FRANCE*

HEADLINE: 'EVERYTHING SHOULD BE BUILT LIKE A SAMSONITE'

CLIENT: SAMSONITE

AGENCY: BBDO, PARIS

PHOTOGRAPHER: GRAHAM FORD

7-8 *PRESS CAMPAIGN, 1987, WEST GERMANY*

CLIENT: KODAK AG

AGENCY: YOUNG AND RUBICAM GMBH

7 *ART DIRECTOR:* KARL HEINZ DANIEL

COPYWRITER: GERO ANLAUF

PHOTOGRAPHER: JEAN LOUP SIEFF

8 *ART DIRECTOR:* HERIBERT BURKERT

COPYWRITER: SUSANNE HESSING

PHOTOGRAPHER: CHRISTIAN VON ALVENSLEBEN

9 *PRESS AD, 1987, HOLLAND*

CLIENT: BRANDSTEDER ELECTRONICS

AGENCY: GGK, AMSTERDAM

HEADLINE: 'SONY UX-PRO SQUEEZES OUT WHAT OTHER TAPES LEAVE BEHIND'

ART DIRECTOR: PIETER VAN VELSEN

COPYWRITER: PETER VAN DER NIJK

PHOTOGRAPHER: CHRIS LEWIS

10 *PRESS AD, 1985, USA*

CLIENT: MAXELL TAPES

AGENCY: SCALI McCABE AND SLOVES, NEW YORK

ART DIRECTOR: LARS ANDERSON

COPYWRITER: PETER LEVATHES

PHOTOGRAPHER: STEVE STEIGMAN

1

2

3

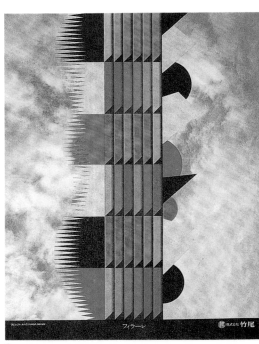

4

5

On devrait tout construire comme une Samsonite.

6

KODACOLOR GOLD FILM. DAS FARBWUNDER.

7

KODACOLOR GOLD FILM. DAS FARBWUNDER.

8

SONY UX-PRO PERST ERUIT WAT ANDERE TAPES LATEN ZITTEN

9

IF THERE'S A MAXELL CASSETTE IN THIS CAR AND IT DOESN'T WORK, WE'LL REPLACE IT.

10

309

1

2

3

4

5

6

7

8

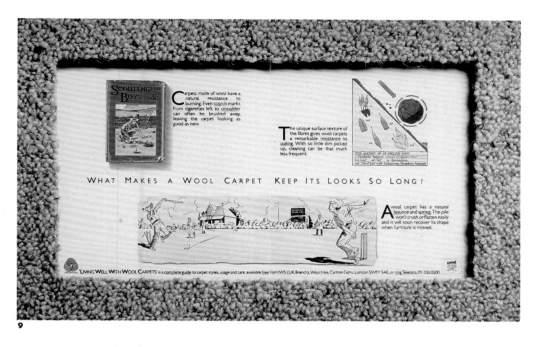

9

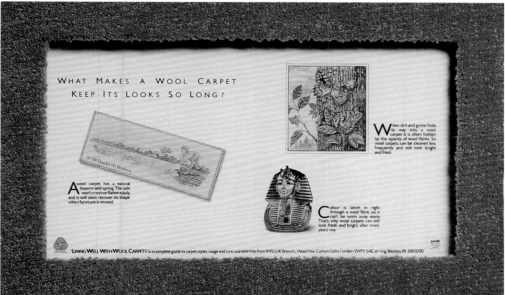

10

11

PRESS CAMPAIGN, 1984-5, UK

CLIENT: WOOL SECRETARIAT

AGENCY: DAVIDSON PEARCE

1 *ART DIRECTOR:* KIT MARR

COPYWRITER: NEIL FAZAKERLEY

PHOTOGAPHER: ANDREAS HEUMANN

ILLUSTRATOR: ALAN CRACKNELL

2 *ART DIRECTOR:* KITT MARR

COPYWRITER: NEIL FAZAKERLEY

PHOTOGRAPHER: TERENCE DONOVAN

ILLUSTRATOR: RAY WINDER

3 *ART DIRECTOR:* JOHN CLIFFORD

COPYWRITER: NEIL FAZAKERLEY

PHOTOGRAPHER: JOHN THORNTON

ILLUSTRATOR: JOHN GORHAM

4 *ART DIRECTOR:* JOHN CLIFFORD

COPYWRITER: NEIL FAZAKERLEY

PHOTOGRAPHER: ROLF GOBBITS

ILLUSTRATOR: CHLOE CHEESE

5 *ART DIRECTOR:* JOHN CLIFFORD

COPYWRITER: NEIL FAZAKERLEY

PHOTOGRAPHER: BRIAN GRIFFIN

ILLUSTRATOR: TONY MCSWEENEY

6 *ART DIRECTOR:* JOHN CLIFFORD

COPYWRITER: NEIL FAZAKERLEY

PHOTOGRAPHER: ROLF GOBBITS

ILLUSTRATOR: CHLOE CHEESE

7 *ART DIRECTOR:* JOHN CLIFFORD

COPYWRITER: NEIL FAZAKERLEY

PHOTOGRAPHER: JOHN THORNTON

ILLUSTRATOR: JOHN GORHAM

8 *ART DIRECTOR:* JOHN CLIFFORD

COPYWRITER: NEIL FAZAKERLEY

PHOTOGRAPHER: BRIAN GRIFFIN

9 *ART DIRECTOR:* JOHN CLIFFORD

COPYWRITER: NEIL FAZAKERLEY

PHOTOGRAPHER: DEREK SEAGRIM

ILLUSTRATOR: MICK BROWNFIELD

10-11 *ART DIRECTOR:* JOHN CLIFFORD

COPYWRITER: NEIL FAZAKERLEY

PHOTOGRAPHER: DEREK SEAGRIM

ILLUSTRATOR: ALAN CRACKNELL

1

2

"Before I'll ride with a drunk, I'll drive myself." —*Stevie Wonder*

Driving after drinking, or riding with a driver who's been drinking, is a big mistake. Anyone can see that.

MIDDLE TAR As defined by H.M. Government
DANGER: Government Health WARNING: CIGARETTES CAN SERIOUSLY DAMAGE YOUR HEALTH

1

MIDDLE TAR As defined by H.M. Government
DANGER: Government Health WARNING: CIGARETTES CAN SERIOUSLY DAMAGE YOUR HEALTH

2

MIDDLE TAR As defined by H.M. Government
DANGER: H. M. Government Health Departments' WARNING: THINK ABOUT THE HEALTH RISKS BEFORE SMOKING

3

MIDDLE TAR As defined by H.M. Government
DANGER: Government Health WARNING: CIGARETTES CAN SERIOUSLY DAMAGE YOUR HEALTH

4

MIDDLE TAR As defined by H.M. Government
DANGER: Government Health WARNING: CIGARETTES CAN SERIOUSLY DAMAGE YOUR HEALTH

5

MIDDLE TAR As defined by H.M. Government
DANGER: Government Health WARNING: CIGARETTES CAN SERIOUSLY DAMAGE YOUR HEALTH

6

MIDDLE TAR As defined by H.M. Government
Warning: MORE THAN 30,000 PEOPLE DIE EACH YEAR IN THE UK FROM LUNG CANCER
Health Departments' Chief Medical Officers

7

MIDDLE TAR As defined by H.M. Government
Warning: SMOKING CAN CAUSE LUNG CANCER, BRONCHITIS AND OTHER CHEST DISEASES
Health Departments' Chief Medical Officers

8

MIDDLE TAR As defined by H.M. Government
DANGER: Government Health WARNING: CIGARETTES CAN SERIOUSLY DAMAGE YOUR HEALTH

9

MIDDLE TAR As defined by H.M. Government
DANGER: Government Health WARNING: CIGARETTES CAN SERIOUSLY DAMAGE YOUR HEALTH

10

ACKNOWLEDGEMENTS

ROBERT OPIE: **pp14-25; 28-30; 38-42; 48-57; 68-70; 73, nos. 2, 3 & 4; 74; 78-80; 88-91; 106, no.3; 107; 114; 115, nos. 4 & 5; 118; 122-129; 132-133; 149, nos. 5, 6, 8 & 9; 150-151; 161; 163, no.7; 171; 185; 198-199; 210-212; 215; 217, no.9; 222-223; 243, no.9; 250.**

KUNTGEWERBE MUSEUM, MUSEUM FUR GESTALTUNG, ZURICH: **pp58-59; 64-67; 75; 84-87; 92-93; 102-103; 106, nos. 1 &2; 116-117; 120-121; 134-135; 142-147; 154-159; 163, no.5; 164-165; 168-169; 178; 179, no.8; 184; 204-205.**

COLIN McARTHUR: **pp71; 100-101; 115, nos. 6, 7, 8 & 9; 119; 140-141; 148; 170; 182-183; 186-195; 200-201; 208-209; 213-214; 216, nos. 1 & 2; 218-221; 224-226; 228-231; 235; 239, nos. 5, 6, 7, 9, 10-13; 240; 246-247; 268.**

SMITHSONIAN INSTITUTION, WASHINGTON, D.C., U.S.A.: **pp 34-37; 43-47; 76-77; 81; 94-99; 108-109; 138-139; 166-167; 202-203; 232-233.**

GRAHAM LINCOLN: **pp238; 239, no.8; 242-245; 248-249; 251; 253; 256-257; 260-261; 282.**

DAVE KING: **pp104-105; 130-131; 163, no.6; 176-177; 179, nos. 5, 6, 7, 9 & 10; 196-197; 258-259.**

LORD'S GALLERY, LONDON: **pp31-33; 62-63; 72; 73, no.1; 149, nos. 5, 6, 7, 9 & 10; 196-197; 258-259.**

ARTHUR GUINNESS, SON & CO: **pp152-153** ARTHUR GUINNESS, SON & CO: **pp172-175** SHELL U.K. LTD: **p216, no.3** ARTHUR GUINNESS, SON & CO: **p217, nos. 4-8** ARTHUR GUINNESS, SON & CO: **p234** LEO BURNETT, CHICAGO: **p254** JOHN HEGARTY: **p255** DOYLE, DANE & BERNBACH; **pp 262-265** DOYLE, DANE & BERNBACH: **p269** DOYLE, DANE & BERNBACH, U.K.: **pp270-271** TONY MURANKA; **p272** CATHY HENG; **p273** DOYLE, DANE & BERNBACH; **pp274-277** GALLAHER LTD U.K.: **p278** ROGER STANIER, LEITH AGENCY, EDINBURGH; **p279** DOYLE, DANE & BERNBACH; **p280** T.B.W.A. LONDON; **p281** COLLETT DICKENSON & PEARCE; **p283** INTERNATIONAL DISTILLERS & VINTNERS LTD; **pp284-285** BRUCE GILL; **p286** DOYLE, DANE & BERNBACH; **p288, nos. 1 & 3** SAATCHI & SAATCHI; **p288, nos. 2 & 4** HALL ADVERTISING, EDINBURGH; **p289** HALL ADVERTISING, EDINBURGH; **p290** COLLETT DICKENSON & PEARCE; **p291** TONY MURANKA; **p294** DOYLE, DANE & BERNBACH; **p295, nos. 5, 7 & 9** SAATCHI & SAATCHI; **p295 nos. 6 & 8** COLLETT DICKENSON & PEARCE; **p298** CLM/BBDO PARIS; **p299** FOOTE CONE & BELDING PARIS; **p300** LEO BURNETT LONDON; **p302** ABBOTT MEAD VICKERS, LONDON; **p303** FCO UNIVAS LONDON; **p304** AMMIRATI & PURIS NEW YORK; **p305** SCALI McCABE & SLOVES NEW YORK; **p306** DOYLE, DANE & BERNBACH; **p307** T.B.W.A. LONDON; **p309** GRAHAM FORD; **p310** COLLETT DICKENSON & PEARCE; **p311** JOHN CLIFFORD; **p312** J. COBY NEILL; **p314** GALLAHER LTD, U.K.

EVERY EFFORT HAS BEEN MADE TO TRACE AND ACKNOWLEDGE ALL COPYRIGHT HOLDERS: QUARTO WOULD LIKE TO APOLOGIZE IF ANY OMISSIONS HAVE BEEN MADE.